Relativity
AND
Redemption

I0148154

A DEVOTIONAL STUDY
OF JUDGES AND RUTH

WARREN HENDERSON

Relativity and Redemption – A Devotional Study of Judges and Ruth

By Warren Henderson
Copyright © 2016

Cover Design: Benjamin Bredeweg

Editing/Proofreading: Keith Keyser,
    Daniel Macy, and David Lindstrom

Published by Warren A. Henderson
3769 Indiana Road
Pomona, KS 66076

Perfect Bound ISBN: 978-1-939770-32-5
eBook ISBN: 978-1-939770-33-2

ORDERING INFORMATION:
Gospel Folio Press
Phone 1-905-835-9166
E-mail: order@gospelfolio.com

Also available in many online retail stores

Table of Contents

Other Books by the Author

Afterlife – What Will It Be Like?
Answer the Call – Finding Life's Purpose
Be Holy and Come Near– A Devotional Study of Leviticus
Behold the Saviour
Be Angry and Sin Not
Conquest and the Life of Rest – A Devotional Study of Joshua
Exploring the Pauline Epistles
Forsaken, Forgotten, and Forgiven – A Devotional Study of Jeremiah
Glories Seen & Unseen
Hallowed Be Thy Name – Revering Christ in a Casual World
Hiding God – The Ambition of World Religion
In Search of God – A Quest for Truth
Knowing the All-Knowing
Lessons For Life
Managing Anger God's Way
Mind Frames – Where Life's Battle Is Won or Lost
Out of Egypt – A Devotional Study of Exodus
Overcoming Your Bully
Passing the Torch – Mentoring the Next Generation
Revive Us Again – A Devotional Study of Ezra and Nehemiah
Seeds of Destiny – A Devotional Study of Genesis
The Bible: Myth or Divine Truth?
The Beginning of Wisdom – A Devotional Study of Job, Psalms, Proverbs, Ecclesiastes, and Song of Solomon
The Evil Nexus – Are You Aiding the Enemy?
The Fruitful Bough – Affirming Biblical Manhood
The Fruitful Vine – Celebrating Biblical Womanhood
The Hope of Glory – A Preview of Things to Come
The Olive Plants – Raising Spiritual Children
Your Home the Birthing Place of Heaven

Preface

Spiritual corruption and idolatry became rampant among the Jews during the era of the Judges, beginning with the generation directly after Joshua's. This angered the Lord who repeatedly punished His covenant people through military invasion. After years of oppression, the Jews would repent and cry out to the Lord for deliverance. On these occasions the Lord raised up judges to remove the oppressors from the land and to guide the nation in righteous conduct. Amidst this long and gloomy backdrop of failure and chastening, a bright ray of redemptive hope is conveyed in the lovely story of Ruth, a young Moabite widow who is sacrificially devoted to her mother-in-law Naomi, also a widow.

Accordingly, from a typological sense, the story of Ruth pictures the fulfilment of all that God's promises in connection with Israel (and no less the Church who is later grafted into such promises), on the ground of sovereign grace, after the nation (portrayed in Naomi) had lost all claims to God's blessing because of moral and spiritual failure (the testimony of Judges). Judges displays the ever increasing depravity of Israel, despite divine chastening and intervention, which ultimately leaves God's people in a thick hue of spiritual deadness. Thankfully, the activities of God's grace are not overcome by human failure; this leaves us with a wonderful scene of joy and blessing at the conclusion of the book of Ruth.

Naomi, representing the chastened nation of Israel, is a backsliding believer, who returns to Lord after experiencing the consequences of departing from God's will. She departed Judah "full," but willing "returns" (a key word in Ruth) "empty," after God stripped everything away by disciplinary action. Having been emptied of all self-ambition and self-fortitude she again experiences God's delight and blessing in her life.

Through her connection with Naomi, Ruth steps forward in faith to reject the deep-seated pagan heritage of her own people to become a Jehovah worshipper. After approaching a potential kinsman-redeemer,

Boaz, and requesting to be redeemed, she receives his pledge to do so. Later, she will experience the redeeming love of Boaz through marriage and be not only brought into the commonwealth of Israel, but also the genealogy of Christ.

Relativity and Redemption is a "commentary style" devotional which upholds the glories of Christ while exploring the books of Judges and Ruth within the context of the whole of Scripture. I have endeavored to include in this book some of the principal gleanings from other writers. *Relativity and Redemption* contains dozens of brief devotions. This format allows the reader to use the book either as a daily devotional or as a reference source for deeper study.

— Warren Henderson

Judges

Introduction to Judges

The Author

While the author of Judges does not personally identify himself, Hebrew tradition asserts that Samuel is the writer of the book. The Babylonian Talmud (Tractate Baba Bathra 14b) states: "Samuel wrote the book which bears his name and the books of Judges and Ruth." The internal evidence mentioned in "The Date" section below also indicates that Judges was written just before the reign of David. If this supposition is correct, this timeframe ensures that Samuel is a strong candidate for authorship. Samuel was the leading prophet at that time, was well-respected in Israel, and also was a renowned writer (1 Sam. 10:25).

The Date

Internal evidence suggests that Judges was written just after the coronation of King Saul in 1051 B.C., but before David overcame the Jebusites dwelling in Jerusalem in 1004 B.C. (1:21). F. Duane Lindsey suggests that there are three pertinent reasons for adopting this conclusion:

> (1) The stylistic motto *"in those days Israel had no king"* is repeated towards the end of the book (17:6; 18:1; 19:1; 21:25) and looks backward from a period when Israel did have a king. (2) The statement about Jerusalem that *"to this day the Jebusites live there"* (1:21) is most clearly explained as written before David's conquest of the city (2 Sam. 5:6-7). (3) The reference to Canaanites in Gezer suggests a date before the time the Egyptians gave the city to Solomon's Egyptian wife as a wedding present (1 Kgs. 9:16).[1]

If Samuel is the author of Judges, the book would have been written in the latter years of his life, just after the appointment of Saul as

Israel's first king. A date of 1050 to 1020 B.C. seems appropriate based on this assumption.

The Interval

While most Bible scholars concur that the book commences with the death of Joshua and concludes with Saul's ascent to the throne, there is much debate as to the actual duration of the book. It is generally agreed that Saul became the first king of the Jewish nation in 1051 B.C.; however, the date of Joshua's death is debatable as it is directly tied to the date of the Exodus. Biblical scholars have placed the date of the Exodus from as late as 1230 B.C. to as early as 1580 B.C. Archeological evidence has been used to bolster various dates in this range.

History records that an Asiatic people called the Hyksos captured and ruled Egypt from around 1720 to 1580 B.C. (corresponding to the time of the Patriarchs and to the 15th and 16th Egyptian dynasties). Some historians believe that the Hyksos, like the Hebrews, were a nomadic people. They were also Semitic (i.e. descendants of Shem), as were the Israelites. It seems logical to conclude that the migration of the Israelites to Egypt and the rise of Joseph to power corresponded with the Hyksos' control of Egypt. Semitic rulers would have been more favorable than the Egyptians to allow a Semitic "foreigner" to be the second in command of Egypt and to permit a migration of other Semitic people to Goshen. The "new king" who did not know Joseph would correspond with the expulsion of the Hyksos from Egypt after the 16th dynasty (Ex. 1:8). With the removal of Joseph and the Hyksos, the Egyptians regained political control and enslaved the Israelites, perhaps in retaliation for Semitic rule.[2] The Pharaoh mentioned in Exodus 1:8 is likely Amenhotep I (1545–1526 B.C.) or Thutmose I (1526-1512 B.C.). Amenhotep II (1450-1425 B.C.) was involved with building projects in northern Egypt and accordingly may have been Pharaoh at the time of the Exodus. In conclusion, a mid-fifteenth century B.C. date for the Exodus is supported by historical evidence.

Solomon states that the Exodus occurred 480 years before he began constructing the temple in the fourth year of his reign (1 Kgs. 6:1). Solomon reigned as king in Israel for forty years, from 971 to 931 B.C. This means that the temple work was initiated in 966 B.C., and 480 years earlier would put the Exodus date at 1446 B.C.[3] Solomon's statements in 1 Kings 6:1 enable us to fix the interval of the Judges with more confidence.

Working forward from the 1446 B.C. date for the exodus and adding forty years for the wilderness experience, seven years for the Canaan conquest, and a few decades for the elders who outlived Joshua to die, the period of the Judges would have commenced between 1390 and 1350 B.C. If the last elder (being less than twenty years of age at the time of the exodus) lived as long as Joshua (i.e. 110 years), then a date nearer to 1350 seems reasonable. Israel entered into idolatry shortly after this time (2:7), thus initiating the cycle of disciplinary action which necessitated the Judges. This evaluation would suggest that the period of the Judges, ended with Saul's ascent to the throne in 1052 B.C. and lasted slightly over three hundred years.

What about Paul's historical overview in Acts 13:18-21, which denotes 450 years for the era of the Judges? The reference is difficult to reconcile with the previously explained Bible chronology, though various explanations have been suggested. It is feasible that Paul is including years of Jewish oppression in Egypt within the scope of oppression during the time of the Judges. But textually speaking, this rationalization does not hold much merit. A more likely explanation is that Paul is speaking of the sum total years of independent judgeships and related oppressions, instead of absolute chronology, as in Solomon's statement.

The narrative indicates that the judges had authority over a particular region of Israel, rather than over the entire nation, thus, some judgeships overlapped. The Jewish response to their oppressors provides credibility to this understanding – not all of the tribes were requested, nor responded to the call to arms. This would mean that the total time of the judges would be less than the summation of each situation (i.e. less than the accumulative 408 years of judgeships and oppressions – see table below).

The Judges

Judges	Years Judged	Oppressors	Years Oppressed	Judges Ref.
1. Othniel	40	Arameans	8	3:7-11
2. Ehud	80	Moabites	19	3:12-30
3. Shamgar	unknown	Philistines		3:31
4. Deborah 5. Barak	40	Canaanites	20	4-5
6. Gideon	40	Midianites	7	6-8
7. Tola	23			10:1-2
8. Jair	22			10:3-5
9. Jephthah	6	Ammonites	18	10:6-12:7
10. Ibzan	7			12:8-10
11. Elon	10			12:11-12
12. Abdon	8			12:13-15
13. Samson	20	Philistines	40	13-16
Total	296+		112+	408+ years

Outline
1:1-3:6: Historical Review and Prophetic Prelude
3:7-16:31: The Era of the Judges
17-21: Examples of Moral and Spiritual Declension

The prelude or preface to the book shows the degeneracy of Israel and their lapse into idolatry after the death of Joshua and his contemporaries (1:1-3:6). The principal narrative of Judges relates to the thirteen distinct judges whom God raised up to deliver His people from their servitude to foreign nations, which resulted from willful idolatry. The last five chapters of the book form an appendix and provide two dramatic examples of idolatry and immorality among the Israelites. These two incidents illustrate the overall condition of the people in the main narrative and occur early in the era of the judges; these events are not chronologically placed.

The Setting

The history of the Jewish nation after the death of Joshua to the reign of King Saul is recorded in the book of Judges. Before his death, Joshua sternly warned his fellow countrymen to drive out the remaining Canaanites in the land and to not intermingle with them (Josh. 24). The Israelites, by Jehovah's power, had defeated the main Canaanite armies and fortifications, but there were many pockets of resistance in their inheritance. By these, the Lord would test the faithfulness of His people. While some like Caleb and Othniel boldly confronted the enemy and gained a pagan-free inheritance, most Jews resorted to either enslaving the remaining inhabitants or benefitting from them through social ties – they did not drive them out. Judges records the consequences of disobedience which eventually led to the greater sins of worldliness and idolatry.

The Theme

Spiritual corruption and idolatry became rampant among the Jews in the generation directly after Joshua's. This angered the Lord who repeatedly punished His covenant people through military invasion. After years of oppression, the Jews would repent and cry out to the Lord for deliverance. On these occasions the Lord raised up judges to remove the oppressors from the land and to guide the nation in righteous conduct. The Hebrew concept of "judge" has wider implications than the English language poses today. The Hebrew judges did much more than merely interpret the Law and issue rulings to its application; they were civil and military leaders also. Unfortunately, after the passing of a particular judge, the Jews would invariably enter into idolatry again and the cycle of rebellion, invasion, repentance, and deliverance would repeat.

It is no coincidence that there were thirteen judges who ministered to Israel during the time when *"every man did what was right in their own eyes"* (17:6). When used metaphorically in Scripture, each of the numbers from one to forty holds a particular meaning; the following are a few examples of how the number thirteen is used in Scripture to show rebellion. The number thirteen is first mentioned in the Bible when five Jordanian kings rebelled against Chedorlaomer (Gen. 14:4). There were thirteen years of silence after Abraham doubted God's promise and fathered Ishmael, after which God reminded Abraham of His covenant thirteen times (Gen. 17). Haman's plot to destroy the Jews was set for the 13th day of a particular month (Est. 3:13). Jeremiah delivered thirteen messages to apostate Judah, whom he calls a "backsliding" people thirteen times. Satan, or the Dragon, is spoken of thirteen times in Revelation. Instead of accepting God's will in the matter, King Saul made thirteen attempts on the life of David, God's chosen man to replace Saul on the throne. Throughout Scripture, the number thirteen is associated with rebellion, and this is likely the determining factor in the number of specific judges in the book.

There is little desire for God or His Word throughout the book of Judges. The main theme of the book is God's abiding love for His people even though they repeatedly forgot Him, embraced false gods, and prompted His chastening hand against them to regain their allegiance and separation. These seasons of rest were short-lived, for abruptly after the instruments of blessing were removed (i.e., the judges), evil quickly redevelops. So while brief and partial revivals do occur in Judges, none reach the full national status that is witnessed in the books of Ezra and Nehemiah. In fact, with each passing deliverance and departure, the condition of Israel grows darker, says J. N. Darby:

> Things have gone from bad to worse. There have been revivals, but still the same principle of unbelief; and the decay of each revival has marked increasing progress in evil and unbelief in proportion to the good which has been thus forsaken. The revival never reaches to the extent of laying hold of what God is, what He revealed Himself as at first from His people, what the first power of revelation and action of the Spirit. When departed from, God is more and more lost.[4]

This era of cyclic and progressive declension predates the time of the prophets, so there were no public calls to repentance or warnings of impending judgment. The long-suffering nature of God would be restrained for a time, but disciplinary judgment would ultimately occur in an attempt to recover His people. Jehovah was jealous for the hearts of His people who repeatedly forsook Him for idols. Yet, He did not forsake them – He sent judges to declare His forgiveness and to govern them in righteousness.

The Chronology of Judges

The following diagram shows major events occurring within five distinct timeframes during the era of the judges.[5]

Chronology of Judges Timeline
The five Indivisible Units of Chronology

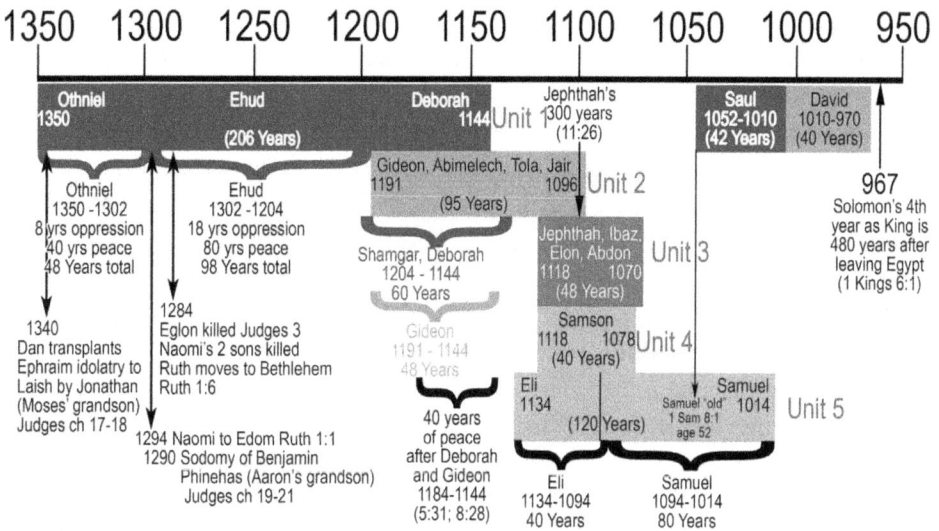

1350	1300	1250	1200	1150	1100	1050	1000	950

Othniel 1350	Ehud		Deborah 1144 Unit 1	Jephthah's 300 years (11:26)	Saul 1052-1010 (42 Years)	David 1010-970 (40 Years)

(206 Years)

Othniel 1350 -1302 8 yrs oppression 40 yrs peace 48 Years total	Ehud 1302 -1204 18 yrs oppression 80 yrs peace 98 Years total	Gideon, Abimelech, Tola, Jair 1191 1096 Unit 2 (95 Years)	967 Solomon's 4th year as King is 480 years after leaving Egypt (1 Kings 6:1)

Shamgar, Deborah 1204 - 1144 60 Years

Jephthah, Ibaz, Elon, Abdon Unit 3 1118   1070 (48 Years)

1340 Dan transplants Ephraim idolatry to Laish by Jonathan (Moses' grandson) Judges ch 17-18	1284 Eglon killed Judges 3 Naomi's 2 sons killed Ruth moves to Bethlehem Ruth 1:6

Gideon 1191 - 1144 48 Years

Samson 1118   1078 Unit 4 (40 Years)

1294 Naomi to Edom Ruth 1:1
1290 Sodomy of Benjamin
Phinehas (Aaron's grandson)
Judges ch 19-21

40 years of peace after Deborah and Gideon 1184-1144 (5:31; 8:28)

Eli 1134

Samuel "old" 1014 1 Sam 8:1 age 52

Samuel 1 Sam 8:1

Unit 5

(120 Years)

Eli 1134-1094 40 Years

Samuel 1094-1014 80 Years

The Problem With Moral Relativity

If moral reckoning is truly derived from developed self-preservation and self-propagating protocol, as evolution postulates, would not the same core of self-focused need be naturally relied on to resolve moral conflict with others? Would not selfishness, abuse of power, manipulation, and violence characterize conflict resolution? Furthermore, if survival is the chief incentive for morality, why would anyone want to show compassion to a retarded child, the elderly, the sick, the injured, the Orpahn, the handicapped, the widow, the poor, the defenseless, etc. *Survival of the fittest* is where moral relativity drives a society, the end result of which is either the Third Reich or social anarchy.

From the atheistic point of view, some actions, such as stealing or murder, may be socially unacceptable, but yet be determined necessary to better promote the survival of the species. So is it morally wrong to steal, or murder someone? Given the atheistic worldview, there is nothing intrinsically wrong with these behaviors – each act might be deemed necessary; whereas, absolute morality condemns both behaviors. It is wrong to steal or to murder.

It stands to reason, that from a theoretical standpoint, a society adhering to absolute moral reckoning rather than moral relativity would be characterized by less violence. If naturalism were true, more aggression would be expected in a society in which each individual pressed for his or her own personal security and survival over the well-being of others. If naturalism were not true, this realization may still be observed, for as a people ignore their moral programming (their consciences), that society will primarily be occupied with pursuing personal gain and selfish indulgences, rather than the good of others. In either case, moral inclinations where self is preeminent and the welfare of others is ignored will lead to the demise of a society, not to its beneficial development.

Historically speaking, this very situation occurred in the Jewish culture during the era of the Judges (11th to 15th century B.C.). After the conquest of Canaan, we read of a new generation which no longer knew or obeyed God. *"When all that generation had been gathered to their fathers, another generation arose after them who did not know the Lord nor the work which He had done for Israel. Then the children of Israel did evil in the sight of the Lord ... and they forsook the Lord God..."* (Judg. 2:10-12). What was the problem? The Jews rejected the divine moral commands imposed upon them and instead chose moral relativity as a guide; *"everyone did what was right in his own eyes"* (Judg. 17:6). Moses had sternly warned them not to do this just prior to their entrance into Canaan: *"You shall not at all do as we are doing here today – every man doing whatever is right in his own eyes – for as yet you have not come to the rest and the inheritance which the Lord your God is giving you"* (Deut. 12:8-10). The Israelites did not heed this warning and through disobedience eventually lost their rest in the land and then their inheritance of land.

Consequently, for several hundred years, the Jews were a splintered people, immorality and paganism were rampant, and they were regularly chastened by God (e.g., conquered and oppressed by other nations). The Bible warns, *"As righteousness leads to life, so he who pursues evil pursues it to his own death"* (Prov. 11:19). *"Righteousness exalts a nation, but sin is a reproach to any people"* (Prov. 14:34). Moral relativity devolves human society into chaos, while pursuing righteousness leads to prosperity – God's blessing.

Application for the Church

While the book of Judges clearly pertains to a specific time of moral relativity in Jewish history, there are important spiritual parallels that may be drawn with the spiritual wherewithal of God's people in the Church Age also. William Kelly encourages us to learn from these instructive lessons in Judges that we might find spiritual help in our present day also:

> The history records repeated instances of Jehovah's deliverances of His chosen people after their successive acts of disobedience to His precepts and departure from His worship. Though that dispensation differs from the present, God as God is unchanged; amid the brazen-faced apostasy and the spiritual lassitude of Christendom the faithful may count that God will as of old raise up some Gideon or Barak and give a season of reviving to those who wait upon His name, as indeed in His gracious sovereignty He has often done at intervals in the past history of His church on earth. The Book of Judges encourages the hope that He will do so again before its final days.[6]

Amen! And amen!

The Joshua-Judges Connection

The English words "rest" and "possession" are key words in Joshua and Judges. Before we can practically understand the meaning of divine rest, we first must understand how we acquire our divine inheritance. The words "possess," "possessed," and "possession" are found twenty-four times in Joshua and nine times in Judges. These references are mainly translated from two Hebrew words *yarash* and *achuzzah*. *Yarash* means "to occupy by expelling the previous tenants," while *achuzzah* conveys the thought of "something (especially land) seized for a possession." Two important lessons are conveyed through the usage of these two Hebrew words.

First, it is observed that *yarash* is found twenty-nine times in Joshua and twenty-seven times in Judges; the only Old Testament book with more occurrences is Deuteronomy. It is translated "to drive out" as well as "to possess." Joshua is the story of God's people relying on His grace to overcome what impedes them from possessing their God-given inheritance. The benefits of that inheritance were only obtained through faithful and obedient acquisition. This is likely why about half of the occurrences of *yarash* in Judges occur in the introduction (1:1-2:9), which recaps the warfare in Canaan after the tribal divisions of the land were complete.

For Christians, our inheritance is the sum total of the blessings of grace available in Christ, yet our possession of these blessings relates only to that portion we make our own. Accordingly, conflict is a necessary aspect of a believer's spiritual development and is inevitable on this side of heaven; it is the means of learning Christ and more intimately identifying with Him. The Kingdom of God advances as believers live for Christ, and they are rewarded accordingly – in this sense there is much ground to be gained.

Second, *achuzzah* occurs six times in Joshua; the only Old Testament books with more occurrences are Leviticus and Ezekiel. The usage of this word in Joshua occurs after chapter 20 (i.e. after the land had been seized by the Israelites from the inhabitants and was available for distribution). Believers must co-labor with the Lord to be victorious in spiritual conflict – we war in response to His wherewithal, not our own. Believers must remain active in faith to fully benefit from their spiritual blessings they already have in Christ. This is probably why *achuzzah* is not found in the book of Judges: the Israelites did not continue on with Jehovah to retain what they had already achieved through faith; in fact, much of it was lost. In summary, *yarash* is the inheritance to be possessed (i.e. labored for), while *achuzzah* is a possession we labor to keep and benefit from now. The Israelites strived to obtain the land (their inheritance) in the first twelve chapters of Joshua and were to continue toiling in faith to secure the life of rest God provided for them. The last twelve chapters of Joshua and the entire book of Judges documents the Israelites' failure to retain that rest.

The Hebrew words *nuwach* and *shaqat* are translated "rest" six times in Joshua to express the Israelites' overall existence of tranquility and peace, despite the necessity of further personal conflict in the land. *Nuwach* is rendered "rest" three times in Judges to convey the same sense of peaceful existence obtained after Jehovah lifted up faithful judges to militarily deliver His people from their oppressors. This restful quality of life was enjoyed by the two and half tribes who settled in the Eastern Plateau after Moses vanquished the warrior inhabitants (Josh. 1:13, 15). Later, rest was apprehended by the nation in general when the whole of Canaan had been conquered after seven years of conflict under Joshua's leadership (Josh. 14:15, 21:44, 22:4, 23:1). Thus, both Joshua and Judges declare that this inward spiritual tranquility of rest could only be realized when the Israelites exercised faith in Jehovah through active conquest.

By faith and obedience the land (their inheritance) was possessed; this accomplishment permitted them the opportunity for rest within the land. Yet, because of their disbelief, the rest Jehovah had for them was never fully realized and, in time, was lost completely (Heb. 4:4-6). Accordingly, the writer of Hebrews uses their failure as an exhortation: *"Let us therefore be diligent to enter that rest, lest anyone fall according to the same example of disobedience"* (Heb. 4:11-12). The matter of victorious living has not changed; continued faith and obedience ultimately translate into obtaining divine possessions and rest. Laboring without faith, or faith without labor, will never translate into divine conquest and spiritual peace, but will rather result in human failure and emotional anxiety.

This is the message conveyed to us in the Hebrew words relating to "possession" and "rest" in the books of Joshua and Judges. By faith and obedience God's people entered Canaan – their inheritance. They could not engage in conquest until they entered the land, they could not possess the land without conquest, and they could not enter God's rest in the land without first possessing it. In the Church Age, believers do not labor for a *place* of rest; our rest and inheritance are in a *Person – "Christ in heavenly places"* (Eph. 1:3). Accordingly, Paul could pray for fellow believers, *"The Lord of peace Himself give you peace in every way"* (2 Thess. 3:16) and also share his life's aspiration with them:

> *Not that I have already attained, or am already perfected; but I press on, that I may lay hold of that for which Christ Jesus has also laid hold of me. Brethren, I do not count myself to have apprehended; but one thing I do, forgetting those things which are behind and reaching forward to those things which are ahead, I press toward the goal for the prize of the upward call of God in Christ Jesus* (Phil. 3:12-14).

Christ is the believer's inheritance and resting place. The practical blessing of those present possessions granted the believer in Christ will be experienced through faith and obedience as one engages in active conquest and is enabled to do so by resurrection power.

There are but a few individuals who through faith and obedience experienced resurrection power throughout the book of Judges. In a book marked by intensifying darkness and spiritual declension, these frail instruments of God's sovereignty shine forth the power of God with tremendous brilliance. Their faith shines out from the shadowy gloom of religious apostasy. May it be so for believers trudging through these latter days of the Church Age, which, as we are told, will also be marked by a deepening darkness (2 Thess. 2:3).

Devotions in Judges

Warring in Review
Judges 1

Judges is a book with two introductions. The first (1:1-2:9) covers the time frame from the division of the land in the days of Joshua until the spiritual decline of the nation after his death. The second introduction (2:10-3:6) poses a theological evaluation of the spiritual state of the Jewish nation, the conclusion of which necessitates disciplinary action, and ushering in the era of the Judges.

The book commences with this statement: *"Now after the death of Joshua it came to pass that the children of Israel asked the Lord"* (v. 1). The phrase *"Israel asked the Lord"* is only found here in Scripture, though a similar expression of *"Israel ... asked counsel of God"* occurs later in Judges 20:18. A similar statement *"inquired of the Lord"* is also found in 1 and 2 Samuel and once in 1 Chronicles. What does *"Israel asked the Lord"* mean in verse 1? This proclamation likely refers to the high priest attempting to determine the mind of the Lord on a particular matter by using the Urim and Thummim, which were stored in his breastplate (Num. 27:21; Deut. 22:8-10). It is unknown how these two stones were actually used, but John Hannah provides the following insight:

> Apparently the Urim and Thummim were two stones. How they were used in determining God's will is unknown, but some suggest the Urim represented a negative answer and the Thummim a positive answer. Perhaps this view is indicated by the fact that Urim (*'urim*) begins with the first letter of the Hebrew alphabet, and Thummim (*tummim*) with the last letter. Others suggest that the objects simply symbolized the high priest's authority to inquire of God, or the assurance that the priest would receive enlightenment (Urim means

19

"lights") and perfect knowledge (Thummim means "perfections") from God.[1]

The high priest asking the Lord as to which tribe should go up first into battle (using the Urim and Thummim) would have been Eleazar. Although the first verse reads *"now after the death of Joshua,"* most of the military engagements recorded in the first introduction occurred before Joshua's death, meaning Eleazar was also still alive. For example, Caleb's seizing of Hebron from the Anakim and Othniel capturing Kirjath Sepher (vv. 9-15) were recorded in the book of Joshua (Josh. 15:13-17).

In reference to Caleb, H. L. Rossier notes the positive impact that one person with unweavering faith has on God's people as a whole:

> Individual faithfulness, even in the most corrupt days of the church, arouses and stimulates spiritual energy in others. Othniel, seeing Caleb's faith, is stirred up to act likewise. He serves his first campaign under him, and acquires for himself a good degree, for he becomes the first judge in Israel. But he is not satisfied with belonging to Caleb's family; he fights for the enjoyment of a new *relationship,* that of the bridegroom with the bride, and he gets Achsah to wife. Joshua 15 relates the fact in the same terms, for individual faith enjoys the same privileges as fully in a time of declension as in the brightest day of the church's history. The church has been unfaithful and has lost the sense of her relationship with Him, who, by His victory had acquired it for Himself; but this relationship may be known and enjoyed today in its fullness by everyone who is faithful.[2]

Judah, the strongest tribe, was to lead the effort to remove the pagans from their own inheritance; their resolve would hopefully encourage the other, weaker tribes to do the same (v. 2). The writer initiates the book on a positive note by detailing some of the successes that Judah had against the Canaanites after Joshua divided the land. Judah was the lion strategically position in the south to guard the nation against its enemies entering the interior. However, this acme is soon marred, for the narrative records that the remaining tribes, except for Simeon who cooperated with Judah, fail to drive the inhabitants from their possessions (vv. 21-36).

While Judah did obey the Lord's command to confront the Canaanites, their request for help from Simeon, who was positioned within their borders, indicates that their faith in Jehovah was somewhat lacking. Brethren working harmoniously together is an expression of God's own character (John 17:20-23); however, if the Lord's people become dependent on each other, instead of the Lord, in executing their calling, failure in some measure is assured. Judah knew that they had been chosen to initiate the confrontation with the Canaanites and instead of fully trusting the Lord, they requested Simeon assist them. Thus, the first step towards national declension, after Joshua divided the land into tribal possessions, was doubt. As shown in this chapter, skepticism in God's wherewithal is often exhibited through self-sufficiency and rationalizing disobedience.

The Israelites had already learned the disastrous consequences of self-sufficiency in their first confrontation at Ai – their only military defeat in seven years of armed conflict in Canaan. Though Simeon helped Judah (v. 3) and Judah assisted Simeon (v. 17) in confronting the Canaanites in their associated inheritances, they experienced restrained success. Limited faith and partial success walk together. Judah drove out the Canaanites in the mountains and hill country, but when it came to fighting the enemy on level ground, the iron chariots proved too much for them (v. 19). There was some success in overcoming the inhabitants of Jerusalem, which was in Benjamin's borders, but not against the Jebusites who resided there (vv. 8, 21). In fact, they would reside there for four more centuries until another with Caleb-like faith, David, a man after God's own heart, would drive them out.

When the faith of Caleb, who wholly followed the Lord, was exercised in battle, fortresses fell and giants fled (v. 20) – no one could withstand the power of God. But when the faith of God's people is weak, we magnify our difficulties, and not our opportunities. At such times, obstacles become stumbling stones, instead of stepping stones, and we settle for much less than what God desires us to achieve. In this case, Judah was satisfied to reside in the rugged hill country instead of the lush fertile valley. May God grant us grace to be victorious overcomers instead of content under-achievers.

One of the notable victories of Judah and Simeon was against Adoni-bezek and his army of ten thousand warriors (vv. 4-5). The battle was fought at Bezek and was a total success. Adoni-bezek, apparently the only survivor of the confrontation, tried to flee from the scene but was captured. He had previously fallen, cut off the thumbs and big toes of seventy Jewish rulers in the land and then forced them to grapple for scraps of food that had fallen from his table (v. 7). The Jews invoked "an eye for an eye, a foot for a foot, a hand for a hand" retribution (Ex. 21:24); Adoni-bezek lost his thumbs and big toes and was brought to Jerusalem (v. 6). He should have been put to death, but perhaps the Jews thought this ongoing humiliation would serve as a greater punishment. Adoni-bezek later died in Jerusalem.

From a practical standpoint, Adoni-bezek's presence in Jerusalem would have served as a good object lesson for the Jews to consider. Thumbs enable us to grasp things firmly and big toes enhance our upright balance while walking or standing. Without our thumbs we lose hold of what is important and without our big toes our walk is unsteady and marked by frequent falls. Believers should be careful not to loosen their hold on biblical truth to instead grip some new social fad or secular philosophy. To do so will hinder our walk with the Lord and cause us to fall into calamity. In considering the wisdom conveyed in Paul's writing, Peter further warns believers that:

> ... *untaught and unstable people twist to their own destruction, as they do also the rest of the Scriptures. You therefore, beloved, since you know this beforehand, beware lest you also fall from your own steadfastness, being led away with the error of the wicked; but grow in the grace and knowledge of our Lord and Savior Jesus Christ* (2 Pet. 3:16-18).

Growth and knowledge accompany our faithfulness which must abide in truth. May we be known by others as those who have a steady spiritual walk, as we go on with the Lord.

Like the tribe of Judah, the Ephraimites did not drive out the Canaanites from their possession – they elected not to obey God's directive. Instead, they sought to profit from their presence by enslaving the inhabitants of Gezer (v. 29; Josh. 16:10) and some of the Amorites in Aijalon and Shallbim (v. 35). This, however, proved to be a costly mistake, for in a few years these roles reversed and the Canaanites would enslave the Ephraimites (4:2). Their victory over the city of Bethel, formally called Luz, is highlighted in verses 22-26. Yet, *"the house of Joseph"* did not fully obey the Lord; they granted freedom to an informant and his family, who rebuilt the city of Luz in the land of the Hittites (v. 26). Letting the enemy escape to refortify himself is never a good idea; that is, when unjudged sin is permitted to survive, it must again be dealt with in a later day, but consequences to do so are greater.

Likewise, Manasseh failed to drive out the inhabitants of chief cities of Beth-shean, Taanach, Dor, Ibleam, and Megiddo and their surrounding towns (v. 27). They too were content to dwell among the Canaanites. Instead of swinging the ax to clear the forest and wielding the sword to appropriate their full possession as commanded by Joshua (Josh. 17:15-18), those in Ephraim and Manasseh thought it better to tolerate and profit by the Canaanites who resided within their territories. What often seems to be the path of least resistance at first becomes the hard and arduous way later; their decision to disobey God's command to drive out all the Canaanites would prove to have painful consequences in future years. May each of us do our best, showing diligence in our God-given duties and opportunities that we may be spared agonizing disappointments and repercussions later!

Zebulun did not drive out the Canaanites from Kitron and Nahalol, but rather enslaved these pagans for profit (v. 30). The tribe of Asher was also content to dwell among the Canaanites in their inheritance (vv. 31-32). Similarly, Naphtali did not drive them out of Bethshemesh and Bethanath, but rather put them to forced labor (v. 33). The tribe of Dan did not drive out the Amorites from their possession. In time, the Amorites became stronger and forced the Danites into the highlands, while they took possession of the fertile farmland in the valley (v. 34). Because of this situation, most of this tribe would later relocate in the far northern part of Canaan (chp. 18).

Moses had sternly warned his countrymen just prior to their entrance into Canaan as to what Jehovah wanted them to do and the consequences if they did not do it:

When you have crossed the Jordan into the land of Canaan, then you shall drive out all the inhabitants of the land from before you, destroy all their engraved stones, destroy all their molded images, and demolish all their high places; you shall dispossess the inhabitants of the land and dwell in it, for I have given you the land to possess. ... But if you do not drive out the inhabitants of the land from before you, then it shall be that those whom you let remain shall be irritants in your eyes and thorns in your sides, and they shall harass you in the land where you dwell (Num. 33:51-54, 56).

Sadly, while God's people are in a spiritually feeble state, the world has more power over them than His Word and promises do: *"When Israel was strong, they put the Canaanites to tribute,"* but that was ruling over for a time, not driving out for good. As a result of deficient faith and partial obedience, much of the Israelite inheritance in Canaan so diligently fought for in the days of Joshua was gradually lost during the era of the Judges. Matthew Henry reminds us that the same type of behavior and consequences still occur today during the Church Age.

The same unbelief that kept their fathers forty years out of Canaan, kept them now out of the full possession of it. Distrust of the power and promise of God deprived them of advantages, and brought them into troubles. Thus many a believer who begins well is hindered. His graces languish, his lusts revive, Satan supplies him with suitable temptations, and the world recovers its hold; he brings guilt into his conscience, anguish into his heart, discredit on his character, and reproach on the gospel. Though he may have sharp rebukes, and be so recovered that he does not perish, yet he will have deeply to lament his folly through his remaining days; and upon his dying bed to mourn over the opportunities of glorifying God and serving the church he has lost. We can have no fellowship with the enemies of God within us or around us, but to our hurt; therefore our only wisdom is to maintain unceasing war against them.[3]

Like the Israelites, when Christians choose to practically forfeit their acquired spiritual possessions in Christ, then the rest associated with those possessions also vanishes (Heb. 4:11). While spiritual declension is often a gradual evil, the world (under the devil's whim) eventually obtains the desired goal – to despoil the children of God of their inheritance, and thereby rendering them miserable and powerless.

How often this tragedy occurs today; the sin that Christians choose to tolerate and manage instead of mortifying grows stronger and, in time, ultimately becomes their master. If the Ephraimites knew their children would one day be slaves to the Gezerites, they would have certainly obeyed the Lord and removed them from their land. Instead, they suffered spiritual regression and the misery of it. H. L. Rossier summarizes the main aspects of this spiritual declension:

> In a word, we may say, *worldliness.* The heart, principles and walk are in unison with the world. This is invariably how declension begins, and we may well understand the "Take good heed to yourselves" in Joshua 23:11. How easily this snare might be avoided, if the hearts of God's children were upright before Him. But instead of dispossessing the Canaanites, Israel is afraid of them, tolerates them, and dwells with them. So, also, the Church, looked at as a whole, is allied with the world. Later on we shall see the disastrous results of this alliance. Suffice it for the present that God's Word establishes the fact, that Israel did not keep separate from the Canaanitish nations.[4]

Worldliness, inappropriate lusting, and self-reasoning will always be at odds with God's will for us (Gal. 5:17). This is one of the valuable lessons for us to learn from the book of Judges: *"For whatever things were written before were written for our learning, that we through the patience and comfort of the Scriptures might have hope"* (Rom. 15:4-5). May we count the cost of disobedience now: a ruined life and testimony and the suffering of future generations is much too high of a price tag.

Meditation

> When we walk with the Lord in the light of His Word,
> What a glory He sheds on our way!
> While we do His good will, He abides with us still,
> And with all who will trust and obey.
> Trust and obey, for there's no other way
> To be happy in Jesus, but to trust and obey.

> — John Sammis

Preamble to the Judges
Judges 2

Israel's spiritual declension was marked by their lack of separation from the world; they had neither the inclination nor power to drive out the enemy. It should be no surprise then that this chapter commences with a rebuke by "the Angel of the Lord" to the entire Jewish nation at Bochim:

Then the Angel of the Lord came up from Gilgal to Bochim, and said: "I led you up from Egypt and brought you to the land of which I swore to your fathers; and I said, 'I will never break My covenant with you. And you shall make no covenant with the inhabitants of this land; you shall tear down their altars.' But you have not obeyed My voice. Why have you done this? Therefore I also said, 'I will not drive them out before you; but they shall be thorns in your side, and their gods shall be a snare to you.'" So it was, when the Angel of the Lord spoke these words to all the children of Israel, that the people lifted up their voices and wept (vv. 1-4).

Two specific violations of the Law are mentioned: first, making covenants with the inhabitants of the land and second, not tearing down their pagan altars. The fact that the Lord does not mention the offense of intermarriages with the inhabitants of the land affirms the early date of this incident. That infraction of the Law is later addressed sometime after Joshua's death (3:6). Because Israel had not obeyed His commands, God would not drive out the inhabitants of the land as He had promised to do in return for their faithfulness. This statement caused the nation to weep before the Lord; ironically, Bochim means "weepers."

When God actually appears to someone, as in this instance in chapter 2, the event is referred to as a *theophany*, which means "God appearance." At such times, the Lord usually emerged as a normal-looking man, but on certain occasions He took other forms to accentuate His message. For example, the Lord spoke to Moses from a bush that appeared to be burning (Ex. 3), and to the Israelites from within a pillar of cloud (Ex. 13).

Whether in human form or in some unusual depiction, the One appearing was normally referred to as "the Angel of the Lord." The title is unique and should not be confused with the expression "an angel of the Lord," which may refer to the manifestation of one of many holy angels. Contextual observation confirms that appearances of "the Angel of the Lord" were *theophanies*. A theophany is a pre-incarnate visit of the second person of the Godhead to the earth as His Father's messenger. The English word "angel" is translated from the Hebrew word *malak* or the Greek word *angelos*; both words mean "messenger." The role of the Son in the Trinity is to do the Father's will, and part of that task involves communicating the Father's will to humanity. When the Son does this in the Old Testament, He is referred to as "the Messenger (Angel) of the Lord." Similarly, in the New Testament, the Son of God is called the Word (John 1:1; 1 Jn. 1:1); the Son became a man to bring the ultimate message of God to humanity. The Lord Jesus was a living message sojourning on the earth; He was both the message and the messenger of God.

In chapter 2, the Lord emerged from His spiritual realm to personally rebuke His people for their disobedience – the Israelites were not driving out the heathen inhabitants from their possession as He had commanded. This is the first of four theophanies in the book of Judges; the call of Gideon is the second (chp. 6), and then the Lord appeared twice to Manoah's wife and then Manoah on His second visit (chp. 13). The theophany in this chapter is unique in that the Lord appeared to and delivered a message to the entire Jewish nation, instead of just one or two individuals.

The divine Messenger confirmed His identity as the One who: had delivered the Israelites out of Egypt, had entered a covenant with them, and had also demanded their complete obedience. It is no accident that the Lord came up from Gilgal to Bochim to rebuke His people. In the spiritual sense, He had been waiting for them to return to Gilgal, but they had not. Gilgal is only mentioned twice in the opening chapters of Judges. This indicates that Jews were no longer aware of its spiritual significance and hence the reason for their own spiritual ineptness. The

Lord now journeyed from Gilgal to where His people were at, the place of weeping, to summon them back to their previous position of communion and power. Unfortunately, it is Bochim, and not Gilgal, which characterizes the book of Judges.

Israelites abode at Gilgal during the entire Canaan conquest led by Joshua. Gilgal, was the place of circumcision, which in type, symbolized the putting away of the flesh, a prerequisite for serving the Lord effectively in any dispensation (Col. 2:11). Gilgal was where God "rolled away" (the literal meaning of Gilgal) the reproach of the nation and began anew with His people after 39 years of aimless wandering. The spiritual benefits gained at Gilgal were the reason for their success in Canaan; the Lord now reminded them of that fact. To enjoy God's blessing, His people must remember and act upon what they previously learned at Gilgal.

Joshua did not mention this national gathering at Bochim in his book, but it may have coincided with one of two final appeals to his countrymen just prior to his death (Josh. 23-24). The location of the Joshua 23 assembling is not stated, but was most likely Shiloh, as the tabernacle was located there; the gathering of Joshua 24 was at Shechem. As the only biblical reference to Bochim is in chapter 2, there are not sufficient references to pinpoint its location. G. F. Moore associates Bochim with Shiloh, while others believe Bochim to be synonymous with Bethel or a location near Bethel.[1] Shiloh lies about ten miles north of Bethel in Ephraim's inheritance.

More important than Bochim's actual location is what the conjunction of Gilgal and Bochim teach us in the spiritual sense. Bochim characterizes the often desperate and sorrowful life resulting from inconsistent faithfulness and worldliness in the book of Judges, whereas Gilgal symbolizes the victorious life of faith which is apart from the world and has no confidence in the flesh. Samuel Ridout elaborates on this symbolic message for all believers:

> God was abiding at Gilgal. He had not moved His abiding place. He was there to meet Israel, the moment they would come to Him. God still abides at Gilgal. He still abides at the place that speaks of the death of Christ as applied to us; and if we want to know in its fullness what it is to have to do with God, we have got to do with Him at Gilgal. ... Oh! how sweet is the cross of Christ! It is the cross that has given you peace with God. It is the cross that we dwell upon every

first-day. It is the badge of our eternal salvation. Are you afraid of the cross? You need be no more afraid of the cross for your pathway, than you are for your salvation.

But the people in Judges are not ready to meet God there. So, in His grace, the angel of the Lord comes up from Gilgal, where God is, from where, I might say, He has an appointment to meet His people, and where he is ever ready to meet them. He comes up to a far different place. Notice that little word "up." It marks the distance between Gilgal and Bochim, and shows the difference between them. The place of lowliness has been forsaken, and high ground and a lofty attitude has been assumed. Ah, it is only too easy, whether as individuals or corporately, to make this ascent. Spiritual pride and self-confidence are in it. There are knives but no bitter tears at Gilgal.[2]

After the Angel of the Lord delivered His rebuke, the Israelites offered sacrifices to Jehovah and then Joshua dismissed the people to possess their inheritance (vv. 5-6).

While Joshua and the elders who outlived him were alive, the Jewish nation refrained from idolatry. These had witnessed *"all the great works of the Lord"* that He had performed on behalf of their nation (v. 7). While the older generation did worship Jehovah, they apparently failed to teach their children about Him, His works, and His commandments, for the next generation *"did not know the Lord, nor the work which He had done for Israel"* (v. 10), *"did evil in the sight of the Lord"* (v. 11), and *"forsook the Lord, and served Baal and Ashtoreths"* (v. 13). Verse 11 begins the actual record of what happened to the nation after the death of Joshua.

Just prior to their entrance into Canaan, Moses solemnly warned the Israelites not to do what they were now doing:

Take heed to yourselves, lest you forget the covenant of the Lord your God which He made with you, and make for yourselves a carved image in the form of anything which the Lord your God has forbidden you. For the Lord your God is a consuming fire, a jealous God (Deut. 4:23-24).

As a result of their idoltary, the Lord's anger burned hot against His people and He delivered them into the hands of "spoilers" (v. 14).

During these periods of chastening, Jehovah would not enable His people to overcome their enemies, but rather they would be conquered, distressed, and enslaved (vv. 14-15). C. A. Coates suggests that believers in the Church Age have the same propensity to forget the works of God and to serve Baal:

> An idol is a master; Baal means master or possessor. The question is, Who is my master? Who possesses me? It is easy to be possessed by the desire to make money. A man who is devoting his energies to making money is a worshipper of Baal; he is serving Baal. This book shows us how easy it is to come under idolatrous influence. It is very solemn that Paul should say to the Corinthians, those in the assembly participating in privileges outwardly: "Some have not the knowledge of God; I speak to your shame." They had fallen under the power of the enemy. If we walk in self-judgment we shall not fall under any influence which is adverse to God, but, if we do not judge ourselves, we shall. We all have to learn to refuse the things that appeal to us.[3]

To this end, believers would do well to observe the progression in verses 10-14: To deny God's Lordship in practice, or to depreciate His past goodness through forgetfulness, can easily result in forsaking Him altogether and engaging in that which He hates.

After His people cried out in repentance, the Lord would show mercy by raising up judges to deliver them; this would conclude a period of chastening and usher in a season of rest (v. 16). The Lord foretold them of their return to spiritual corruption after the death of a delivering judge and also His renewed chastening until the process of repentance and rescue would be repeated again (v. 17). Why would the Lord choose to intervene at such times to deliver His people? It was because His compassion could no longer endure the groanings of His people (v. 18). Yet, even after experiencing the tender mercies of God, the next generation would regress back into idolatry and again prompt His chastening hand:

> *And it came to pass, when the judge was dead, that they reverted and behaved more corruptly than their fathers, by following other gods, to serve them and bow down to them. They did not cease from their own doings nor from their stubborn way (v. 19).*

30

Why does this cycle of **rebellion (sin)**, **retribution (suffering)**, **repentance (supplication)**, **rescue (salvation)**, and **rest (security)** continue throughout the book of Judges? It was necessary because the Jews *"did not cease from their own doings nor from their stubborn way."* They were a stiffed-necked people, but they were the Lord's people and He loved them too much to let them go their own way. Pondering the practical ramification of the text, F. C. Jennings sounds the alarm for the second generation of believers:

> Does it not add a kind of extra solemnity to our lot if we are living after a "first generation" has passed away? Does it not give stronger grounds for heart searching; for strong crying to God; for increased watchfulness; for clustering together in mutual love and exhortation?[4]

The interim between the division of the land and Joshua's death had been characterized by rest. There were certainly regions in the land that remained unconquered, but apparently the Canaanites had no stomach for waging war with the Israelites after seven years of being trounced. Their resolve to fight, at least for the present time, had waned. Jehovah had defeated the main forces of the Canaanites (Josh. 23:3-4), but had allowed pockets of resistance to remain in the land to test His people (vv. 20-23). F. C. Cook offers some assistance in following the chronology of events through this portion of the chapter:

> Verse 20 is connected with verse 13. The intermediate verses refer to much later times; they have the appearance of being the reflections of the compiler interspersed with the original narrative. But Judges 2:20 catches up the thread only to let it fall immediately. All that follows, down to the end of Judges 3:7, seems to be another digression, closing with words like those of Judges 2:13.[5]

Verse 22 explains why the Lord permits His people to experience trials and to be tested, He must know if *"they will keep the ways of the Lord ... or not."* Each tribe and clan would be responsible for cleansing the remaining inhabitants from their possession. If the Jews would be faithful to confront them, the Lord would prove Himself a noble ally by driving their enemies from the land (Josh. 23:5). If, however, His people settled into a peaceful coexistence with their pagan neighbors, there would be drastic consequences ahead – thus, the record of Judges.

31

God longs to labor with His people to accomplish the impossible for His glory, but if His people do not desire to work with Him for this cause, He has ways of making them wish they had!

Meditation

Does it grieve you, my friends, that the name of God is being taken in vain and desecrated? Does it grieve you that we are living in a godless age?... But we are living in such an age and the main reason we should be praying about revival is that we are anxious to see God's name vindicated and His glory manifested. We should be anxious to see something happening that will arrest the nations, all the peoples, and cause them to stop and to think again.

— D. Martyn Lloyd Jones

Idolatry Ensures Slavery
Judges 3:1-7

We are told twice in the first four verses that God allowed a contingency of Canaanites to remain in the land after the main conquest under Joshua's leadership was complete in order to "test" the resolve of His people. Would they obey His commandment to rid the land of the remaining pagans? God had made an unconditional promise to Abraham to build up a nation in His name and He was bound by the power of His name to keep it. Yet, God is able to accomplish His word and still test and prove each generation in the corridors of time leading to culmination of His promise. Each generation will either have His blessing or judgment depending upon their obedience or disobedience, respectively, to His revealed will.

For example, God gave Noah a token of His new covenant with humanity, the rainbow, which is a product of both storm and light and is hung in heaven for all to see and appreciate. Thus, the rainbow is a portrait of God's unfailing grace during times of testing. To the believer, God's grace and peace settle our hearts during life's storms – for He will not test us above what we are able to bear without providing the way of escape (1 Cor. 10:13). To the unbeliever, the rainbow is an invitation to find peace with God and escape the wrath to come: *"For the grace of God that brings salvation has appeared to all men"* (Tit. 2:11). Thus, testing is a normal part of the Christian experience; testing shows us where we are at spiritually (God already knows), it builds up our faith, and also declares the grace of God to those who need to experience it. Practically speaking, faith cannot be trusted unless it has been tested; character cannot be validated until circumstances verify it. How else do we really know what is in our heart? So, by the remaining Canaanites, Jehovah would test the faithfulness of His people (vv. 1, 4).

Unfortunately, after Joshua died, the Levites apparently quit instructing the people and parents became apathetic in teaching God's

Law to their children. As a result, the Jews comfortably dwelt alongside the Canaanites, Hittites, Amorites, Perizzites, and Hivites (v. 5). In time, their complacency led to compromise and they disobeyed God's command forbidding intermarriage with the heathen of the land (v. 6). The Jews' comfort, complacency, and compromise then resulted in carnality – and the next generation forsook the Lord and embraced the false gods of the land (v. 7). Centuries later, John would remind the Church of this hazard: impurity and immorality are strongly connected with idolatry; therefore, *"keep yourselves from idols"* (1 Jn. 5:19, 21). What controls the affection of one's heart will determine his or her conduct.

Hence we see in the opening pages of Judges a principle which is paramount throughout Scripture: Separation from evil is fundamental, and nothing can be maintained for God except on that basis. God's people dwelt among the Canaanites instead of driving them out of their inheritance and in time developed social connections with them. The longer such associations with the world remain, the less God's people think about their separation inwardly, and eventually they open the door to what God hates outwardly.

The aftermath of Joshua's death illustrates the fallacy of depending upon any spiritual influence outside the family to maintain your family's spiritual welfare. How did God respond to His people's departure from Him to embrace other gods?

> *Now these are the nations which the Lord left, that He might test Israel by them, that is, all who had not known any of the wars in Canaan (this was only so that the generations of the children of* **Israel** *might be taught to know war, at least those who had not formerly known it)* (Judg. 3:1-2).

God seized the role of the parent in order to teach the new generation about Himself. He loves His people too much to leave them void of truth and the knowledge of His presence. What was God's instrument for making His presence known? The disciplinary rod of military invasion and conquest. Israel did not remember God's awesome means of delivering them from slavery and from Egypt, so God used death, invasion, and servitude to awaken them again to His presence and their essential need of depending on Him. All this occurred because the Levites and the parents failed to instruct the

34

children of Israel in the ways of the Lord. Instead of driving out the heathen from their possession through direct conflict, they became content to dwell among them – they regressed from active duty to willful concession. Jehovah would force them to reengage the enemy; spiritual warfare is an inescapable ongoing reality for God's people in any dispensation.

What is the lesson in this for us? In the New Testament, Paul used Israel's past foolishness as an object lesson to teach the Corinthian believers about proper behavior. He warns, *"now these things were our examples"* (1 Cor. 10:6); Christians should learn from the mistakes of Israel. Human history inevitably repeats itself when man fails to acquire wisdom from his past failures. Children must be trained up for the Lord.

This means that Christians are not to neglect the assembling of themselves in the local church; this is where the Word of God is to be administered (1 Cor. 14:22-31; Heb. 10:25). The Lord Jesus Christ has provided the Church with teachers and the indwelling Holy Spirit to guide believers into a deeper understanding of divine truth. Christian parents must know the Lord and His Word to properly teach their children to know and love Him too. The Bible should never be neglected, but rather should be the rulebook for all family matters.

A Christian family is not a household of Christians, but a Christian household. It is more than Christ dwelling within the hearts of family members; it is a family that is pursuing the heart of God. If the Bible is not at the center of family life and all home affairs, that home cannot be called a true Christian home.

Untrained children, not surprisingly, remain foolish (Prov. 22:15) and predictably absorb from outside influences what seems appropriate to fill their void of understanding. Children are natural sponges: they are compelled to learn and to develop an understanding of the world in which they live. The next generation in Israel did not know God, so they embraced false gods, and God had to judge His covenant people – a bitter chastening resulted because the parents neglected to raise spiritual children.

The same travesty is occurring today. *What* our children are being taught will directly affect their understanding of God and, consequently, the course of our nation, and even more importantly, how God regards this country. *Who* is training our children directly impacts *what* they are being taught. God's choice instruments to train children are their parents (Prov. 22:6; Eph. 6:1-4). Our children must know God. The Jews painfully learned that the Lord was faithful to demonstrate His presence to their children despite their parental negligence.

Although, as a nation, God's covenant people would repeatedly stray from God's Law through the centuries, the prophet Ezekiel informs us that during the Millennial Kingdom of Christ this will not be the case. The Levites will again teach their brethren God's Word and, through the power of the Holy Spirit, they will never abandon it again (Ezek. 44:23-24). This reminds us of the statement: *"For the gifts and the calling of God are irrevocable"* (Rom. 11:29); His calling for the Levites to establish His Word in the land of Israel will ultimately be fulfilled. May we parents likewise fulfill our divine calling and train up our children for the Lord now.

The Lord punished His people by permitting Cushan-Rishathaim, the king of Mesopotamia, to enslave the children of Israel for eight years. Cushan-Rishathaim's name means "doubly wicked one." Why would God use such a wicked king to punish His people? Centuries later, the prophet Habakkuk had a similar quandary when God informed him that He would use the wicked Babylonians to severely chasten His people for their idolatry (Hab. 1:6). Habakkuk reasoned that even in their backsliding, the Jewish people were more righteous than the Babylonians (Hab. 1:13).

Understanding God's response to Habakkuk's question is foundational to comprehending the workings of God among humanity. He told the prophet, *"The just shall live by faith"* (Hab. 2:4). This verse is repeated three times in the New Testament (Rom. 1:17; Gal. 3:11; Heb. 10:38) and conveys one of the central themes of the Bible. It suffices here to say that trusting in God and His Word results in life and that pride and rebellion lead to death. The lesson for Habakkuk was not to trust in his feelings or emotions, but rather to have faith in God's choices and doings: God would chasten Judah, judge Babylon, and in the process exalt His great name in all the earth. The greatest good is accomplished when man lives by faith and trusts God with his fate – this would be the lesson God would repeatedly teach His people in Judges.

Meditation

God is most glorified in us when we are most satisfied in Him.

— John Piper

Faith does not eliminate questions. But faith knows where to take them.

— Elisabeth Elliot

Othniel, Ehud, and Shamgar
Judges 3:8-31

Before introducing the first judge of Israel, an important observation as to how God works among His covenant people during this apathetic time of declension should be noted. When the spiritual vitality of God's people is of a pitifully low condition, God usually responds by using instruments which in themselves are imperfect and weak. H. L Rossier summarizes this observation in connection with some of the Judges:

> Othniel sprang from a younger branch of the family; he was *"the son of Kenaz, Caleb's younger brother."* Ehud was weak through his infirmity, Shamgar through his weapon, Deborah from her sex, Barak by his natural character, Gideon on account of his relations, Jephthah by his birth (he was the son of a harlot).[1]

The point is that God's people were no longer beneficiaries of His goodness as in the days of Joshua. At that time, God's energizing power was evident in faithful men, such that there was no need for the weakness of the vessels to be known. Such was the outshining of God's goodness through the apostles in the infancy of the Church Age. William Kelly further elaborates on this principle and its application to our present day:

> This feature [using imperfect and weak instruments], however, belongs characteristically to the ways of God in a broken state of things. The instrument that He employs when His people are fallen is not according to the same pattern as when all things are orderly in His sight. In short, when the people of God depart from Him, He marks it, not by withholding a deliverer, but by the kind of deliverance given them. I am persuaded that there is a fitness in His choice of instruments, and that the same men that He employed, say, to found and form the Church, are not of the class which suits His thoughts

38

when all things are fallen into confusion. When the Church was brought into being, when the ecclesiastical air was clear and bright, then it was simply a question of God working by the Holy Spirit upon earth in answer to the glory of Christ in heaven; then He raised up witnesses in accordance with the glory of Christ and the reality of His victory as man over Satan, as well as of His love in caring for His body, the Church. When on the contrary the Christian profession had quite failed as a witness to Him, there could not but be God's answer to the cries of distress that went up from His saints; but none the less has each instrument a marked weakness in some particular or other.[2]

It should then be no surprise that God may use those of less than admirable character, but yet have faith to accomplish feats of sovereign grace during this present day of ruined testimony.

Accordingly, in Judges, the frailty and imperfections of those whom God would use to reveal His glory is normally quantified prior to His using them. This practice would illustrate to the Israelites that they were never too low nor too far gone to receive God's help. The Lord is quite able to use *"the things which are not, to bring to nothing the things that are"* (1 Cor. 1:28). This idea epitomizes God's method for delivering His distraught people from oppression after they repented of their waywardness. The power was from above, not in the instrument itself, and it was thus available for anyone exercising genuine faith in Jehovah.

The First Judge - Othniel

After eight years of servitude, God called Othniel, the son-in-law and nephew of Caleb, to be a judge and deliverer of Israel (v. 9). Being a man of faith and courage, it was no doubt challenging for Othniel and his wife Achsah (Caleb's daughter) to see God's people suffer in disbelief and then walk with them in their affliction, but he did so patiently. He knew that until the hearts of his people were exercised to repentance, any effort to avert their chastening would be meaningless. Othniel had a good example of lingering patience in such matters; his uncle Caleb faithfully endured a similar situation for forty years before revival came. The faithful must learn to wait with God for those who have lost their way to return to the path of righteousness and of faith.

Othniel means "the lion of God," an indication that the power of God would be with him. He is the first person in Scripture of whom it is said *"the Spirit of Jehovah"* came upon him. Empowered by the Holy Spirit, Othniel led the Jews into victorious battle against the Mesopotamians (v. 10). Afterwards the Jews enjoyed forty years of rest under his leadership (v. 11). This forty-year period would be a time of testing for God's covenant people – would they remain loyal to Jehovah after experiencing His divine deliverance from their oppressors? As long as the energy of faith and the good moral condition of the people remained, the enemy was held in check.

In general, the number forty is used in Scripture to represent *probation* and *testing*, which explains its frequent occurrence. At times, God extended the nation of Israel forty-year probationary periods to test or prove them: The Israelites were tested in the wilderness forty years before Jehovah brought them into Canaan (Deut. 8:2-5). He sent the prophet Jeremiah to call them to repentance for forty years before expelling them from Canaan because of their deep-seated idolatry. During the era of the judges, God's people would enjoy forty years of rest while Othniel, then Barak, and then Gideon judged Israel (v. 11, 5:31, 8:28).

The Second Judge - Ehud

Unfortunately, after the days of Othniel, *"Israel did evil again in the sight of the Lord"* – they again flunked the test (v. 12). Jehovah responded by strengthening Eglon, the king of Moab, who solicited the help of Ammon and Amalek to invade Canaan (v. 13). The Jews were defeated; the city of the palm trees, Jericho, was seized (v. 14). It is striking that the king of Moab barely enters the territory of God's people, but yet is able to hold and control them from that location for 18 years. Jericho is a place of fragrance and attraction, and represents the world, the very first enemy that Joshua had to conquer after entering Canaan.

Now, the people of God were again being controlled by the enemy located at Jericho. Yet, the Jews responded appropriately to God's chastening via the Moabites:

> But when the children of Israel cried out to the Lord, the Lord raised up a deliverer for them: Ehud the son of Gera, the Benjamite, a left-handed man. By him the children of Israel sent tribute to Eglon king of Moab. Now Ehud made himself a dagger (it was double-edged and

a cubit in length) and fastened it under his clothes on his right thigh (vv. 15-16).

The Word of God is likened to a sharp sword several times in Scripture (e.g., Eph. 6:17; Heb. 4:12). Hence, it would seem a legitimate application to apply the imagery in this situation, for Ehud told Eglon, *"I have a message from God for you"* (v. 20). It was of the pointed kind. Ehud, whose name means "praise" was the son of Gera, meaning "meditation." When God's people engage in proper meditation and praise, the Eglons of the world fall prey to the two-edged sword (i.e., the proper application of God's Word). The unregenerate may mock the Word of God because they do not understand that it is a living sword. But be faithful to keep skillfully poking them with it; eventually they will get the point. The fact that God would use a left-handed man from the smallest tribe to deliver Israel again shows His ability to use the weak and foolish things of the world to demonstrate His power.

It is somewhat ironic that Israel, in their miserable state, sends the very one whom God was about to employ as their deliverer, to deliver their tribute to King Eglon. The tribute confirmed Israel's loyal subjection to the one who had dominion over them. How many resources, abilities, and spiritual gifts in the Church today through disobedience and faithlessness are being willfully surrendered to one who longs to have dominion over such things? The many Eglons in the devil's domain will always attempt to rob God of the glory due His name. This can be accomplished by seizing whatever wherewithal God's people have to worship and serve Him. Though Israel was content to be under Eglon's dominion, there was one man of faith who was not, Ehud.

Ehud fashioned a foot-and-a-half-long two-edged dagger and secured it to his right thigh under his raiment (v. 16). He entered into King Eglon's presence with others who bore him the heavy tribute, paid the tribute, and then departed from Eglon. After reaching the sculptured stones at Gilgal, he allowed his fellow countrymen to continue their journey home, but he turned back to visit Eglon again (vv. 17-18). These "graven images" (ASV) at Gilgal were a well-known landmark which may have been connected with the memorial of twelve stones Joshua erected there years earlier after crossing the

Jordan River. If so, this would have been a lovely reminder of what resurrection power can accomplish in God's people through faith.

By turning back, Ehud's plan accomplished two things: First, it would save the lives of his companions if his assassination plan was discovered. Second, because the tribute had already been paid, it would appear Ehud's second appearance was of a genuine nature. He was likely searched by Eglon's guards before coming into Eglon's presence to pay the tribute; perhaps they were not as diligent the second time. In any case, right-handed soldiers normally secured their swords to their left leg, thus Ehud's dagger was not discovered and he was able to come armed into the king's presence on a "secret errand" (v. 19).

King Eglon told Ehud to remain silent until all of his attendants were removed from his summer parlor, to ensure privacy (v. 20). It was at this time that Ehud delivered his message from the Lord: he rose from his seat and thrust the entire dagger into Eglon's belly (v. 21). Because he was a very fat man, the hilt of the dagger was swallowed up in the folds of fat, so that Ehud could not withdraw the dagger (v. 22). Ehud then departed the parlor and locked the door behind him (v. 23). Finding the door locked, Eglon's servants chose not to disturb the king, believing that privacy was desired; this delay permitted Ehud to escape to Seirah (vv. 24-26). Eventually, Eglon's servants discovered their slain king, while at the same time Ehud was blowing a trumpet to rally the Jews in Ephraim; he then led an attack against the unsuspecting Moabites (v. 27). Ehud's battle cry was *"follow after me, the Lord has delivered your enemies"* (v. 28). The Lord was with His people and they slew ten thousand valiant men of Moab and under Ehud's leadership that region of Israel enjoyed rest for eighty years (vv. 29-30).

The Third Judge - Shamgar

One verse introduces us to Shamgar and also describes his doings:

After him was Shamgar the son of Anath, who killed six hundred men of the Philistines with an ox goad; and he also delivered Israel (v. 31).

Some commentators refer to Shamgar as a "minor judge," while others hold to the position that his story was added to the text sometime later, thus implying that he was not a judge at all. However, C. T. Lacey reminds us to be careful in undermining the value of another's ministry in the kingdom of God:

> It is as well that the assessment of a believer's service does not rest in the distorted and ill-formed opinions of men, but in the righteous estimate of the Lord! Whatever unjustified conclusions men might have reached in relation to Shamgar, the record of Scripture remains, *"he also delivered Israel"* (v. 31). His achievements for the Lord have an abiding message of encouragement for all servants of the Lord.[3]

How long the Lord used Shamgar to oversee the Lord's people after conquering the Philistines in the far west is not known, nor do we know what region of Israel he resided over as judge. What is revealed is that one man empowered by the Spirit of God used an ox goad, an instrument used to herd animals, to defeat six hundred Philistine soldiers. F. Duane Lindsey describes for us what an ancient ox goad looked like: "His [Shamgar's] weapon was a sharp metal-tipped stick about 8 or 10 feet long used to direct animals. The other end usually had a chisel-like blade for cleaning a blow."[4] Whether he used this crude weapon to fight all six hundred Philistines at once or during the period of his judgeship is unknown.

Later in the book we will find Samson slaying a thousand Philistines with the jawbone of an ass (chp. 15). Jehovah had already demonstrated at the fall of Jericho that His ways were not man's ways. As previously mentioned, the Lord often uses what is deemed feeble and indeed laughable to confound the might and intelligence of men. God was teaching His people not to rely on their physical strength to conquer their enemies, but rather His. Paul explains why the Lord chooses to work this way to accomplish the spectacular:

> But God has chosen the foolish things of the world to put to shame the wise, and God has chosen the weak things of the world to put to shame the things which are mighty; and the base things of the world and the things which are despised God has chosen, and the things which are not, to bring to nothing the things that are, **that no flesh should glory in His presence** (1 Cor. 1:26-30).

It makes no sense to use an ox goad to fight men armed with shields, spears, and swords, yet that was what God used to accomplish the spectacular. This would serve to keep His people humble and to incite fear in their enemies. The Israelites would repeatedly learn in the era of the judges that the land was a gift from God that had been received by faith and must be maintained in faith; it could not be conquered through human effort.

As believers in the Church Age, we too must realize that all our engagements with the enemy are the Lord's battles. We have no strength against the devil, other than what the Lord provides. Thus, we need a supernatural work of God's grace in our lives to pull down the strongholds in our minds and overcome the enemy's evil tactics and power against us:

> *For though we walk in the flesh, we do not war according to the flesh. For the weapons of our warfare are not carnal but mighty in God for pulling down strongholds, casting down arguments and every high thing that exalts itself against the knowledge of God, bringing every thought into captivity to the obedience of Christ* (2 Cor. 10:3-5).

Though Paul is speaking to the Corinthians about the threat of being mastered by false teachers, the provision of deliverance he mentions has much broader ramifications. John highlights this wonderful principle in his first epistle: *"For whatever is born of God overcomes the world. And this is the victory that has overcome the world – our faith. Who is he who overcomes the world, but he who believes that Jesus is the Son of God?"* (1 Jn. 5:4-5). Though there will be satanic opposition to hinder the work of God that we are engaged in, the solution is before us. In faith, the Israelites daily marched around Jericho until God miraculously delivered the city into their hands. In faith, David ran towards an armored giant with a sling and five stones. In faith, Shamgar charged six hundred Philistines with an ox goad. These victories and more were not accomplished through carnal weapons of war, but in divine response by faith and obedience to God's Word. This is the pathway to victorious Christian living!

Meditation

Don't be surprised if there is an attack on your work, on you who are called to do it, on your innermost nature – the hidden person of the heart. It must be so. The great thing is not to be surprised, nor to count it strange – for that plays into the hand of the enemy. Is it possible that anyone should set himself to exalt our beloved Lord and not instantly become a target for many arrows? The very fact that our work depends utterly on Him and can't be done for a moment without Him calls for a very close walk and a constant communion of spirit. This alone is enough to account for anything the enemy can do ... Don't be surprised if you suffer. It is part of the way of the cross ... So rejoice! You are giving Him what He asks you to give Him: the chance to show you what He can do.

— Amy Carmichael

Deborah and Barak
Judges 4

Up until this juncture, the judges have been in southern Canaan; now the focus switches to the northern tribes. Israel again did evil in the sight of the Lord after Ehud died (v. 1). God responded by permitting the Canaanite nations to unify and come to power under the leadership of Jabin; Sisera was Jabin's captain of the Canaanite army (v. 2). The Canaanites severely oppressed God's covenant people for twenty years. Because they possessed sophisticated weapons of warfare, i.e., iron chariots, the Israelites saw no possibility of overcoming their oppressors except through supernatural deliverance – thus they cried out to the Lord (v. 3).

Apparently, there was no man in all of Israel with the faith to step forward and be used of God to remedy the situation. However, there was a woman of faith, Deborah, who was deeply grieved over the humiliating condition of God's people. Deborah was not the choice vessel for the task at hand, but she was available and willing and God therefore used her in such a way to deliver His people and also rebuke the men of Israel for their shallow confidence in Him.

Deborah's name means "a bee" and she lived up to her name – there was nothing half-hearted about her. She was an industrious woman, who through tirelessly caring for her people had gained their respect and admiration. However, as H. L. Rossier surmises, Deborah knew that "it would be to the *shame* of the leaders in Israel, that God should entrust a post of public activity to a woman in their midst. She says to Barak: "I will surely go with thee."[1] So in God's solution, He would use a wise, courageous woman who was already providing counsel and direction to the nation as a catalyst to stir up faith in others that Israel might experience deliverance.

We read in verse 4 that *"Deborah, a prophetess, the wife of Lapidoth judged Israel at that time"* (v. 4). There are other

46

prophetesses noted in the Bible: Miriam (Ex. 15:20), Huldah (2 Kgs. 22:14), Anna (Luke 2:36), and the four daughters of Philip (Acts 21:9). The Lord did not often use a woman to express His mind to His people, but sporadically did so in times of spiritual declension, usually as a means to awaken men of their lack of spiritual fortitude in fulfilling their God-given role as leaders. Such was the situation in Israel at this time. Scripture records that Deborah was the wife of Lapidoth. C. A. Coates suggests that this shows that Deborah recognized proper headship in the things of God:

> Any vessel raised up of God would recognize divine order. God could not raise up a prophetess to traverse His own order. If the Lord gives prominence to a woman, she will be prominent in a way suitable to the position, and will recognize headship.[2]

Deborah was not a presumptuous woman; she knew her proper place, but also understood God's ways when His people were in a desperate way. She did not sit, as rulers often did, at the gate of a city, (i.e., in a place of public prominence) to serve the Lord, but rather remained at home.

Additionally, we learn that Deborah abode in Mount Ephraim under a palm tree (v. 5). She lived between Ramah, which means "high places," and Bethel, "the house of God." The narrative provides a symbolic pattern for how spiritual battles must be fought. Paul states that "the house of God" in the Church Age is composed of all believers (1 Tim. 3:15), who during their earthly sojourn must boldly approach Christ in the heavenlies to receive resources to engage the darkness of this world and the wickedness in high places (Eph. 1:3, 3:10, 6:12). Only then can we be *"strong in the Lord and in the power of His might"* (Eph. 6:10). Deborah was heavenly-minded, an overcomer in Canaan, which means "lowland"; she appropriately dwelt in the "high position" that all believers should, under a palm tree, which signifies victory.

Deborah's entire ministry was centered at home, both in caring for her family and in helping her people. She did not abandon this sphere of responsibility; the people came to her for wisdom. One day Deborah summons Barak, the son of Abinoam **to come to her,** for she had a message for him from the Lord:

> *"Has not the Lord God of Israel commanded, 'Go and deploy troops at Mount Tabor; take with you ten thousand men of the sons of Naphtali and of the sons of Zebulun; and against you I will deploy Sisera, the commander of Jabin's army, with his chariots and his multitude at the River Kishon; and I will deliver him into your hand'?"* (vv. 6-7).

Barak cringed at this prophetic declaration. He recognized that Deborah was an honorable woman that God was using to provide hope and help to all those who came to her, so he responds: *"If you will go with me, then I will go; but if you will not go with me, I will not go!"* (v. 8). Hebrews 11:32 accredits Barak as being a judge in Israel, but clearly he lacked spiritual energy and confidence in the Lord at this juncture. To call him a coward would not be in keeping with Scripture, but he was, as other judges, an imperfect instrument in the hands of a great God. To request Deborah's presence as a condition for obeying God's revealed will was not a God-honoring response. There were two main negatives associated with Barak's caveat: First, it showed that his reliance was, at least partly, in Deborah, and not fully in the Lord. Second, he sought to pull Deborah from her place of ministry and calling.

Deborah agreed to accompany Barak, but also confirmed that because his confidence was not in the Lord alone, God would not bestow him the full honor in the victory he could have received. Deborah then foretold how the Lord would glorify Himself in the situation through a most unlikely means: *"for the Lord will sell Sisera into the hand of a woman"* (v. 9). Barak's faith was in its infancy, and required someone to come alongside him to urge him on in his calling. We see a similar situation with Moses before God at the burning bush in Exodus 3 and 4.

Moses first rejected the idea of him being God's chosen deliverer to rescue the Jewish people from Egypt. After raising objections, and sensing the overwhelming nature of what he was being asked to do, Moses pleads, *"O my Lord, please send by the hand of whomever else You may send"* (Ex. 4:13). This self-centered frankness angered God, but His wrath was tempered by mercy and His foreknowledge had already provided the solution – Aaron, who even then was already en route to Moses. God's gracious response to Moses' lack of faith resulted in a sign with which to enrich his faith. The coming of Aaron would be another sign to Moses of God's wisdom and control. God did not choose to send someone else to Egypt, nor did He give Moses a persuasive tongue, but He did transfer some of the honor offered to a hesitant Moses to a willing Aaron.

The Lord Jesus told the Church at Philadelphia, *"Behold, I am coming quickly! Hold fast what you have, that no one may take your crown"* (Rev. 3:11). His reward, which He bestows at His Judgment Seat, will be with Him when He comes to the clouds to snatch away His Church from the earth (1 Thess. 4:13-18; Rev. 22:12). In light of the Lord's imminent return, the saints at Philadelphia were to be attentive and faithful, lest they lose their reward (crown); this would allow someone else to earn it. This is what happened to Moses: God had given him a service opportunity, but he complained and wavered, so the Lord transferred part of the prospect, and the accompanying honor, to Aaron. God has a work to do and it will be accomplished by those who are willing to serve Him, and God shall recompense them accordingly.

Like Moses and Barak, we too, when facing a daunting situation, are prone to rely on that which is visibly tangible rather than on the vast resources of an infinite God. Such situations serve as a reality check as to the quality of our faith. It is good to remember at such times that God can use our weak faith to affect His glory, but the honor we acquire in doing so will be of the same diminished quality. Weak faith leads to diminished glory (1 Cor. 15:41-42; 2 Cor. 4:17).

Deborah does accompany Barak, but she realizes that it is not her place to organize and lead the Jewish army into battle. So it is Barak who gathers ten thousand men from the northern tribes of Zebulun and Naphtali to battle against the Canaanites (v. 10). He will lead this army into battle, and Deborah will watch and rejoice in the victory. This narrative upholds the sanctity of the genders which God put into order at the beginning of creation (Gen. 1:27, 2:24; 1 Tim. 2:11-14).

God instituted creation order over the genders when He fashioned the first man and then created the first woman from that man. Genesis 2 informs us that the woman came from the man, was made for the man, and was brought to the man by God to be his helper. The general principle in creation is that men are to lead and women are to support. God's creation order is further depicted in biblical authority structures for other spheres such as home order, civil order, and church order. In marriage, husbands are to love and care for their wives and wives are to submit to and respect their husbands (Eph. 5:22-33). In the realm of civil authority, it is notable that nowhere in the Bible do we find any example of God appointing a woman to lead His people. Although Deborah was a wise prophetess who provided personal counsel to the people, she would not lead Israel's army into battle against the Canaanites because she knew that would be inappropriate.

The same pattern for gender roles is also witnessed in the Church; only men were called to be apostles of the early Church, only men served as church elders (Titus 1:6; 1 Tim. 3:1-2), and only men are to be appointed as deacons in the local church (1 Tim. 3:11-12; Acts 6:3). Likewise, there are also ministries reserved for women, into which men cannot intrude. The Bible is full of examples of godly women who served and assisted others through various means and methods. For example, the sisters, like the Kohathites of old, have been entrusted with the ministry of the coverings within the house of God. They are to cover and conceal all glories that compete with God's glory.

As the assembly gathers in the presence of the Lord Jesus, each woman who covers her head ensures that she (the glory of man, 1 Cor. 11:7) and her long hair (her own personal glory, 1 Cor. 11:15) do not compete with God's glory, as symbolically portrayed in the man's uncovered head (1 Cor. 11:7). This earthly activity patterns the heavenly reality where only God's glory is observed and where even the cherubim and the seraphim use their wings to cover their own intrinsic glories in His presence. As Lucifer (a covering cherub) learned, God does not tolerate any competing glories in His presence (Ezek. 28:12-17).

The Church faithfully obeyed this command for nearly two millennia, but the practice was widely rejected in the 20th century as a result of the feminist movement, although even today most men still remove their hats to pray. The practice of the head covering is a visible salute by believers to show submission to God's authority and order for the Church. It is like a soldier who salutes a commanding officer who has come into his or her presence; the salute indicates to all present that the soldier is in agreement with the authority over him or her. The same Scripture that commands the head covering practice also explains its application: it is to be used when God's people come into His presence to talk with Him in prayer or to learn from Him through the teaching of

His Word. The uncovered head of the man and the covered head of the woman indicate to God and to all who observe (including the angels, see 1 Cor. 11:10) their willing submission to God's authority. God wants there to be distinctions between the genders as a testimony of His order in creation.

Believers would do well to refuse to listen to cultural arguments or humanistic reasoning which spiritualize away the clear teaching of God's Word. Man continually works to undermine God's testimony of order. The Church has been given a clear pattern to follow: only men are to lead and teach in the local church and women are to remain silent (1 Tim. 2:11-12; 1 Cor. 14:34-35).

Returning to the narrative, Sisera had forded the Kishon River, which flowed northwesterly through the Jezreel Valley, south of Harosheth. He then moved southeasterly to gather the Canaanite forces near Megiddo (5:19). After learning that Barak had gathered his ten thousand troops on the southern slopes of Mount Tabor, Sisera moved his army, with a compliment of 900 iron chariots, in a northwesterly direction towards Tabor (vv. 12-13). Mount Tabor rises 1,843 feet above sea level and is the highest mount in Lower Galilee. Because of its height and lone stature in the valley, other writers have compared Mount Tabor to Mount Carmel in the west (Jer. 46:18) and to Mount Hermon in the far north (Ps. 89:12), which are the two most prominent peaks in the Holy Land.

The Canaanite army again forded the Kishon River and assembled in the Plain of Esdraelon; they knew better than to engage the Jewish army positioned on Tabor. Deborah confirmed God's will to Barak: *"Up! For this is the day in which the Lord has delivered Sisera into your hand. Has not the Lord gone out before you?"* (v. 14). Barak obeys the word of the Lord and leads a surprise attack against the Canaanites. From a strategy perspective, this bold assault made no sense at all; indeed the Canaanites were not expecting the Jews to attack them. So, Barak and his ten thousand ill-equipped infantry bravely departed the safe haven of their rocky fortress and charged down Tabor to assault a much larger Canaanite army who had 900 iron chariots. On flat ground, these mobile chariots were the most lethal weapon of war known to man at that time. But the Jews had an advantage that the Canaanites were unaware of – Jehovah God!

Deborah told Barak that the Lord had gone out before them – meaning that He was fighting in advance of the Jewish army. How did Jehovah go out before them? This question is answered by examining another: Why did Sisera and his soldiers leave the safety of his chariots? While it is possible that the Lord simply caused the chariots to break down, the text seems to indicate that He invoked nature's fury to accomplish this task: *"The torrent of Kishon swept them away, that ancient torrent, the torrent of Kishon"* (5:21). The Kishon River was known for its swift current and also to be enclosed by a wide marshy area which was dangerous to cross. A sudden and unseasonable downpour caught the Canaanite army by surprise. Perhaps their chariots became stuck in the bogs near the Kishon and then the soldiers were swept away and drowned by a flashflood when they attempted to escape westward by re-crossing the river.

Early in the nineteenth century, Edward Robinson described Kishon River as a channel which in some places sunk 15 or 20 feet below the level of the plain. Another early explorer to Palestine, John Newman (1876), put the depth of the Kishon during the rainy season from 4 to 8 feet and said that it was from 10 to 40 feet wide.[3] Kishon was not a large river, but it served God's intended purpose of dislodging the Canaanites from their chariots.

Barak and his ten thousand men pursued the fleeing Canaanites westward and they were soon joined by troops from Ephraim and Manasseh from the south (5:14). The Lord used Barak and his men to rout Sisera and his Canaanite army as they fled along the Kishon northwesterly even as far as Mount Carmel (about 20 to 25 miles from where the battle originally commenced). By capturing the enemy-controlled Jezreel Valley, Barak succeeded in uniting the northern and southern tribes against their Canaanite enemy.

A group of Kenites of the family of Heber (descendants of Hobab, Moses' brother-in-law) were encamped near Kedesh (v. 11). This location was likely just a few miles east of the battlefield and is probably not a reference to the town of Kedesh some thirty miles northeast in Naphtali. Judges 1:16 records that these Kenites chose to depart from the pleasantness of the city of palm trees to live among the tribe of Judah in their inheritance. Joshua had put a curse on anyone who sought to rebuild and fortify the city of Jericho, which Jehovah had destroyed. Perhaps this fact alone caused the Kenites to depart from Jericho. For some unknown reason, the family of Heber had separated from his Kenite brethren and resettled in the north. In this unconsecrated position, Heber had peaceful interaction with Jabin, the enemy of God's people. This situation proves that it is possible to identify with God's people in name and even associate with them without truly being converted by the truth that binds them together. This same phenomenon can be witnessed in many local churches today.

Because the Kenites were at peace with Jabin, Sisera fled several miles eastward to their location (v. 17). Seeing Sisera coming, a woman named Jael, the wife of Heber, invited Sisera into her tent. He welcomed this opportunity to rest. After entering her tent, Jael covered him with a mantle (v. 18). An exhausted Sisera requested something to drink. Jael opened a skin of milk, which Sisera drank of (v. 19). F. C. Cook suggests that this was curdled milk, probably a fermented and intoxicating drink, which demonstrated friendship and further lulled Sisera into security. [4]

Sisera asked Jael to stand watch for him. After she confirmed that no one was pursuing him, Sisera quickly drifted off to sleep. Observing his deep slumber, Jael quietly approached Sisera with a hammer and a tent stake. She must have landed a powerful and well-coordinated blow to not awaken Sisera in time for him to protect himself. Jael drove the stake through his temples and fastened his head to the ground. The narrative confirms the obvious: *"so he died"* (v. 21). The Lord continued to empower the military campaign of His people until Jabin with his Canaanite army was destroyed (vv. 23-24).

The prophecy of Deborah had been precisely fulfilled; though thousands of Canaanites were slain by Barak and his army, Scripture bestows the honor of slaying the opposition's leader to a woman. She is the heroine of the day, but no more than a homemaker, equipped with only those instruments to which she was accustomed in her nomadic lifestyle (i.e., she knew how to put up and take down tents). Jael knew that it was wrong for her clan to enjoy peace with the enemy of God's people; it was a grievous alliance to the Lord and when He gave her the opportunity to revoke it, she smote Sisera. Hence, brave Jael accomplished a grand feat for God without abandoning her sphere of ministry in the home. He knew the integrity of her heart and brought the opportunity to serve Him directly to her front door. Accordingly, some of the honor which Barak might have received was bestowed to Jael, the wife of Heber.

In God's design, the woman was created to be a helper for the man (Gen. 2:18). Hence, Jael should not have been put in such an ominous position; her ghastly deed thus was a rebuke of the male complacency in Israel at that time. God's work will be accomplished by one means or another; if we are hesitant because of weak faith, He is faithful to enhance our faith, usually by involving those with faith in His purposes. Such individuals will then receive the reward that we might have earned for eternity; deficient faith has many consequences. May God help us when our faith is weak to do those good works in which He has graciously predetermined for us to walk in for His glory (Eph. 2:10).

Meditation

Dear Lord, increase my faith, I pray,
While on this earth I roam;
Banish my every doubt away,
And guide me safely home.

Give me the faith to trust Thy power,
Even where I cannot see;
The faith to yield this very hour,
My life, my all, to Thee.

To yield the whole and not a part,
Is my most earnest prayer;
Come, Thou, and cleanse my froward heart,
And reign forever there.

— Flora McLean

The Song of Deborah and Barak
Judges 5

This song is significant in being the only one of Judges. Their victory over the Canaanite kings is used to highlight God's ability to rescue His people at all times, despite the overwhelming nature of the situation. It is His prophetic Word alone which determines the how and the when God will exalt His people in the presence of their enemies and end their oppression. Because God alone had orchestrated their monumental success, it was most appropriate for His people to promptly praise Him, says Matthew Henry:

> No time should be lost in returning thanks to the Lord for his mercies; for our praises are most acceptable, pleasant, and profitable when they flow from a full heart. By this, love and gratitude would be more excited and more deeply fixed in the hearts of believers; the events would be more known and longer remembered. Whatever Deborah, Barak, or the army had done, the Lord must have all the praise. The will, the power, and the success were all from Him.[1]

In the previous chapter, Jehovah had secured a tremendous Jewish victory through the most unlikely instruments: two brave women (homemakers), and a man of ability but who lacked character. This is God's calling card throughout Judges; He uses illogical and unusual instruments to magnify His grace and power to awaken His people from spiritual slumber. Praise should follow deliverance and that is the paramount resolve of this chapter. It is a grand review of how the prophetic word spoken by Deborah was carried through to complete God's purposes.

When God's appointed leaders follow Him, God's people are blessed by following them: *"When leaders lead in Israel, when the people willingly offer themselves, bless the Lord!"* (v. 2). For this cause the Lord Jesus, who never departed from the right way, implores His disciples to follow Him:

> *If any man will come after Me, let him deny himself, and take up his cross, and follow Me. For whosoever will save his life shall lose it: and whosoever will lose his life for My sake shall find it* (Matt. 16:24-25).

It is only by following the Lord that a disciple of Christ is able to lead others into a life of blessing and fruitfulness. The Lord finished His course on earth after living a life which completely shunned and rejected what God opposed. Hence, just hours before His crucifixion, He could rally His disciples to also finish their journey in triumphant faith: *"These things I have spoken to you, that in Me you may have peace. In the world you will have tribulation; but be of good cheer, I have overcome the world"* (John 16:33). Godly leadership then follows the Lord's example of consecration, obedience, and victorious faithfulness.

The victory hymn of Deborah and Barak over the Canaanites underscores this statement. Because both the leaders (v. 9) and the people freely offered themselves, God avenged them and ended their subjugation. Hence, the motive for praising God was for what His grace had produced in their leaders, and among themselves. He was worthy of praise: He had shown them mercy and moved powerfully against their enemy (v. 3). The writer, likely Deborah herself, first highlights some of Jehovah's previous feats to ensure that there would be no confusion as to the One she was speaking of: He is the God that shook Mount Sinai in the days of Moses, and then led His people in victories against Seir and Edom before bringing them into Canaan under Joshua's leadership (vv. 4-5). Deborah acknowledges that she was raised up as *"a mother in Israel"* to nourish her people during these desperate circumstances (v. 7). God had permitted this because His people *"chose a new god"* to worship (v. 8). Despite the profound position bestowed to her, Deborah maintains her character as *"a mother in Israel,"* and manifests remarkable awareness of the province of her gender.

The oppressive condition under the Canaanites is described in verses 6-11. No one was safe in Northern Israel unless they resided in walled cities. Traveling by roadways or residing in unwalled villages was dangerous. Canaanite snipers apparently hid near wells to ambush the Jews when they came to draw water (v. 11). However, with the death of Sisera everything changed; those sitting on rare white asses (i.e., the rich), those rulers sitting in city gates to judge, and also anyone traveling through the land could do so safely (v. 10).

The song of victory begins with the divine call of Deborah and Barak to action (v. 12). A blessing is then pronounced on the tribes who answered their appeal and engaged the Canaanites in battle: Ephraim, Benjamin, Makir (a division of the tribe of Manasseh), Zebulun, Issachar, and Naphtali (vv. 13-15, 18). Zebulun and Naphtali receive special recognition for hazarding their lives for Jehovah. The battle was intense and despite the spoils of silver available to them, they remained engaged in the conflict until the enemy was totally defeated. This is a splendid example that we would do well to imitate – the work of God and His association with it is more important than the personal benefits received for being obedient to it.

Christians today can prosper against spiritual enemies even as the Israelites did centuries ago against physical foes in Canaan. How is this possible? Believers already have the authority of God to labor with Christ in effecting His will and power, but we must choose to walk with Him in truth (1 Jn. 1:6-7). If we choose to walk the path of darkness and disobedience, we do so alone, for the Lord cannot abide with us there. At such a time, He does not leave us, but we, rather, depart from His fellowship. However, if we walk in accordance to revealed truth we will appreciate the Lord's communion, for He has promised: *"I will never leave you nor forsake you"* (Heb. 13:5).

As the writer of Hebrews pondered the blessed solace of the Lord's abiding presence, he concluded: *"So we may boldly say: 'The Lord is my helper; I will not fear. What can man do to me?'"* (Heb. 13:6). Though conscious of his own deficiencies and the dangerous conflict ahead, Barak knew what his divine calling was and chose to move forward to fulfill it. So although Deborah was wonderfully used of the Lord, it is Barak who is commended for his faith by the writer of Hebrews (Heb. 11:32). When believers know what they have been called to do and yield themselves as a channel of mercy for that cause, they become invincible until their work is finished!

Sadly, there were several tribes that for various reasons chose not to get involved in Israel's desperate fight for liberation. These valued their personal interests above the name of Jehovah, His work, and the welfare of His people and consequently did not receive the rewards or the praise of victory, but rather the Lord's condemnation. The tribe of Reuben, for example, had *"great thoughts of heart,"* (i.e. sincere deliberations) but chose to remain among their sheepfolds rather than to join the conflict (vv. 15-16). Likewise, Dan remained engaged in lucrative commerce – they lingered in their ships. Asher decided it was better for them to enjoy the refreshing costal breeze, rather than to interrupt their comfortable good life (v. 17). Gilead (referring to the tribe of Gad) chose not to cross over the Jordan River to engage in battle; perhaps they surmised it would be too much work or even dangerous to ford the river.

C. A. Coates suggests that the phrase *"Gilead abode beyond Jordan"* refers to the two and a half tribes in the Transjordan region (Reuben, Gad and part of Manasseh), not just Gad. He asserts that these tribes represent the "people who have not taken heavenly ground; they have no interest in heavenly conflict, and do not care anything about it; they stay beyond Jordan."[2] There are many believers in the Church today who also refuse to enter into the heavenlies where Christ is seated to gain a spiritual advantage against principalities, powers, and spiritual wickedness in high places. William MacDonald reminds us that the Lord knows who is really serving Him and who is faking it:

> Scripture notes carefully those who fought in the battle and those who stood passively by, unwilling to risk their safety in Jehovah's cause. And so it is today: The Lord knows who is actively confronting the world and the devil and who is sitting back and simply watching. There is a time of reward coming, but it is also a time of loss (1 Cor. 3:10-15).[3]

As in the days of Deborah and Barak, materialism, professions, comfortable lifestyle, and imagined difficulties have always hindered the Lord's people from doing what they know they should do and, thus, from being victorious. The time is short and the battle intense; may the Lord awaken the pampered elect to rise above their vanity and imagined deterrents to serve the Lord faithfully!

Reuben, the firstborn of Jacob, should have been the leading tribe and the recipient of the double blessing bestowed by Hebrew birthright custom to the eldest son. However, Reuben committed adultery with Bilhah, his father's wife; this led to the loss of his position (Gen. 35:22). In his final prophetic statement, Jacob likened Reuben's lusts and impulses to turbulent boiling water, saying these would result in his failure as a leader (Gen. 49:4). Indeed, by the time of the Judges, the tribe of Reuben was characterized by indecision and a lack of resolve to go on with the Lord. They heard the call to battle, but despite the desperate situation, did nothing but ponder the matter within their own hearts. If God's Word had been permitted to deeply penetrate their thinking, no doubt their response would have been God-honoring.

David realized that every aspect of his life was searched out, planned, and meticulously controlled by the Lord; hence, it would be wrong for him not to act when required to uphold God's righteousness (Ps. 139:17-22). For this reason, David could trust the Lord to thwart his enemies, those who despised the Lord's name, and also to further examine and refine his inner man (Ps. 139:1, 23-24). Hamilton Smith reminds us that godly saints desire this type of spiritual scrutiny and enhancement:

> The godly man welcomes the searchings of God into the inmost recesses of his heart, desiring that he may be delivered from every evil way and led "in the way everlasting." In the experience of the psalmist, the consciousness of the omniscience of God at first plunges his soul into the deepest distress as he thinks of his own broken responsibilities towards God. When, at length, he realizes that God's "works" and God's "thoughts" are toward him in grace, the omniscience of God becomes the source of his deepest comfort.[4]

The Reubenites merely searched their own hearts and did nothing else; however, divine inspection of David's heart both proved his loyal devotion to the Lord and permitted God to further test and enrich his character. He knew that he could not hide his thoughts and doings from the Lord, so David desired to transform all his contemplations and deeds to be pleasing to God. This is the proper response to the omnipresent, omniscient, omnipotent God. David shows us that there is no middle ground in devotion to the Lord; what God opposes is what we must reject, and what God approves is what we should desire also.

A mature believer wants what God wants. Today, we might hear a Christian say, "I will pray about that" in order to shun his or her responsibility for confronting obvious sin. But silent neutrality condones sin – it is a sin not to reprove what one knows is morally wrong (Eph. 5:11)!

God forbid that we should be like the tribes of Reuben, Dan, Gad, and Asher and not stand with God and His people against evil and its brutal oppression. Rather, when we are reviewed at the Judgment Seat of Christ, may we be identified with the tribes Zebulon and Naphtali who jeopardized their lives and shunned earthly spoil to achieve a great victory for the Lord and to have His approval (v. 18).

The Canaanite confederation was ruled by Jabin of Hazor, whose army was commanded by Sisera. The most intense part of the battle occurred north of Taanach near the waters of Megiddo. The song speaks of celestial bodies descending to cause an unseasonable downpour of rain; this poetically depicts God's intervention in the conflict. The nearly dry riverbed of the Kishon was transformed into an impenetrable torrent of water with a vast marshy bog surrounding it. Some of the Canaanites were swept away by the mighty current of the swollen Kishon. Many more were entrapped by the bog and thus forced to abandon their chariots and flee the scene on foot (vv. 19-22).

Those of Meroz were cursed for not assisting the Lord and His people in the conflict; however, a blessing was pronounced on Jael for slaying Israel's enemy, Sisera (vv. 23-27). Meroz, located in the plains of Galilee north of Mount Tabor, was strategically located to benefit the Jewish cause, but the men of the city remained neutral when help was desperately needed. Commenting to the unqualified malediction on Meroz, H. L. Rossier remind us of our allegiance to Christ:

> *"Curse ye Meroz, said the angel of the Lord, curse ye bitterly the inhabitants thereof; because they came not to the help of the Lord, to the help of the Lord against the mighty."* Those who in these troublous times do not take sides with Christ; those who identify themselves with His name and that of God's people, and whose hearts are at the same time indifferent to Himself, let them be cursed. *"If any man love not the Lord Jesus Christ, let him be Anathema Maranatha"* (1 Cor. 16:22).[5]

Thankfully, the purposes of God cannot be thwarted, but those who passively ignore His calling will suffer the consequences of their willful desertion.

The colorful account of the Canaanite general's demise is further amplified by the ironic description of Sisera's mother waiting and wondering when her son would return with the spoils of war. The various excuses for his delay suggested by Sisera's mother and her maidens further amplify the irony of the situation – Sisera was never coming home (vv. 28-30).

It would have been strange to conclude this lovely song of praise at Sisera's palace, with the false hopes of Sisera's mother; rather this satire is contrasted with the hope of all those who truly love Jehovah in verse 31. Those who oppose Jehovah's rule and His covenant people will always suffer eventual defeat, but those who faithfully love Him will be exceedingly blessed, *"like the sun when it rises."* Those who love the Lord obey Him and long for His appearing (John 14:15; 2 Tim. 4:8).

Benefiting from Deborah's wisdom and Barak's tactical efforts, the Jews in that region enjoyed forty years of peace (v. 31). Yet, this would be a mere foreshadowing of a future day in which the Lord will vanquish all His people's enemies and then commence a timeless era of peaceful bliss and unconstrained blessing. This is truly the blessed hope of all God's people (Tit. 2:13).

Meditation

You call me Master and obey me not,
You call me Light and see me not;
You call me Way and walk not;
You call me Life and desire me not;
You call me Wise and follow me not;
You call me Fair and love me not;
You call me Rich and ask me not;
You call me Eternal and seek me not;
You call me Gracious and trust me not;
You call me Noble and serve me not;
You call me Mighty and honor me not;
You call me Just and fear me not;
If I condemn you, BLAME ME not!

— Unknown

61

The Call of Gideon
Judges 6:1-16

Despite all of the joyous praise and triumphant fanfare of Judges 5, that season of blessing was not to last; the Jews again forsook Jehovah and returned to paganism. He in turn chastised His people for their unfaithfulness by delivering them into the hands of the Midianites. An expression similar to the one in verse 1, *"the children of Israel did evil in the sight of the Lord,"* is found seven times in Judges to introduce a season of corrective punishment. Then, at the appropriate time, Jehovah would conclude the discipline and raise up a new judge to deliver them from their oppression.

Each cycle initiated after God's people turned from their idols and cried out to the Lord for deliverance: *"when the children of Israel cried unto the Lord"* (v. 7). Although these two expressions are not explicitly stated at each advent of a new deliverer, the idea is certainly apparent.

In this chapter, Gideon is chosen to rescue his countrymen from the seven-year tyranny of the Midianites and the Amalekites (v. 3). The Midianties were related to the Israelites in that Midian was a son of Abraham, born of Keturah whom he married after his wife Sarah's death (Gen. 25:1-2).

The situation was bleak; the Jews had taken refuge in caves, dens, and mountain strongholds to evade the Bedouin marauders raiding their livestock and crops (vv. 4-7). Because the Midianites rode camels, they could travel vast distances quickly and without water; this permitted the raiding parties to venture even as far west as Gaza (v. 4). This meant that no one was safe anywhere in Israel; there was nothing preventing the Midianites from stripping the land like locusts. Accordingly, God's people were barely surviving: they were *"greatly impoverished"* because the Midianites took whatever they could and left them *"no sustenance."* In desperation they pleaded with the Lord for liberation, but the Lord knew His people well, and their past regressions had shown their faith in Him to be fickle.

The Lord responded by sending them a prophet to test their motives and to remind them of three things (vv. 8-10). First, they were to remember His past faithfulness to deliver them from their bondage in Egypt, to safely conduct them to Canaan, and to give them that land for an inheritance. Second, they were to extend no credence to the false gods of the land. Third, they were suffering because they had not obeyed the Lord's commandments. Were they pleading for His deliverance because they were truly repentant or were they just self-centered children who wanted their painful discipline alleviated? After confirming the conditions for relief and restoration, the prophet departed, leaving the people under the weight of personal responsibility, but also with the promise of mercy. They chose to obey, and God responded by calling Gideon, the next judge of Israel, to deliver them.

The story of Gideon is more fascinating than any of the previous judges, in the respect that we are permitted to observe his personal experiences relating to his calling. Of particular interest is how his thinking was conformed to Jehovah's will. His growth in leadership is remarkable, first leading his father's house against idolatry, then an entire city, and finally much of the Jewish nation.

Gideon, the son of Joash, was secretly threshing wheat at a winepress in Ophrah (v. 11). This was an unusual scene; wheat was normally threshed in an open area on the top of a hill. This permitted the threshing carriages to pass over the grain to separate out the chaff and then the wind to blow the chaff away. However, a winepress was often hewn out of bedrock and at a lower location in a vineyard to ensure accessibility to carts and wagons. To avoid being discovered by the Midianites, Gideon was beating out grain for his people in an obscure pit. Although being inconspicuous, this was still a bold move by just the kind of man that Jehovah was looking for, says C. A. Coates:

> The first part of this chapter shows Israel's public position. The people of God generally are influenced by what they have in common with men naturally, and they have lost the enjoyment of the produce of the land. God takes up Gideon, a man personally exercised. He was concerned about the state of things; he felt it and was doing his best to

save a bit of the produce of the land from the Midianites. He wanted a little food for Israel. That is the kind of man God can take up; he is presented as feeling the situation.[1]

The Angel of the Lord interrupts Gideon's threshing by his sudden appearance and declaration: *"The Lord is with you, you mighty man of valor!"* (v. 12). The latter statement was a fact not known to Gideon, or anyone else for that matter, but the Lord knew Gideon was a man of valor. Was Gideon surprised by the abrupt incursion into his secluded workplace or by the profound accolade? Perhaps, but the narrative does not record those details; rather, it reveals Gideon's response of immediate intercession on behalf of God's covenant people: *"O my lord, if the Lord is with us, why then has all this happened to us? And where are all His miracles which our fathers told us about, saying, 'Did not the Lord bring us up from Egypt?' But now the Lord has forsaken us and delivered us into the hands of the Midianites"* (v. 13). Gideon realized that the one that was speaking to him officially represented Jehovah in some capacity, perhaps a prophet, hence, his first concern was to identify with God's suffering people and intercede for them.

The Lord is delighted when those in fellowship with Him stand in the gap and intercede for those who are not or for those in dire need. This is what the Lord Jesus did at Calvary; He willingly hung between heaven and earth on a cross in order to mediate between a holy God and rebellious sinners in desperate need of salvation (1 Tim. 2:5). In Genesis 18, we observe Abraham, the friend of God, interceding for wicked Sodom; in Exodus 32, we find Moses engaged in the same ministry for the rebellious Israelites. In Judges 6, Gideon intercedes for his people and the Lord promptly responds by commissioning him as the next judge of Israel – he was to deliver the Jews from the Midianites (v. 14).

Gideon was surprised by this statement and attempted to negate his calling by telling his honorable visitor something that he apparently did not know: he was of the smallest tribe, Manasseh, and the least in his father's house (v. 15). In the presence of this heavenly representative, Gideon was conscious of his own littleness in a way that he never had been before. He felt insignificant; he had no social clout and no inherent power or authority to accomplish such a feat against the

Midianites. Yet, Scripture repeatedly demonstrates to us that this is exactly the type of person that the Lord uses to manifest His awesome power. Paul explains the matter to the church at Corinth:

> *For you see your calling, brethren, that not many wise according to the flesh, not many mighty, not many noble, are called. But God has chosen the foolish things of the world to put to shame the wise, and God has chosen the weak things of the world to put to shame the things which are mighty; and the base things of the world and the things which are despised God has chosen, and the things which are not, to bring to nothing the things that are, that no flesh should glory in His presence* (1 Cor. 1:26-30).

Contrite Gideon was concerned for his fellow countrymen. If he obeyed the Lord and ventured forward in the power of faithfulness and humility, he would be able to save the Jews from their oppressors, for God promised to be with him (vv. 14, 16). Gideon's apparent weakness and meekness stand in stark contrast with the obvious imperfections of several others who were chosen by God to judge Israel.

The Old Testament contains a number of examples of individuals, like Gideon, who received direct instructions from God concerning their calling in life. God personally spoke to Abraham, Moses, Samuel, Isaiah, Jeremiah, and Ezekiel to convey their calling. Saul, David, and Elisha received God's message for their lives from prophets. The means by which their callings were given are quite unique also: Abraham saw the God of glory, Samuel heard a still quiet voice, Isaiah and Ezekiel witnessed the majestic throne of God, and Moses bowed before a burning bush.

The New Testament also records the direct and specific calls of the disciples to ministry. So, how should a Christian today expect to understand God's personal call for him or her to serve? Should believers expect a voice from heaven, a vision, or a prophetic utterance to confirm God's calling for them? During the early days of the Church Age, prophets were given to the Church as a check against false teachers – they confirmed the oral transmission of the Word of God before it was written down. Since believers have a divine anointing to understand truth (1 Jn. 2:20, 27) and the Word of God is now complete (Jude 3; 1 Cor. 13:9-10), modern Christians should not expect a prophetic confirmation of their ministry, at least in the normative sense.

God may reveal Himself directly, but it should not be expected of Him to do so.

The fact is that the apostles, whom the Lord directly commissioned, have long since died, thus the apostolic age closed two millennia ago. This fact is also witnessed in Scripture in that the use of sign gifts (tongues, interpreting tongues, commanding miracles, etc.) steadily decreased in frequency as the New Testament was written. In fact, there is no recorded occurrence of these supernatural gifts after about 58 AD, although over half of the New Testament was written after that time. The book of Acts reveals a clear transition from "apostles" to "apostles and elders" to just "elders" (speaking of local church leaders) through its record of early Church history. All of this is to say that today we should not expect specific revelation to confirm God's calling for us in ministry.

Practically speaking, how would you know a supernatural sign or a prophetic utterance was from God anyway? It might be from the devil to lead you astray. Moreover, we tend to read into situations that which we want to be true – we are not very objective when we want something to be a certain way. For example, a young man once thought he was called by God to plant churches. After explaining this fact to a preacher, the preacher asked him, "How did you come to know your calling?" The young fellow said, "I was plowing in a field one day and saw two clouds floating overhead: one was shaped like a 'P' and the other like a 'C' and realized God wanted me to **p**lant **c**hurches." The preacher responded, "How do you know God wasn't telling you to 'plant corn'?" It is hard to be objective if we really want something to be a certain way.

In summary, every believer should be faithful to complete whatever responsibilities he or she has already been assigned before desiring or expecting additional opportunities to serve the Lord:

> *Let each one remain in the same calling in which he was called. Were you called while a slave? Do not be concerned about it; but if you can be made free, rather use it. For he who is called in the Lord while a slave is the Lord's freedman. Likewise he who is called while free is Christ's slave. You were bought at a price; do not become slaves of men. Brethren, let each one remain with God in that state in which he was called* (1 Cor. 7:20-24).

The Lord provides greater opportunities for service as His people are faithful to what they have already been asked to do (Luke 16:10-11; Acts 13:1-3). There is no example in Scripture of the Lord calling a lazy person to serve Him. Elisha was plowing behind twelve yoke of oxen when he received his call through Elijah. Moses and David were shepherding sheep when God beckoned them to service. Four of the disciples were fishing when they were told by the Lord Jesus, *"Follow Me."* And as we have just noticed, Gideon was summoned while threshing wheat. The Lord calls working people to serve Him.

Meditation

Take my life and let it be
consecrated, Lord, to Thee.
Take my moments and my days;
let them flow in endless praise.

Take my hands and let them move
at the impulse of Thy love.
Take my feet and let them be
swift and beautiful for Thee.

Take my love; my Lord, I pour
at Thy feet its treasure store.
Take myself, and I will be
ever, only, all for Thee.

— Frances Ridley Havergal

Gideon's Call Confirmed
Judges 6:17-40

Was this impromptu meeting a dream or had Jehovah really called him to deliver Israel from the Midianites? Gideon seems unsure, and therefore asks for a sign to validate the discussion (v. 17). Gideon does not yet seem to realize that he is speaking face to face with the Lord, not merely a prophet. He addresses the messenger as *Adown* (v. 13), meaning "Master," and by this word's emphatic form in verse 17, *Adonay*, which is rendered "my Lord." However, it is not until the sign is witnessed that Gideon realizes that his visitor is a heavenly messenger – *"the Angel of the Lord"* (v. 22).

Gideon sought to refresh his visitor and gains permission to prepare a meal for his guest, who has agreed to wait for it under an oak tree (v. 18). Gideon quickly prepares a kid and unleavened bread. Clearly, such a sacrifice during abject poverty and need was very costly. Gideon placed the cooked meat, freshly baked bread, with a pot of broth in a basket and brought it to God's messenger, who tells him to place the meat and bread on a rock, and to pour out the broth (vv. 19-20).

God accepts those offerings and sacrifices which rightly portray various aspects of His Son's character and sacrifice. The Levitical "drink offerings" were of wine and poured over certain sacrifices, but there was no ritual which used meat broth. We are not told where Gideon poured out the broth: it may have been on the offering to enhance the forthcoming miracle (e.g., Elijah soaked his offering on Mount Carmel with barrels of water), or it may have been poured out on the ground because it did not scripturally reflect the Lord.

The goat's flesh pictures the unblemished body of the Lord Jesus freely given at Calvary for a sacrifice (Heb. 10:5-10). The unleavened bread symbolizes the sinless and impeccable qualities of the Lord's life (1 Cor. 5:7-8; 2 Cor. 5:21). For this reason the meat and bread were to be positioned on a particular foundation, "this rock," which can be none other than Christ. The overall representation of Gideon's sacrifice, then, metaphorically represents all the foundational truths of salvation for Israel and indeed for all humanity found in Christ alone (Ex. 17:6; Matt. 16:18). In comparison to their enemies' wherewithal, Moses affirmed to Israel, *"their rock is not like our Rock"* (Deut. 32:31). Amen! Only that which centers in Christ has value to God and will deliver man from himself and divine judgment for sin.

The Angel of the Lord then touched the meat and the unleavened bread with the end of his staff and fire promptly came out from the rock and consumed all. The life of an innocent victim, the unleavened quality of a sinless life, and the foundation rock of truth are all accurate presentations of Christ in Scripture. Hence, Gideon's sacrifice was accepted, despite his ignorance concerning the broth. Having completed His message, the divine messenger then vanished from sight (v. 21).

At that moment, Gideon realized that his visitor was "the Angel [Messenger] of the Lord" and is arrested with fear; he surmises that such an intimate encounter with God must result in his imminent death (v. 22). But the Lord consoles His chosen deliverer with words of reassurance: *"Peace be with you; do not fear, you shall not die"* (v. 23). Despite all the spiritual chaos and human sorrow about Him, the One who perfectly controls all things could extend peace to the one that was presently fearful and doubtful of the future.

Gideon's reaction to the Lord's presence and words of assurance should be our response also – he worshipped God. Prior to commissioning His disciples and on the eve of His crucifixion, the Lord instructed His disciples what the solution was to all their troubles: *"Let not your heart be troubled; you believe in God, believe also in Me"* (John 14:1). Genuine faith is fostered in adoration, appreciation, trust, and awe for the Lord; without such qualities our service for Him will fail miserably and nothing will be gained for eternity.

Gideon responds by erecting an altar at that location and worshipping the Lord – calling Him, *Jehovah-Shalom* or *"The Lord is Peace"* (v. 24). It is a tremendous blessing to be told that you have peace with your Creator, especially when you know His brilliant holiness demands your death. Likewise, Paul confirms that every true believer in the Lord Jesus Christ has peace with God: *"Therefore, having been justified by faith, we have peace with God through our Lord Jesus Christ"* (Rom. 5:1). Praise the Lord!

Jehovah-Shalom is one of several compound terms in Scripture which combine God's name, Jehovah, with some description of His divine work. Other augmented names of God include:

Jehovah-Jireh, "The Lord Will Provide" (Gen. 22:14)
Jehovah-Nissi, "The Lord Our Banner" (Ex. 17:15)
Jehovah-Sabbaoth, "The Lord of Hosts" (1 Sam. 1:3)
Jehovah-Maccaddeschem, "The Lord Thy Sanctifier" (Ex. 31:13)
Jehovah-Tsidkenu, "The Lord Our Righteousness" (Jer. 23:6)

The Lord then tested Gideon's loyalty by commanding him to tear down his father's altar to Baal and to cut to pieces the Asherah pole (a wooden pole or tree honoring the goddess Asherah) next to it (v. 25). Why was God permitting the Midianites and Amalekites to repeatedly raid the stores of His people? The reason was their idolatry. So before Gideon could successfully lead a military campaign to rid Israel of their oppressors, he first had to remove what had prompted the Lord's anger against His people. Samuel Ridout suggests that, in the practical sense, the divine test put to Gideon is not too different than what believers face today:

What a heart-searching test is applied to him. He is to exalt Jehovah in his own home. After his own personal relation with God had been established, we might say, after he had won his victory in private, he is to establish those relations in his own home circle. Does he worship and obey God for himself? Then that same obedience must be claimed for the entire circle of his responsibilities. Is a man going to be a deliverer for all Israel, while his own family is in bondage? Is he to lift up the altar of Jehovah for all Israel, and are those who are nearest and dearest to him to bow to Baal? The circle of divine influence expands from the center. How many are tempted to invert this order. They may be jealous enough for God's altar for all Israel, and yet have never set it up in their own homes.[1]

Obedience and service to the Lord must begin in one's own house. Hence, Gideon is instructed to pull down his own father's public altar to Baal, erect a proper altar to Jehovah in its place, and then offer one of his father's young bulls on it. The Lord specifically chose a bull of seven years of age, which suggests that this same bull may have been previously designated to be an offering to Baal. C. T. Lacey explains the spiritual significance associated with this particular bull, i.e., the "second bull":

> The fact that it was the "second" points to Christ as, "the second man"…the Lord from heaven (1 Cor. 15:47). It is also written of Him, "He takes away the first, that He may establish the second" (Heb. 10:9). The bullock was seven years old, corresponding to the seven years of Midianite oppression for which it was to make atonement. God cannot tolerate any rivals and therefore the two altars could not possibly exist side by side.[2]

Not only did Gideon take the "second bull," but he also took men to assist in the work, as this was a huge task which must be accomplished at night to avoid a confrontation with Baal worshippers trying to protect their pagan altar.

The fire for the burnt offering was to be kindled with the wood from the hewn down Asherah pole(s) (vv. 26-27). Today, believers frequently demonstrate mixed allegiance to the Lord because they do not rid from their lives what God opposes; however, Gideon burned what God hated as part of the acceptable burnt offering. Jehovah would not accept two altars, nor an altar for Himself with wooden idols about it – true worshippers must hold to the truth and sanctify their affections (John 4:23).

Gideon's actions show us that religious rubbish and worldly dissipations must be disposed of before God's people can erect a true testimony of His greatness. Before we build up for God, we must first peer inward, and evaluate ourselves downward. Religious smugness, careless attitudes, coldness of heart, misplaced affection, and pride in any form must be removed before we can effectively serve the Lord. His Word alone is the Rock that we can build on. Foundations laid on personal glory, false doctrine, and humanism will crumble away (Luke 6:46-49; 1 Cor. 3:11-15). It would have been easier for Gideon to offer a sacrifice on an altar that already existed rather than tear it down and rebuild a new one, but ultimately only what is founded on God's Word will stand the test of time and eternity. Despite the arduous task and the threat of conflict, Gideon did exactly what God commanded – and so should we.

The next morning the men of Abiezer were stunned to find their pagan altar and images destroyed and the remains of a burnt offering smoldering on a new altar erected to Jehovah (v. 28). An investigation was launched and soon all fingers pointed to Gideon – the men of Abiezer demanded Joash deliver his son to be put to death for the offense (vv. 29-30). Joash is apparently brought to repentance, after witnessing his son's zeal for Jehovah and wisely denies their request; rather, he decrees that anyone interfering with Baal's own vengeance should be put to death. Joash asserts: *"'If he [Baal] is a god, let him plead for himself, because his altar has been torn down!' Therefore on that day he called him Jerubbaal, saying, 'Let Baal plead against him, because he has torn down his altar'"* (vv. 31-32). Gideon's bold testimony had convinced his father of the nothingness of Baal. Joash had less faith than his son Gideon, but yet enough to respond and to defend his son's actions. Gideon destroyed Baal's altar because he trusted Jehovah; Joash turned to the Lord, seeing the utter powerlessness of Baal. Before us is a good example as to how one individual acting in faith to God's revealed will can awaken others of weaker faith to do the same.

Furthermore, the fact that Baal did nothing against Gideon, a Jehovah worshipper, aroused the entire city to consider their own degeneracy before Jehovah. Thus, when the Midianites and Amalekties united in the Jezreel Valley to launch raiding parties in Israel, Gideon, having the Spirit of God, blew a trumpet and all of Abiezer came to him (vv. 33-34). By doing so, they were siding with Jehovah and not Baal. Messengers were sent out to gather more troops for battle and the tribes of Manasseh, Asher, Zebulun, and Naphtail readily responded; in all, 32,000 men came to assist Gideon (vv. 35, 7:3).

Having gathered an army, Gideon now seeks to determine how and when the Lord would defeat their enemies. As confirmed by a miraculous sign, Gideon already knew the will of God on the matter from his earlier encounter with the Angel of the Lord. Therefore, the fleece test was not for guidance, but rather for divine confirmation. Gideon was fully aware of the immense task he had been assigned, but he wanted to confirm God's presence and enablement in accomplishing it. He therefore asks God:

"If You will save Israel by my hand as You have said – look, I shall put a fleece of wool on the threshing floor; if there is dew on the

fleece only, and it is dry on all the ground, then I shall know that You will save Israel by my hand, as You have said" (vv. 36-37).

Early the next morning Gideon squeezed the fleece and was able to wring out a bowl full of water, yet the threshing floor was completely dry. To be absolutely sure that the threshing floor had not naturally dried out before the fleece, Gideon asked the Lord for one more confirmation: *"Do not be angry with me, but let me speak just once more: Let me test, I pray, just once more with the fleece; let it now be dry only on the fleece, but on all the ground let there be dew"* (vv. 38-39). It might seem strange that a man listed in Faith's Hall of Fame of Hebrews 11 would test God in this way, but the Lord accommodates both of Gideon's requests. The next morning Gideon found the fleece completely dry but the ground was moist with dew (v. 40). As a wool fleece naturally absorbs moisture, the second sign was more compelling than the first.

Sometimes people refer to a naturally occurring event as being their fleece, so to speak, in guiding them into some life-changing decision. However, this is a misapplication of the story on two accounts: First, the fleece was a confirmation to Gideon concerning what God had already told him to do – there was no new revelation imparted. Second, if a decision was based on a naturally occurring phenomenon, how would someone know whether it was the Lord or some random improbable event? Gideon had asked for something supernatural to endorse his assigned task, not some natural phenomenon. The Lord granted his request. Let us be careful to not read too much divine direction into natural occurring events.

Did Gideon have weak faith or did he just want to know that the Lord was with Him going forward? We are not told the answer to this question, but rather God patiently worked with His chosen deliverer in such a way that he was prepared to hazard his life and those of his men against an army four times as large. It would be wrong to fault Gideon in this matter; after all, David, *"a man after God's own heart,"* requested something similar of the Lord:

You, O Lord, are a God full of compassion, and gracious, longsuffering and abundant in mercy and truth. Oh, turn to me, and have mercy on me! Give Your strength to Your servant, and save the son of Your maidservant. Show me a sign for good, that those who hate me may see it and be ashamed, because You, Lord, have helped me and comforted me (Ps. 86:15-17).

With his marching orders divinely confirmed, Gideon steps forward in faith despite being greatly outnumbered. He assembles his volunteer army at the spring of Harod (7:1).

Meditation

A perfect faith would lift us absolutely above fear.

— George MacDonald

Satan is so much more in earnest than we are – he buys up the opportunity while we are wondering how much it will cost.

— Amy Carmichael

Too Many for God
Judges 7

Thirty-two thousand Jewish volunteers gather to Gideon at the spring of Harod (or Ain Jalud), probably located on the eastern base of Mount Gilboa (v. 1). The Midianite force of 132,000 was in the Jezreel Valley at the Hill of Moreh situated about five miles directly north of their position. Just south of the Hill of Moreh was the city of Shunem. This is where the Philistines would later gather to fight King Saul, whose army would also assembly at Mount Gilboa (1 Sam. 28:4, 31). Shunem was also the town in which Elisha would later raise up the widow's son from the dead (2 Kgs. 4:8-37).

The Lord informed Jerubbaal, that is, Gideon, that too many Jews had assembled for Him to vanquish the Midianites; to do so with such a complement would only cause Israel to be lifted up in pride (v. 2). The solution was to tell all who were afraid to return to their homes, and 22,000 men did just that (v. 3). H. L. Rossier explains why it was necessary for those who were afraid to depart from the upcoming battle:

> Moses had formerly given this command to the children of Israel: "What man is there that is fearful and fainthearted? Let him go and return unto his house, *lest his brethren's heart faint as well as his heart*" (Deut. 20:8). The same passage (vv. 5-7) teaches us that those who were fearful and afraid, were those who had *something to lose.* A servant of God is full of courage for his work, when he has nothing to lose here, because the excellency of Christ has made him despise what the world values. ... God wants undivided hearts for the accomplishment of His work; hearts that have nothing to lose, that are afraid of nothing, and who cannot exert a baneful influence over those who have gone out to the war unentangled with the affairs of this life. The twenty-two thousand came in for the spoil, but were unequal to the effort required to get it. Those that are fearful will profit by the testimony, but have not the qualification necessary to maintain it.[1]

When the Lord's servants have nothing to lose and everything to gain for the excellence of Christ, then wonderful feats are accomplished for the kingdom of God. Dear believer, what you are afraid of losing is what will keep you from winning, that is, being victorious in Christ (Luke 9:24-25).

The Lord wanted there to be no question in anyone's mind that He had intervened to bring about a miraculous deliverance of His people, thus, Gideon's army must be further reduced in size. The solution was to have the remaining 10,000 men venture down to the spring and be observed while they drank its water. This is a good reminder that the Lord often tests His people in the ordinary activities of daily life to determine their availability for service. We may not think that the Lord is particularly concerned as to how we respond in the mundane affairs of life, but clearly God notices every detail – even the way we drink water.

While commentators differ in respect to what drinking styles are described, the main distinction seems to be between those who got down on their hands and knees to aggressively slurp up the water (these were set aside) and those who scooped up the water in their hand(s) to drink while in an upright position (vv. 4-5). The three hundred men drinking from their hands became Gideon's new army; this meant that they were now outnumbered 450 to 1 (vv. 6-7). These are not good odds for a normal conflict, but this campaign was atypical from the start by design; in fact, Gideon's small fighting force would not be provided conventional weapons of war to initially engage the enemy. The three hundred men received provisions and trumpets from those told to return to their homes (v. 8).

Why were the men who drank water in an upright position permitted to remain and be used in God's deliverance? The application seems to be that those who drank in moderation were able to remain alert and in readiness. They were better prepared for the Lord's work than those who momentarily took their eye off the enemy to drink (i.e., facing down while on their knees and elbows, they would not be cognizant of their surroundings). However, those scooping up the water to their lips would still be able to scan the area for a possible enemy incursion, perhaps even holding a trumpet in one hand while drinking with the other in order to quickly sound an alarm, if necessary.

Peter warned the Christians of his day to be alert because the enemy of their souls, the devil, was constantly prowling about to devour them: *"Be sober, be vigilant; because your adversary the devil walks about like a roaring lion, seeking whom he may devour"* (1 Pet. 5:8-9). Many believers have become spiritual casualties because they underestimated the resolve of the enemy to confront the work and the people of God. The devil is despicably brutal and relentless to do evil – believers will do well to learn from his past tactics and be on full alert for the redeployment of such devices. On this side of glory, there are no vacations from spiritual warfare, only brief reprieves of rest after victories and seasons of recovery and healing after defeats.

The text seems to indicate that Gideon and his men moved to the northern slope of Gilboa, where they could see below them an innumerable host of Midianites, Amalekites, and Arabs with all their camels (vv. 8, 12). That same evening, the Lord spoke to Gideon:

Arise, go down against the camp, for I have delivered it into your hand. But if you are afraid to go down, go down to the camp with Purah your servant, and you shall hear what they say; and afterward your hands shall be strengthened to go down against the camp (vv. 9-10).

The Lord did three things that prepared Gideon for battle. First, He caused Gideon to be aware of his own frailty. He told Gideon, *"if you be afraid"* go down with Purah to the enemy's camp. This forced Gideon to admit the honest truth – he was afraid and hence no different than the twenty-two thousand that confessed the same. Second, God would affirm the victory to come through a spectacular means. Gideon and Purah descended Gilboa and stealthily entered the outer fringe of the enemy's camp (v. 11). There Gideon heard one Midianite tell another of his dream: a barley cake tumbling into their camp, striking and overturning a tent such that afterwards it laid flat (v. 13). The other interpreted the dream: *"This is nothing else but the sword of Gideon the son of Joash, a man of Israel! Into his hand God has delivered Midian and the whole camp"* (v. 14). Jehovah would use something as insignificant and lowly as a barley cake (Gideon) to smash the entire Midian army. Third, when Gideon heard the interpretation of the dream, he worshipped God. Only sincere worshippers can be true warriors. Despite his fears and reservations, Gideon would faithfully obey the prophetic word of God.

Gideon returned to his own camp; he was now convinced that Jehovah had delivered the Midianites into his hand, and declared as much to his men (v. 15). He mobilized his troops and divided them into three separate groups of one hundred men. Each man was to carry a trumpet (*showphar* – a ram's horn) and a torch; the torches were to be hidden in earthen jars which were to be broken on command in order that all the burning lamps would shine out at once (vv. 16-17). Gideon instructed his troops, *"Look at me and do likewise; watch, and when I come to the edge of the camp you shall do as I do"* (v. 17). This is the mark of a powerful leader: he not only tells others what they must do to serve the Lord, but exemplifies it in his own life also – he practices what he preaches. Once in place, all eyes were on their leader as they waited for his signal. Once recognized, each man was to simultaneously sound his trumpet and then shout, *"The sword of the Lord, and of Gideon"* (v. 18). While the Midianites feared *"the sword of Gideon,"* the battle cry of the Jews proclaimed the real power of their confrontation – *"the sword of the Lord."*

Given the direction of the Midianites' flight, it is assumed that Gideon circled the enemy's camp in a clockwise rotation and placed his men on the southwest, the northwest, and the northeast side of the Hill of Moreh. Just after the Midianites had changed their first watch (likely sometime between 10 p.m. and midnight), the alarm was sounded and suddenly 300 trumpets were blown simultaneously and 300 torches lit up the countryside surrounding the enemy's camp. The Jews stood still, but yelled out their assigned battle cry: *"A sword for the Lord and for Gideon"* (v. 19-20)!

Pandemonium quickly swept through the enemy's camp, so much so that as each band of soldiers ascended Moreh to try to discern what was happening they met others doing the same. The darkness served to enhance the chaos and the Midianites began slaughtering each other thinking that the Jews were charging them (vv. 21-22). Why did the Midianites devour one another with such insane fury and then flee their camp in utter terror? Because the Lord caused them to believe that they were being attacked by an enormous Jewish force; normally one man in a division of troops carried a lamp and a trumpet. Thus, it seemed to them that they were suddenly surrounded by 300 divisions of soldiers.

It is also possible that the allies (the Midianites, the Amalekites, and the Arabs) suspected treachery along ethnic associations with their own alliance. Surprise, suspicion, confusion, and the darkness were all integral components of the mayhem.

According to Numbers 10 two silver trumpets were used to declare God's mind to His covenant people. The sound of the trumpet represents God's Word and was used to call the Jews to an assembly, to journey, to war, and to worship (e.g., the trumpets were blown over sacrifices, on Feast days, and in the year of Jubilee). Today, God speaks to His people through canonized Scripture to convey His directions for their assembling, their walk, their warfare, and their worship.

> This method of defeating the Midianites may be alluded to, as exemplifying the destruction of the devil's kingdom in the world, by the preaching of the everlasting gospel, the sounding that trumpet, and the holding forth that light out of earthen vessels, for such are the ministers of the gospel (2 Cor. 4:6-7).[2]

May we, like Gideon and his men, shine brightly for the Lord Jesus and sound out loud and clear the revealed Word of God, so that we might also see the victorious hand of God in all that we do.

The greatest part of the slaughter was over without one Hebrew raising a sword, but now others were needed and summoned for the cleanup operation. The tribes of Naphtali to the north, Asher to the northwest, and Manasseh to the south were the first to respond; they chased down the Midianites as they fled southeastward to the Jordan Valley (v. 23). Because of their strategic location, Gideon also requested that the tribe of Ephraim quickly charge eastward and retake Beth-barah and other nearby fords of the Jordan River; this would cut off the escape route of the fleeing Midianites (v. 24). Centuries later, this would be the location that John would baptize those repenting of their sins in anticipation of their coming Messiah (John 1:28). The Ephraimites did so and captured and executed two Midianite princes, Oreb and Zeeb, in the process. Their heads were brought to Gideon who was preparing to ford the Jordan to pursue the bolting enemy into Gilead (v. 25, 8:4).

Gideon's incredible victory teaches us something about godly leadership and the necessity of brokenness in the work of God. William MacDonald summarizes what we can learn from Gideon:

> The leader must be thoroughly convinced about what he is doing before he can lead others. He must be a worshiper first of all, giving God His rightful place (v. 15). He must lead by example (v. 17). He must be careful that the credit goes where it belongs – to God first, then to the instruments of His choosing (v. 18).[3]

Normally, when something breaks, it loses value. For example, a collision decreases the worth of an automobile, and the shattered keepsake is remorsefully discarded as a total loss. Within the physical realm, the laws of nature work to depreciate the value of our possessions, but this is not so in the spiritual realm – in fact, the opposite is true. Scripture poses a number of metaphoric examples to show that in God's reckoning, things, and especially people, become more valuable for service after being broken. In this chapter we observed that the torches showed forth their light only after the jars were broken. Light speaks of divine truth or a God-honoring testimony (e.g., Matt. 5:14-16; 1 Jn. 1:6-7). The narrative shows us that the believer's testimony for Christ becomes more intensely brilliant through brokenness.

Some might say, "What a waste to break 300 perfectly fine jars." But the 300 broken pitchers were an integral part of God's plan for victory. These earthen vessels were not strong; in fact, they only benefitted the work of God because each was fragile. Similarly, believers are likened to earthen vessels bearing the precious contents of the gospel message: *"But we have this treasure in earthen vessels, that the excellence of the power may be of God and not of us"* (2 Cor. 4:7). Believers can only further the kingdom of God by understanding their own weakness to affect spiritual warfare. However, God prizes brokenness and consecration in His people and invigorates such fit vessels for service.

Furthermore, the noise of the breaking jars enhanced the element of confusion and the blazing torches made suddenly visible enhanced the ruse that an enormous Hebrew army was rushing upon the Midianites. The Lord shows us that He controls the dreams and the sanity of men, and may use simple and foolish things to accomplish His sovereign purposes. What might the Lord accomplish in your life through brokenness?

Meditation

We must be really brought to the end of everything with which self has ought to do; for until then God cannot show Himself. But we can never get to the end of our plans until we have been brought to the end of ourselves.[4]

— C. H. Mackintosh

Towards himself a Christian should have a broken spirit, but towards God it should be one of rejoicing always in Him. He rejoices not for its own sake nor because of any joyful experience, work, blessing or circumstance, but exclusively because God is his center.

— Watchman Nee

Victory, Rest, and Confusion
Judges 8

During the process of distributing tribal inheritances a few decades earlier, the children of Joseph exhibited an arrogant and jealous spirit (Josh. 17:8-14). They do so again with Gideon, accusing him of wrongdoing because he had not initially involved them in the confrontation (v. 1; also see 12:1). Since the time of Deborah (5:4), the tribe of Ephraim had suffered further declension. Gideon, being led by God, does not involve them in the initial contest, but only the mop-up activity. This secondary distinction caused them to be jealous of what Jehovah had entrusted to their fellow countrymen.

It is good for believers to realize that a single victory over the enemy is not enough; other trials and tests are needed to build up our faith and to honor God. Such was the case with Gideon; the festive exhilaration of victory was quickly dampened by self-focused men from Ephraim looking to exalt themselves. Apparently, these men did not realize the principle of God's sovereignty in obtaining victory, and were sore that they had been passed over. It is good for us to remember that God will use whomsoever He will to do His work, and that it is not the vessels He uses in the work that are anything, but what He accomplishes for His glory that has value.

Additionally, we should expect that carnal people will be preoccupied with their own importance and needs and hence be prompted to jealousy by the energy of faith in the Christ-focused spiritual man. Matthew Henry further expounds this point:

> Those who will not attempt or venture anything in the cause of God, will be the most ready to censure and quarrel with such as are of a more zealous and enterprising spirit. And those who are the most backward to difficult services will be the most angry not to have the credit of them. Gideon stands here as a great example of self-denial; and shows us that envy is best removed by humility. The Ephraimites

had given vent to their passion in very wrong freedom of speech, a certain sign of a weak cause: reason runs low when chiding flies high.[1]

As Paul acknowledges, this type of carnality is a frequent source of strife between brethren: *"For you are still carnal. For where there are envy, strife, and divisions among you, are you not carnal and behaving like mere men?"* (1 Cor. 3:3). After admonishing the believers at Corinth, Paul tells them how to resolve their carnality and strife:

> *So then neither he who plants is anything, nor he who waters, but God who gives the increase. Now he who plants and he who waters are one, and each one will receive his own reward according to his own labor* (1 Cor. 3:7-8).

Believers must realize that we are nothing in affecting the work of God; it is God alone who brings about anything good from our laboring. With that mindset, Christians are to labor together with God in their individual callings and for the common cause of exalting Christ, not themselves. The self-focused Ephraimites sought their own honor, rather than the good of the nation and the glory of Jehovah. Unfortunately, their contentious fervor continued to escalate through the centuries and ultimately resulted in the division of the nation, as instigated by Jeroboam, an Ephraimite, after the death of King Solomon (1 Kgs. 11:26).

The battle was not yet over, and conflict among God's people would only benefit the escaping enemy and minimize Israel's victory. Hence, a weary Gideon exercises restraint and wisely answers the Ephraimites by praising their accomplishments and minimizing his own at Moreh in comparison: *"What have I done now in comparison with you? Is not the gleaning of the grapes of Ephraim better than the vintage of Abiezer? God has delivered into your hands the princes of Midian, Oreb and Zeeb. And what was I able to do in comparison with you?"* (vv. 2-3). Gideon assumed the low place in meeting the Ephraimites; He confronted the spirit of self-importance with the opposite demeanor. Gideon diminishes his own accomplishments and amplifies those of the Ephraimites. This gentle answer pacified the quarrelsome Ephraimites and civil war was averted. The entire situation likely explains why Gideon did not summon the Ephraimites to battle in the first place; they were high on themselves and Gideon knew that this victory must be achieved through humility and brokenness before the Lord. Having resolved the issue, Gideon and his three hundred weary men then forded the Jordan River and resumed chasing the Midianites in Gilead.

Their next difficulty pertained to experiencing the fatigue and weariness of their own frailty; they were *"exhausted but still in pursuit"* (v. 4). Gideon and his men were faint, yet not satisfied with what had been accomplished; they were still eager to do more against their enemy. This is the reality of things that every child of God must learn: the outward man, who we are naturally, must perish daily to enjoy God's strengthening of the inner man. No sustaining or effective power for spiritual warfare can be found in our flesh (2 Cor. 10:3-4). Rather, the believer is to remain faithful by relying on the infusing power of the Holy Spirit to engage the enemy: *"Therefore we do not lose heart. Even though our outward man is perishing, yet the inward man is being renewed day by day"* (2 Cor. 4:16). There is nothing in the flesh that can please God (Rom. 7:18), and the sooner the spiritual man learns that truth, the more quickly he or she is able to engage the enemy effectively for the Lord.

To emphasize this point, the Lord Jesus told His disciples the night before His crucifixion: *"For without Me you can do nothing"* (John 15:5). Thankfully, Paul knew from practical experience that the flipside was also truth: *"I can do all things through Christ who strengthens me"* (Phil. 4:13). Paul understood that humble purity and the energy of faith were inseparable in the work of God. This is what Gideon and his men were also learning: They were weary, but in faith they charged onward and were divinely strengthened for the task.

Gideon and his men had now traveled over thirty miles southeast to the town of Succoth in pursuit of Zebah and Zalmunna, the kings of Midian. They were famished and faint and asked provisions of the inhabitants of Succoth. C. A. Coates suggests this was the next test for Gideon and his men: Would they remain in the Lord's work even though many of His people were complacent in it?

> Gideon gets another test by brethren of even a worse character than the men of Ephraim, that is, the men of Succoth; and at Penuel he finds Israelites with no interest in what is going on. They were quite

84

neutral; they were totally unsympathetic with those fighting the Lord's battles. That is another test. Are we prepared to go on in spite of that? Gideon had a right to count on sympathy and support, they were Israelites, and his men were faint and weary; but he finds a total lack of sympathy. Nothing is more trying to the spirit than to be engaged in the Lord's battles and to find no support from those who profess to be His people.[2]

The men of Succoth refused to aid their brethren, fearing that the Midianites might retaliate against them, if Gideon failed to capture the kings and secure a complete defeat (vv. 5-6). After all, they were outnumbered 15,000 to 300 (or 50:1). This attitude marks carnal believers and false professors; they are not able to clearly identify a true work of God even when it is staring them in the face and, consequently, do not become a part of it. Matthew Henry reminds us that faithful servants of the Lord should expect to be hindered in accomplishing the things of God by those who are not servants of the Lord:

> The active servants of the Lord meet with more dangerous opposition from false professors than from open enemies; but they must not care for the behavior of those who are Israelites in name, but Midianites in heart. They must pursue the enemies of their souls, and of the cause of God, though they are ready to faint through inward conflicts and outward hardships. And they shall be enabled to persevere. The less men help, and the more they seek to hinder, the more will the Lord assist.[3]

Was Jehovah with the 300? Yes. And that was the only question that the men of Succoth needed to answer correctly. Yet, despite all the evidence, their complacent response indicated, "No, Jehovah is not doing anything spectacular through His people at this time." They chose to be indolent while their fellow brethren hazarded their lives to accomplish a great feat for God.

Because Succoth allied with the Midianites instead of Jehovah, Gideon pronounced judgment on them after the Midian kings were captured: *"I will tear your flesh with the thorns of the wilderness and with briers"* (v. 7). This expression is understood to be an idiom meaning to strike with violence. The act of dragging them over thorns similar to a threshing sled over grain or perhaps pulling a sled of briers over them to punish them was meant as a severe threat, one that they may not survive.

Following the brook Jabbok eastward, they came to the town of Penuel about five miles from Succoth. This location was named by Jacob centuries earlier, after he wrestled all night with the Lord there (Gen. 32). It was here that Jacob learned brokenness, and ironically, Jabbok means "to empty" and that is what God accomplished in Jacob's life. The townspeople of Penuel also declined to aid Gideon; he therefore promised to return and tear down their tower, likely referring to the town's stronghold of defense (v. 9).

The two Midian kings gathered all their remaining troops, about 15,000 men, at Karkor to mount a counterattack. The narrative records that 120,000 soldiers in their original army had already perished (v. 10). Karkor may have been located about one hundred miles southeast of Penuel, which meant Gideon and his men had faithfully pursued the fleeing Midianites for many days before the confrontation at Karkor. Gideon used a caravan route east of Nobah and of Jobbehah, which was located about 15 miles southeast of Penuel (v. 11). Gideon launched a surprise attack on the unsuspecting Midianite camp and was able to capture the two fleeing kings and destroy the remainder of their army (v. 12).

Beginning the long trek home, Gideon headed northwest through the Ascent of Heres (v. 13). A young man of Succoth was caught and then interrogated. From this informant, Gideon obtained the names of the seventy-seven elders of Succoth (v. 14). These men had mocked Gideon earlier about his ability to capture Zebah and Zalmunna, whom he now had in his custody and would parade before them. The elders were found and punished as Gideon had threatened to do previously; likewise the tower of Penuel was demolished and the men of that city were put to death for their offense, perhaps because they tried to resist Gideon's retribution (vv. 15-17).

Was this punishment too harsh for merely refusing to aid those honoring Jehovah's name through faithful obedience? Apparently not. Neutrality in the things of God is the same as worldliness and God hates it (Jas. 4:4). By not assisting Gideon they were choosing to aid the enemy; the men of Succoth and Penuel feared the wrath of the two Midian kings more than Jehovah's retribution. Believers are instructed to *"have no fellowship with the unfruitful works of darkness, but rather expose them"* (Eph. 5:11). Silence in the presence of sin condones evil, but hindering the proper service of God's people by neutrality is even a weightier offense!

By interrogating the kings about raids conducted near Mount Tabor (probably before the events of this chapter), what Gideon suspected was affirmed: these kings were responsible for killing several of his brothers (vv. 18-19). In answering the question on this matter, the captured kings praised Gideon: *"As you are, so were they; each one resembled the son of a king"* (v. 18). The child of God should always be distrusting of the world's flattery, understanding that our lost humility and dependence on the Lord equate to defeat in what is important to Him.

Both justice and family revenge necessitated that both kings be immediately executed. Gideon permitted Jether, his oldest son, to do the honor, but the lad was not prepared for such a callous task (v. 20). This was a mistake; those who are fearful and young in the faith must grow in courage and learn proper warfare before being entrusted with such responsibility (Josh. 10:22-27). This high honor was Gideon's alone and even Zebah and Zalmunna preferred that Gideon slay them. They reckoned that it would be more honorable to die by the hand of a victorious warrior than that of a timid youth (v. 21). Gideon, the appropriate avenger of blood, obliged their request and slew both of them; he then took the ornaments that were on their camels' necks as spoils of war (v. 22). F. C. Cook notes that the custom of adorning the necks of camels with gold chains and ornaments prevailed among the Arabs up until the time of Mahomet.[4]

Thus far, Gideon has been an overcomer in every trial, but another test presents itself on the heels of this victory. The men of Israel made a request of the one who had led the uprising that liberated them from the Midianites: *"Rule over us, both you and your son, and your grandson also"* (v. 22). So enthralled was Israel with Gideon that they wanted him to be the fountainhead of a long-lasting royal dynasty. The people wanted a king and a royal line that they could admire. Gideon refused, saying, *"the Lord shall rule over you"* (v. 23). Neither he, nor his sons, would intrude on Jehovah's rulership of His people.

A few centuries later, a similar demand by the people during Samuel's prophetic ministry would be made. The request angered the

Lord, because His people had higher regard for a human king to reign over them than Himself. They wanted to be like the nations, and have a visible head over them, rather than submitting to their God alone (1 Sam. 8:5-7). Gideon was the most respected man in Israel at that time and he could have effortlessly been exalted over the people, if choosing to, but he wisely does not take what was not his to have – only Jehovah ruled Israel. He was merely God's appointed judge and deliverer. H. L. Rossier suggests that the flattery of the Lord's people after some accomplishment is just as devastating to the man and woman of faith as the flattery of the world:

> It is no longer the flattery of the world, but that of the people of God. The men of Israel said unto Gideon: "Rule thou over us, both thou and thy son and thy son's son also, for *thou* hast delivered us from the hand of Midian." They put their leader in the place of Jehovah and offer him the scepter. "Rule thou over us." None are more prone to clericalism than the people of God. It is not only the bane of Christendom, it is also the innate tendency of the natural heart of believers. The fact of ministry being blessed is apt to lead us to make of the servant a "minister" in the human sense, thus losing sight of God. By the grace of God, the faith of Gideon escaped this danger. He said resolutely, "I will not rule over you, neither shall my son rule over you; *Jehovah shall rule over you.*" The object of his ministry was that God should have the pre-eminence and lose nothing of His authority over His people.[5]

Although Gideon did not directly supplant Jehovah's rule in Israel, he did make a foolish request that in time would lead the people away from Him nonetheless. Gideon bids those involved with the battle to donate to him all the gold earrings seized from the defeated army as a gesture of thankfulness for his efforts (v. 24). F. C. Cook suggests that the reference is actually to nose-rings, rather than earrings:

> The custom of wearing nose-rings prevails in Eastern countries to the present day. The circumstance of Job's friends each contributing a nose-ring of gold (Job 42:11) is a remarkable parallel to the incident in Gideon's history. Rings of gold were also used as money in Egypt, as appears on several early monuments, and by the Celts.[6]

Regardless of which type of gold jewelry was actually referred to, Gideon's request was granted. A garment was put down to collect the spoil which equated to 1700 shekels (vv. 25-26). The entire activity was a terrible blunder! The gold earrings of the Ishmaelites were connected with paganism and Gideon in turn used the gold to craft an ephod which was publicly displayed in the city of Ophrah.

With the Levitical system in disarray, perhaps Gideon thought a memorial would be beneficial for the people to recall how God had miraculously delivered them from the Midianites. Despite what may have begun with good intentions, no one should create something that challenges God's revealed will: *"You shall not make for yourself a carved image – any likeness of anything that is in heaven above, or that is in the earth beneath"* (Ex. 20:4). The ephod became a national idol, and Ophrah, not Jerusalem, the place of worship. So while Gideon had rightly refused the kingship of Israel, his actions effectively intruded into God's priesthood and introduced a different form of idolatry to God's people.

In Genesis 35, God calls on Jacob to get rid of the idols that were among them. Jacob's family obeyed this command: *"They gave Jacob all the foreign gods which were in their hands, and the earrings which were in their ears; and Jacob hid them under the terebinth tree which was by Shechem"* (Gen. 35:4). The fact that Jacob quickly discarded this evil paraphernalia and did not attempt to melt it down and reuse the metal for other legal uses is admirable. He realized that God's people must *"Abstain from all appearance of evil"* (1 Thess. 5:22). This, in principle, is good counsel for new converts that may be tempted to sell tokens (magazines, music, movies, etc.) of the old life, which ought to be destroyed as not to stumble others. Why did Jacob's family give him their earrings? As we observe in the narrative before us, earrings were frequently used in the manufacturing of idols or to support other immoral idolatrous practices (Ex. 32:2-4; Hos. 2:13). Thus, not only was Jacob ridding his family of their idols, but he was also ensuring that they did not have a provision to create new ones. What wisdom!

Unfortunately, Gideon did just the opposite of what Jacob did – he gathered gold earrings to fashion that which would later became an idol. This unfortunate exercise of connecting what is spiritual with what is not occurs often in Scripture and always results in something which is contrary to the mind of God. Instead of resting in the promises of

God, Abraham took Hagar as a concubine, and Ishmael was born; he is then rightly displayed as a symbol of the flesh, that which opposes the things of God throughout Scripture.

In the beginning, Gideon tirelessly labored to rid Israel of pagan oppression; sadly, by his own hand it regained a foothold under a different guise – for in time Gideon's golden ephod became a religious snare to his own house, and the entire nation (v. 27). God's people must learn that misplaced affection leads to misdirected allegiance which ultimately results in chaos and judgment. Gideon had answered God's call; he pulled down Baal's altar and destroyed his images, erected an altar for Jehovah, and then was used to defeat an immense invading army. Like Gideon, we too may remove some evil from our lives only to replace it with a less conspicuous idol because it is a work of our own hands.

Christendom is no stranger to golden ephods! It has often been the case that what was received by divine appointment later becomes a reproach to Christ through humanized religion. Separated from their source, religion can transform meetings of the church, personal ministry, believer's baptism, the Lord's Supper, prayer, etc. into ephods before which people prostrate themselves. For example, believers are to remember the Lord through the breaking of the bread, yet if believers begin worshipping their worship in doing so, what was once special to the Lord becomes idolatrous.

When religious form displaces God, a subtle form of idolatry occurs. Even the place of suffering and shame of our dear Savior, the cross of Christ, has become a decorative symbol, an idol, to be profited from and esteemed. Yet, the cross has no value apart from Christ. Is it not dishonoring to the Lord to venerate a meaningless token and neglect honoring the Lord of Glory and acknowledging what He has done? Like the bronze serpent on the pole, sometimes familiarity results in religious blindness; we can never be too careful – to esteem our own handiwork is often the first step leading us away from the Lord.

An idol of the mind is as offensive to God as an idol of the hand.

— A. W. Tozer

Gideon returned to Abiezer to live out the remainder of his days; he lived to be a *"good old age"* (vv. 29, 32). He had many wives who bore him seventy sons (v. 30) and at least one concubine who lived in Shechem; she bore him a son named Abimelech, who is a prominent character in the next chapter (v. 31). It is likely that Abimelech's mother was a Canaanite; this would explain the strong animosity between himself and his half-brothers in the next chapter.

The golden ephod aside, Gideon's faithfulness secured forty years of peaceful existence in Israel (v. 28). This is the last reference in the book of Judges of God granting Israel peace after a victory of a particular judge. Because of their increased wickedness and repeated rebellion, this normal quality of Jehovah's deliverance was not conferred to His people after Gideon's judgeship.

Gideon died and was buried with his father Joash in Ophrah. After his death, Israel forgot Jehovah and how, through Gideon, He had rid their land of foreign invaders (vv. 33-34). The Jews sadly returned to idolatry, specifically Baal worship; furthermore, they no longer esteemed Gideon's family for what he had accomplished for them (v. 35). Despite God's goodness, His covenant people again chose to provoke His jealousy by committing spiritual adultery. Consequently, chapter 9 is a sorrowful chapter, but God will send another man named Tola to rightly lead and judge His people.

Meditation

What God says is best, indeed is best, though all men in the world are against it. Seeing, then, that God prefers His religion; seeing God prefers a tender conscience; seeing they that make themselves fools for the kingdom of heaven are wisest; and that the poor man that loves Christ is richer than the greatest man in the world that hates him: Shame, depart, thou art an enemy to my salvation.

— John Bunyan

Am I a soldier of the cross, a follower of the Lamb,
And shall I fear to own His cause, or blush to speak His Name?
Must I be carried to the skies on flowery beds of ease,
While others fought to win the prize, and sailed through bloody seas?

Sure I must fight if I would reign; increase my courage, Lord.
I'll bear the toil, endure the pain, supported by Thy Word.

— Isaac Watts

The Career of Abimelech
Judges 9

The son of Gideon's concubine, Abimelech, visited his kin (i.e, brothers of his Canaanite mother) living in Shechem. He asked them if it were not better for him, one of their own, to rule over them than the seventy sons of Gideon (vv. 1-2). His appeal was not made in connection with Gideon, but rather through his mother: *"as your bone, and your flesh."* Like Ishmael, Abimelech derived his nature from his mother, and Abimelech's mother was a pagan – he was a product of the flesh and likewise represented the carnal appetites and desires of the flesh nature. The fact that he referred to his father as Jerubbaal, instead of Gideon, would surely invoke the disgust of Baal worshippers in Shechem. Abimelech, a carnal man, knew just how to appeal to proud pagans and gain their cooperation.

A few decades earlier the Shechemites had pleaded that Gideon and then his sons would rule over them, but Gideon would not be their king, declaring that Jehovah alone would rule over them (8:23). However, the men of Shechem now included a strong Canaanite presence, and they did not value Gideon and his sons. Instead, they were inclined to agree with Abimelech and his brothers; they would do well to have a robust ruler over them. It is significant that the Hebrew word *ba`al*, meaning "a master" is used to refer to "the men" or literally "the masters" of Shechem throughout this chapter (e.g. 2-3, 6-7, 18, 20, etc.). These men were filled with a spirit of self-exaltation and felt Abimelech's proposition could gain them a higher status than what they presently enjoyed. The "lords" of Shechem therefore bestowed Abimelech seventy pieces of silver of pagan treasury to demonstrate their approval (v. 3). Hence, the devil's resources were put into an opportune position to accomplish his evil work, i.e., into the hands of a proud, arrogant man.

With this money, Abimelech hired worthless men to follow him; his first task was to find and murder Gideon's seventy sons, his half-brothers, to ensure that there would be no rivals to his rule (v. 4). Abimelech brutally murdered sixty-nine of Gideon's sons on one rock, but the youngest son of Gideon, Jotham, hid himself and could not be found (v. 5). A. R. Fausset suggests that the sixty-nine sons that were slain were:

> Intended to be expiatory victims to Baal for the sacrilege done to him by Jerubbaal their father. As Jerubbaal had sacrificed to Jehovah upon the altar rock, using the sacred bullock and the Asherah grove associated with Baal worship to consume this burnt offering, so the Baal worshippers, who had been offended at his act…offer them all together upon an altar-like stone.[1]

Clearly, Abimelech was not a God-appointed judge; rather, he was a wolf desiring to have preeminence over others and after obtaining it would devour his own subjects. C. A. Coates likens the self-exalting tactics of Abimelech with those of Diotrephes in the New Testament.

> Abimelech is not presented to us as one who delivered Israel, but as representing a principle that has been very much in evidence among the people of God. Like Diotrephes in the New Testament, he seems to be governed by the one desire to be prominent and to rule. He entirely lacked the brotherly spirit; he was so lacking in it that he slew all his brethren. We do not see in Abimelech a single spiritual feature from the beginning of his course to the end; so he is a warning rather than an example.[2]

The men of Shechem responded to Abimelech's brutal act by crowning him their king, a title of authority among pagan nations, but not in Israel (v. 6). What the nations represented to Israel is what worldliness resembles to the Church today. It would be good to remember that worthless men want titles of honor and the esteem of others; not so for devoted servants of Christ. The New Testament identifies callings, but accredits no titles of status to any believer – all such titles are Christ's alone (Matt. 23:7-12).

Hence, Abimelech was successful and evil was apparently triumphant, but such mockery of justice and goodness will never result in peace among men. Treachery and struggles for supremacy have their eventual end, but disturb the tranquility of God's people during their diabolical interim. Yet, H. L. Rossier reminds us that at such dismal times, God permits a ray of light in the darkness to provide hope for the faithful:

> *He does not leave Himself without testimony;* this we may reiterate with confidence, as we pass through difficult times. And should there be, as here, only a single witness left for God in this world, may we be that one, that despised Jotham, the last of all, but standing steadfast for God. Preserved by the providential goodness of Jehovah, "he went and stood on the top of Mount Gerizim" (v. 7).[3]

Upon hearing the news of Abimelech's kingship, Jotham came out of hiding and ventured to the top of Mount Gerizim. From this location he lifted up his voice and delivered a stern warning to the men of Shechem (v. 7). Shechem was a city which guarded the entrance to the valley between Ebal and Gerizim. The sterile slopes of Ebal, the sentinel to the north, sharply contrasted its twin-giant to the south, Mount Gerizim, with its fruitful beauty, picturesque foliage, and natural limestone ledges (which often served as benches during congregational gatherings). The lush valley below measures only five hundred yards across, though the two mountain summits are nearly two miles apart. This location is a natural amphitheater and capable of containing a vast audience of people as demonstrated when Joshua read the Law of Moses to the entire nation (Josh. 8:30-35). All this to say that the men of Shechem would have had no difficulty hearing Jotham's rebuke.

Jotham represents the faithful remnant who provide a clear testimony of the truth and suffer for it. He was the last survivor of Gideon's sons and had a clear and decisive testimony against the dominant evil of that day. In short, Jotham's foliage allegory accuses the men of Shechem of making a self-exalting and self-serving man their king, while maligning a man, Gideon, who had served them selflessly for years and had risked his own life to deliver them from oppression (vv. 8-17). Irving L. Jensen summarizes the meaning of the foliage allegory:

> Using a figure of a republic of trees electing a king, he pictures Israel's conduct. He spoke of Gideon and his sons as the olive tree,

the fig tree, and the vine, who wisely refused to leave their God-appointed places of usefulness in order to go and reign over the trees. But he likened Abimelech to a bramble, who not only eagerly accepted the invitation but warned that he would destroy the cedars of Lebanon if the trees did not elect him king.[4]

In summary, the noble Gideon and his worthy sons had declined the offer of the kingdom; however, the vile son of a Canaanite, Abimelech, was determined to have it, but such a position would cause his own ruin and that of his followers in the end. Abimelech was a worthless man who wanted the preeminence in Israel and threatened destruction if he was not recognized as their king (v. 15). However, Jotham's warning reminded the men of Shechem that there was no occasion for the trees to choose their own king; they were all merely trees that the Lord had planted. Nor was there any cause for Israel to set a king over themselves; the Lord alone was their King.

The content of Jotham's foliage allegory is well chosen to represent three distinct aspects of Israel's existence and fruitfulness which have been consistently opposed by satanic authority: the vine, the fig tree, and the olive tree. The nation of Israel, as a political reality, is likened to a noble vine (a grape vine; Jer. 8:13), which God planted in the world (Jer. 2:21, 12:10). Yet, the prophet Jeremiah told his fellow countrymen that Israel's selfish shepherds had made God's beautifully planted vineyard desolate (Jer. 12:10). When Israel is spoken of as a fig tree in Scripture, the metaphor relates to the religious element of Israel, which often was fruitless for God (Jer. 8:13; Matt. 21:19-21). The olive tree is a symbol of spiritual vitality which results in a true testimony for God (Zech. 4:6). With Christ's Second Advent to earth, the spiritual blindness of the Jewish nation will come to an end and they will trust in the Lord Jesus Christ, their Messiah (Zech. 12:10). In this spiritually fruitful state, the Jews will be known as the olive tree which provides a testimony of God's goodness to the entire world (Hos. 14:6; Rom. 11:17-24). The enemy has always sought to prevent Israel from being a true lampstand for God in the world. However, Jotham's parable highlights how Jehovah would cause His people to flourish in every aspect of aspiration: political, religious, and spiritual.

Jotham's message accused the men of Shechem of being treacherous in condoning Abimelech's slaughter of Gideon's sons (v. 18). If this was a just deed, then blessings and rejoicing would follow the union between Abimelech and the people of Shechem, but if not, Jotham decreed that Abimelech and the men of Shechem (especially the house of Millo) would devour each other (vv. 19-20). After finishing his speech and announcing his curse, Jotham fled some thirty miles northeast to the town of Beer, for he was afraid of Abimelech (v. 21). He departed from the congregation of Israel in Canaan; he abandoned them to suffer the chastising to come, and indeed was nearly upon them.

The amenable relationship between Abimelech and the men of Shechem lasted three years, at which time the Lord intervened by causing an ill-will between them (vv. 22-23). Both parties were guilty for the murder of Gideon's sons and the Lord now commenced the process of extracting justice for their crime (v. 24). Men choose their sin, but God determines the consequences of their sin. The inhabitants of Shechem devised a scheme to kill Abimelech: they robbed those who traveled the trade routes through the central highlands near Shechem in the hopes that Abimelech, who controlled the commerce in the region, would hear about it. He then would be drawn out to investigate and be caught in their ambush (v. 25).

They also put their confidence in Gaal and his brethren to assist them in getting rid of Abimelech (v. 26). Nothing else is known about Gaal, but no doubt he was a smooth talker who saw an opportunity to advance himself amid the contentious situation. While in the sanctuary of Baal-berith, Gaal, in a drunken stupor, curses Abimelech and boasts of besting him and his men in battle, even destroying them (vv. 27-29). Zebul, the ruler of Shechem and an Abimelech sympathizer, is enraged by Gaal's foolish insults and sends messengers to Abimelech that Gaal is fortifying the city against him (vv. 30-31). Zebul further advises Abimelech to take advantage of the nighttime hours by traveling to Shechem and surrounding the city in order to spring a surprise attack on Gaal in the morning (vv. 32-33). Abimelech does this and positions his men in four divisions around Shechem (v. 34).

Early the next morning Gaal and Zebul are both at the entrance of the city's gate, which had likely just been opened after being securely shut for the night (v. 35). As Gaal looks out, he thinks he sees people rushing down the slopes of nearby hills, but Zebul suggests that he is just seeing the shifting shadows caused by the early morning sun (v. 36). However, as Abimelech's forces near the city, Gaal realizes that indeed these are companies of troops (v. 37). Zebul, who had summoned Abimelech, then taunted Gaal to honor his bold threat from the previous day; he should go out and fight those he had vehemently scorned (v. 38). Gaal does, but the confrontation goes poorly for him and many of his men are killed or wounded before the city's gate (vv. 39-40).

Gaal was able to flee back into and secure himself in Shechem after this loss, but Zebul later expels Gaal and his men from the city (v. 41). The next day the people of Shechem went out to work in the fields and to take spoil from those killed in battle. Abimelech was enraged that many in Shechem had been influenced by Gaal to rebel against him. After learning about the Shechem scavengers being outside the protection of their city, Abimelech sends three companies of troops against the city in a surprise attack (vv. 42-44). The city is destroyed and its inhabitants slaughtered, except for those who had taken refuge in the tower of Shechem, the stronghold of the house of Baal-berith (v. 46). Matthew Henry observes that when God uses men to work His purposes, they rarely understand His ways:

> Abimelech intended to punish the Shechemites for slighting him now, but God punished them for their serving him formerly in the murder of Gideon's sons. When God uses men as instruments in His hand to do His work, He means one thing, and they another. That which they hoped would have been for their welfare, proved a snare and a trap, as those will certainly find, who run to idols for shelter; such will prove a refuge of lies.[5]

Abimelech led his troops to the forest at Mount Zalmon, where he chopped down a tree and carried the firewood back to Shechem; his men did the same (vv. 47-48). The wood was used to set the stronghold on fire in order to finish off the last inhabitants of Shechem; Abimelech's plan succeeds and about a thousand people perished in the fire (v. 49).

It is unknown why Abimelech then attacked the city of Thebez, about ten miles to the northeast of Shechem; perhaps he became aware of an alliance with Shechem against him (v. 50). The city fell to Abimelech except that some men and women had taken refuge in a strong tower (v. 51). Abimelech attempted to gain access by burning the gate of the tower (v. 52). Having punished the city of Shechem for its evil against the house of Gideon, Jehovah would now execute justice on Abimelech, as Jotham had pronounced.

A woman in the tower threw down a piece of a millstone which cracked open Abimelech's skull (v. 53). The Hebrew word used for millstone suggests that it was an "upper millstone." The "upper stone" or "rider" was much smaller than the one it was placed on top of, varying in shapes and in diameter from a few inches to nearly two feet and having a width of two to six inches. This particular millstone likely weighed several pounds. Rather than suffer the disdain of being killed by a woman, Abimelech orders his armor-bearer to draw his sword and finish him off, which he does (v. 54). The death of Abimelech ended the conflict and everyone returned to their own homes; God's vengeance was full for the brutal murders of Gideon's sons (vv. 56-57). The same influences of the world that disturbed Israel, namely, the ambition of Gaal, the deceit of Zebul, the fickleness of Shechem, and the violence of Abimelech were all used to secure their combined destruction.

This chapter affirms a reality that we observe throughout Scripture: there will always be legitimate consequences for engaging in corruption. Paul explains that what *"a man sows, that he will also reap; for he who sows to his flesh will of the flesh reap corruption"* (Gal. 6:7-8). The Jews were quite aware of the "sowing and reaping" principles of the harvest, but needed to learn that these applied to sin also. The three laws of the harvest are as follows. First, you reap what you sow. Second, you reap more than what you sow. Third, you reap later than you sow. All the suffering that the inhabitants of Shechem experienced resulted from their sinful behavior three years earlier. The consequences of their sin, destruction of their city and death for its inhabitants were much more than they could have ever imagined at the juncture when they aligned with Abimelech to do evil. Whether others know of our sins or not, the laws of the harvest still apply to us too; hence it is better to repent, come clean, and suffer the consequences willingly than to continue in sin and be devastated by it.

Meditation

One great power of sin is that it blinds men so that they do not recognize its true character.

— Andrew Murray

It is because of the hasty and superficial conversation with God that the sense of sin is so weak and that no motives have power to help you to hate and flee from sin as you should.

— A. W. Tozer

Tola, Jair, and Slavery Again
Judges 10

After the devastating escapades of Abimelech, the Lord summoned Tola, the son of Puah, to be Israel's seventh deliverer (v. 1). We are not informed much about Tola other than that he was from the tribe of Issachar (Gen. 46:13), lived at Mount Ephraim, and was buried at Shamir. His judgeship over Israel lasted twenty-three years (v. 2).

The narrative is almost as brief in disclosing information about the next deliverer, Jair, a Gileadite who judged Israel for twenty-two years (v. 3) and was then buried in Kamon (v. 5). Concerning the judgeships of Tola and Jair, Matthew Henry concludes:

> Quiet and peaceable reigns, though the best to live in, yield least variety of matter to be spoken of. Such were the days of Tola and Jair. They were humble, active, and useful men, rulers appointed of God.[1]

Yet, we should not think of Tola and Jair as minor judges, as some commentators have concluded. C. T. Lacey suggests that to treat these two judges in this manner is to do them grave injustice:

> The very fact that their service spanned a combined total of forty-five years is enough in itself to raise them above the level of being termed, "minor men of God." No service for the Lord, however small it might appear to be, should be devalued or dishonored by referring to it as "minor."[2]

Jair had thirty sons who ruled over thirty cities in Gilead which formed a collective called Havoth-jair. The reference to each of his sons riding on ass colts may indicate that Jair's judgeship was characterized by peace and prosperity. Throughout Jewish history, kings typically rode donkeys during times of tranquility, but mounted horses to engage the enemy in war. The Lord Jesus illustrates this

101

symbolism in His own ministry: During His first earthly sojourn He rode the foal of a donkey while declaring His heavenly message of peace (Matt. 21:1-10); this fulfilled Zechariah's prophecy (Zech. 9:9). At His second advent to the earth, He will be riding a white horse to execute fierce wrath and vengeance against the wicked (Rev. 19:11-16). Additionally, owning donkeys for private transportation is much like families owning several automobiles today – it was a sign of affluence (5:10).

After the passing of Jair, Israel unfortunately suffered spiritual declension and returned to paganism. This resulted in eighteen years of intense chastening at the hands of the Philistines and Ammonites; Jews on both sides of the Jordan River were immensely distressed by the raiding (vv. 7-9). The list of false gods honored is extensive: Baalim and Ashtaroth of Syria, the gods of Sidon, Ammon, and of the Philistines (v. 6).

The chastisement of God's people served its intended purpose in bringing them to repentance. They sincerely confess their twofold sin: serving Baal and forsaking Jehovah (v. 10). Matthew Henry explains the principle of chastening, repentance, and restoration that we witness here is one that is prevalent throughout Scripture:

> God is able to multiply men's punishments according to the numbers of their sins and idols. But there is hope when sinners cry to the Lord for help, and lament their ungodliness as well as their more open transgressions. It is necessary, in true repentance, that there be a full conviction that those things cannot help us which we have set in competition with God. They acknowledged what they deserved, yet prayed to God not to deal with them according to their deserts. We must submit to God's justice, with a hope in his mercy. True repentance is not only for sin, but from sin.[3]

The Lord replies to their sorrowful confession by acknowledging His past faithfulness to deliver and protect His people in Egypt, while wandering in the wilderness, and throughout the seven-year Canaan conquest (v. 11). Furthermore, during the era of the Judges, the Lord has responded to the bitter cries of His people to deliver them from the Sidonians, Amalekites, and the Maonites (perhaps referring to the Midianites). This probably refers to Jehovah's intervention during the days of Ehud (3:13) and Gideon (7:1-8:12).

The injury that Israel inflicted on God's heart is dramatically displayed by satire in verses 13-14: *"Yet you have forsaken Me and served other gods. Therefore I will deliver you no more. Go and cry out to the gods which you have chosen; let them deliver you in your time of distress."* The children of Israel responded to this decree by confessing their sin and expressing a willingness to accept whatever punishment Jehovah determined was appropriate for their offense. Yet, they did plead with the Lord to remove the rod of their discipline (i.e., the oppression of the Philistines and the Ammonites) because it had served its purposed (v. 15). The Lord, citing previous instances of their short-lived repentance after His past deliverances, chose not to abruptly respond to the petitions of His people.

Jehovah's chastening had been severe as *"Israel was greatly distressed"* (v. 9). Verse 16 reveals that Jehovah also suffered with His people during this time of discipline: *"His soul could no longer endure the misery of Israel."* It grieved the heart of God to see His people suffering for their sin. To demonstrate that they were truly repentant and were not just rendering lip-service to God, Israel willfully put away their foreign gods and began serving Jehovah again (v. 16). This act of true repentance and the continued suffering of His people did prompt Jehovah to call another deliverer, Jephthah, in the next chapter. But chapter 10 closes with Ammonites gathering their army together at Gilead, to confront the leaderless Israelites who have gathered their meager forces at Mizpah (v. 17). We read in verse 18 the question that was on everyone's mind: *"Who is the man who will begin the fight against the people of Ammon? He shall be head over all the inhabitants of Gilead."* Jehovah had yet to reveal his choice for the next judge of Israel. Hence, chapter 10 concludes with the Lord's people waiting on Him to appoint their deliverer who will lead them into battle and liberation.

In application, this chapter teaches us much about what true repentance is and is not, a topic that David explains a few centuries later in Psalm 38 through personal experience: Suffering severely under the chastening hand of the Lord, David petitions the Lord to temper His anger with mercy and to pardon him for his offense. David did not attempt to hide his sin, but readily confessed his foolishness; he was miserable night and day, and was also suffering from a debilitating illness because of his transgression. He knows that his pitiful state, brokenness, and deep sighing were fully visible to the Lord.

The psalmist does not deny his sin, nor that he is justly suffering because of it, but rather confesses it before the Lord and pleads for God to rescue him from his vicious enemies who are planning his destruction. The situation was desperate, God's discipline had served its purpose, and David now entreats the Lord to not forsake him, but instead be his Savior. Both chapter 10 and David's example teach us not to ignore sin, but to confess it to God, and to not complain about His just recompense for our stupidity. Such repentance should never be repented of, for restored fellowship with God should be cherished (2 Cor. 7:10).

Meditation

> Unless you have made a complete surrender and are doing God's will it will avail you nothing if you've reformed a thousand times and have your name on fifty church records.
>
> — Billy Sunday

> We all want progress, but if you're on the wrong road, progress means doing an about-turn and walking back to the right road; in that case, the man who turns back soonest is the most progressive.
>
> — C. S. Lewis

Jephthah Victory and Tragic Vow
Judges 11

Jephthah was a man of valor, the son of Gilead and a prostitute (likely a local Canaanite woman; v. 1). Gilead demonstrated love towards Jephtath by including him in his family and caring for him as one of his legitimate sons. When Gilead's lawful sons became of age, they promptly severed Jephthah's family ties, claiming he had no share in his father's inheritance because he was the son of "a strange woman" (v. 2; KJV). This language seems to confirm what Josephus the Jewish historian states: Jephthah's mother was not a Jew (Antiq. 5.7.10).

While it is true that the Law prevented an illegitimate son from being a part of the congregation of Israel (Deut. 23:2), the real reason for Jephthah's discharge was because of greed – Gilead's sons wanted to maximize their portion of their father's inheritance. Apparently, the elders of Gilead agreed and consented to his expulsion (v. 7). Jephthah permitted himself to be despoiled of his rights and, to avoid a possible hostile confrontation, departed to the town of Tob, some fifteen miles east of Ramoth-Gilead and just outside of Israel's territory.

We read that worthless fellows joined with Jephthah while in Tob and that they raided and plundered the Ammonites dwelling in that region (v. 3). Sometime later Gilead was under the imminent peril of an all-out Ammonite invasion. The men of Gilead desired a mighty warrior to confront the threat and lead them into battle; they petition Jephthah to return and be their captain (vv. 4-6).

Jephthah had been wrongly despised and rejected by his brethren and yet behaved honorably and perhaps for this reason alone God chose him. In this sense, Jephthah foreshadowed the One who also would be slurred as being the product of fornication and be hated and rejected by His own people – God's own Son and Israel's Messiah (Isa. 53:3-6; John 8:41). Samuel Ridout affirms the pattern – it is only the despised and rejected One who can deliver man from the bondage of sin and the grip of evil:

> It is a despised and rejected one who can affect deliverance. I think that, with many reservations and additions, you have certain things in the life of Jephthah that are very suggestive of our Blessed Lord. His brethren cast him out. They would not have anything to do with him. They refuse him as a disgrace to themselves, and when they saw him, there was no beauty that they should desire him. In that way he reminds us of Him who was rejected by His brethren as Joseph before, when he came to his brethren, was rejected and cast out by them, and David, in later years, when he was sent on a message of love to his brothers in the camp, in the very face of the enemy, was despised and set at nought by them. …The only deliverer, then, of the people of God from the power of evil and evil doctrine, is one who himself has been rejected by his brethren. So it points us in this way to Christ as the only One who can deliver.[1]

Though Jephthah's escapades at Tob seemingly foreshadowed his future role in defeating the Ammonites altogether, there is nothing in the text to suggest that Jephthah was a spiritually-minded man. Indeed, he was an able combatant and did demonstrate humility in dealing with his brethren, but no divine appointment is confirmed, nor do we witness a ministry of mercy towards God's people prior to his judgeship. Rather, the people selected him as their champion out of necessity, and fortunately for them, God had chosen him too.

Hence, the spiritual revival occurring at the conclusion of the last chapter was marred by this presumptuous action of God's people seeking their own means of rescue. While it was true that Jephthah would be the next judge of Israel, the men of Gilead sought a deliverer of their choosing apart from knowing the will of God. During periods of spiritual declension, God's people are prone to meddle in the affairs of God, usually to their own detriment. Providentially for Gilead, God was working in the situation despite their intrusion and self-seeking ignorance. The point is that the call of Gideon stands in blunt contrast to the choosing of Jephthah. C. A. Coates further clarifies this point:

> Jephthah comes to the front simply by the necessity of the case. … It seems as if God would humble His people even by the character of the deliverer He used; He humbles them by driving them to have

recourse to one who had been hated and expelled as an illegitimate son, a man with no status at all. There is a humbling character about the very deliverer that God was pleased to use. Jephthah represents men whom God has used to deliver His people, but who are not spiritual men; men who have had faith to do what was needed in the necessities of the time, and who had the power of the Spirit to do it, but yet were not spiritual. To have the power of the Spirit does not make a man spiritual; he may still do things which are not according to the mind of God.[2]

Jephthah exercised faith in overcoming the Ammonites and for that he is mentioned among the faithful saints of Hebrews 11, but though the Spirit of God powerfully used him, he was not a spiritually-minded man.

Although hesitant at first, because of their past offense, Jephthah agreed to Gilead's proposition, with the stipulation that he would remain their leader after victory was achieved (vv. 8-11). Here we witness Jephthah's carnal desire for headship and honor among his people and his determination to take full advantage of the situation to gain what he covets. This was agreed to and the matter was stated before the Lord at Mizpah. The phrase *"before the Lord"* designates the presence of the tabernacle, or at least the Ark of the Covenant, or of the high priest with the Urim and Thummim (Judg. 20:26, 21:2; 1 Sam. 21:7). In any case, Jephthah publicly recognized Jehovah's authority over Israel and the Ammonites and his reliance on Jehovah to vanquish their enemy.

Jephthah became the ninth judge in Israel, likely overseeing the northeastern region of the nation. In an attempt to avert war, Jephthah initially assumes a meek and non-hostile demeanor towards the Ammonites. He sent messengers to the king of Ammon to respectfully pose the following reasons as to why the Ammonites had no just claim on Gilead (v. 14):

- The region of Gilead was never theirs in the first place; Israel had seized it from the Amorites before entering Canaan because King Sihon would not allow the Israelites to pass through their land, but instead chose to engage them in battle (vv. 15-22).
- Jehovah God had determined to rid the land of the Amorites and bestow to the Israelites (vv. 23-24).

- The Ammonites were not stronger than the Moabites, and Balak, their king chose not to engage Jehovah's people in conflict (v. 25).
- Even if the Ammonites did have such a just claim on Gilead, why did they wait three hundred years to assert it? Clearly, their forefathers did not hold that assessment (v. 26).

In his concluding remarks, Jephthah stated that Israel had not wronged the children of Ammon and that if war was pressed in this matter, Jehovah would render justice to uphold the good of His people (v. 27). Israel was in a pitifully weak condition to wage war, but Jephthah is not constrained by that fact in speaking to Ammon; rather, in faith he correctly affirms God's Word and His authority in the situation. This is how the child of God is to confront the enemy; we are to humbly and faithfully stand fast in the infallible Word of God (Jas. 4:7). We should not threaten, taunt, or mock the enemy, but rather resist him faithfully with divine truth. God will choose His own means for defending His name and achieving victory. We need not be concerned about confronting the devil – we are to do our part in affirming truth and God will do His part in conquering the enemy. The king of Ammon rejected Jephthah's logical arguments and warning; war was now inevitable (v. 28).

Concerning biblical historicity, Donald Campbell explains why the information in verse 26 is helpful to confirm the date of the Canaan invasion to be 1406 B.C. (which Jephthah mentions to be three hundred years earlier):

> According to 1 Kings 6:1 the Israelites left Egypt 480 years before the fourth year of Solomon, that is, before 966 B.C. Adding these figures gives an Exodus date of 1446 B.C. The beginning of the Conquest was 40 years later (after the wilderness wanderings) or 1406. The evidence from Judges 11:26 confirms this. Jephthah said the period from the Conquest to his time was 300 years (Judg. 11:26). Adding 140 years to cover the period from Jephthah to the fourth year of Solomon gives a total of 480 years, which agrees with 1 Kings 6:1.[3]

After the negotiations with the Ammonites faltered, we read that *"the Spirit of the Lord came upon Jephthah"* (v. 29). It is only a man who is empowered by the Spirit of God who can successfully lead Israel in the name of Jehovah and accomplish His work (Zech. 4:6).

Jephthah then mobilizes the Hebrew troops and travels south to engage the Ammonites (v. 30). As mentioned previously, in his holy zeal to obtain victory, Jephthah utters a foolish vow to God:

> *And Jephthah made a vow to the Lord, and said, "If You will indeed deliver the people of Ammon into my hands, then it will be that whatever comes out of the doors of my house to meet me, when I return in peace from the people of Ammon, shall surely be the Lord's, and I will offer it up as a burnt offering"* (vv. 30-31).

Though the Spirit of Jehovah had come upon Jephthah, he evidently still had some doubts and felt he needed to leverage God's favor to ensure victory, so he enters into an unspiritual vow. This vow would later spoil Jephthah's triumph. As we have already witnessed when Gideon created the gold ephod after his tremendous triumph, being endowed with the power and wisdom of the Holy Spirit does not prohibit willful foolishness. The only difference is that Jephthah was imprudent before achieving victory.

Jephthah did not adequately understand God's true character – he had God's power available to him, but did not have the wisdom needed from God's Word to guide his conduct. If he did, he would have known that Scripture forbid him from doing what he foolishly vowed to do. He apparently undervalued God's grace and power at work in the situation and felt that he needed to make an arrangement with God, as if to guarantee His faithfulness. God was silent in the matter; His Word would stand sure despite the religious mutterings of Jephthah. Hence, Jehovah did not approve or disapprove the vow, nor did He even acknowledge it, but merely left the responsibility and consequences of its folly with Jephthah. William Kelly overviews the fallacy of Jephthah's vow and the sad consequences of it:

> Here the rashness of the man enters the scene, the consequence of which is a display of what was painful in the extreme. We have had the power of God acting in deliverance, but man alone is incapable even of a safe vow to Jehovah; and who could fail to foresee the bitter fruit of rashness here? Man is as weak and erring as God is mighty and good: these two things characterize the book from beginning to end. ... As the vow was without God, so an issue was permitted most offensive to the Holy Spirit. We can easily therefore comprehend how

> the holy wisdom of Scripture avoids details on a fact so contrary to the mind of God, as a man dealing thus with a human being, yea, with his own daughter. It seems to me then that the reserve of the Holy Spirit is as strikingly according to God as the rashness of Jephthah is a solemn warning to man.[4]

Jehovah was about the real business of delivering His people from oppression, not responding to humanized religiosity. To this end, Jehovah is with Jephthah and His Spirit invigorates this man of faith despite his shortcomings.

Jephthah and his men engaged the Ammonites in a conflict that spanned a region containing twenty cities between Aroer and Minnith. Aroer was located about 15 miles east of the Dead Sea and just north of the Arnon River. The location of Minnith is unknown, but was probably near Abel Keramim. The Ammonites suffered a horrendous slaughter and were subdued (vv. 32-33). Jephthah returned home to Mizpah as Israel's champion, but his rejoicing quickly turned to sorrow when *"his only child"* (a term of endearment) came out of the house to greet him with shaking tambourines and celebratory dancing (v. 34). Remembering his early vow, he tore his clothes and then sadly told his daughter of his vow and that he could not evade honoring it (v. 35). Despite Jephthah's rash vow, it is noteworthy that he was committed to monogamy, which cannot be said for most of Israel's judges and future kings. He was content to have only one child, rather than engage in polygamy in an attempt to acquire more children, as Jewish men often did (e.g., 1 Sam. 1).

The devotion of Jephthah's daughter to her father is also commendable; she consoles him by saying that the Lord had granted him a great victory and that he must honor his vow despite the consequences to her (v. 36). What was her death in comparison to the tremendous victory that Jehovah had granted her father?

Indeed, Jephthah's vow was tragic, on two fronts. First, he was wholly wrong in his conception of the character of God – he valued what God did not, and it cost him terribly. Second, if Jephthah had only known the Word of God, he would have been aware that there was a remedy for the situation. He could have offered atonement and been forgiven of his foolish vow, thus sparing his daughter the repercussions of his impulsive religiosity. Leviticus 5:4 permits a lamb to be used as a sin offering for someone who uttered a rash oath, or perhaps a forgotten vow, and wanted to be forgiven for doing so. Furthermore, there was a viable option of redeeming individuals who had been dedicated to the Lord by paying specific amounts of silver (Lev. 27:1-8). One trip to the tabernacle to amend for the error would have settled the issue.

Did Jephthah actually offer his daughter as a burnt offering to the Lord? As the narrative is not explicitly clear on the matter, commentators are split on the answer to this question. Yet, it is hard to sidestep the plain language of verse 39: *"He carried out his vow with her which he had vowed."* Human sacrifices were forbidden by Levitical Law (Lev. 18:21, 20:2-5), but during the era of the judges, God's Law was mostly unknown and unobserved by His people. Jephthah had vowed to offer a burnt offering (an *olah*) of *"whatever comes out of the doors of my house to meet me"* (v. 31). Clearly, he was determined to offer a human sacrifice, but probably thought one of his servants would be first to greet him after returning from battle, not his daughter. Jephthah's vow demonstrates how much paganism had influenced the Jewish culture during this near lawless period. His brutality of the Ephraimites in the next chapter (slaughtering 42,000 of them) shows that he had the rudimentary wherewithal to do such an abhorrent act. Given that Jephthah was greatly distressed over the outcome of his vow and that he claimed he must do what he promised to do no matter the cost to him personally all indicates that he did sacrifice his daughter (v. 35).

With that said, it hard to believe that Scripture would elsewhere present Jephtath in such a positive way, if he had offered to God what God clearly detests, a human sacrifice (1 Sam. 12:11; Heb. 11:32). It is therefore plausible that Jephthah dedicated his daughter to the Lord in lifelong celibacy and service, perhaps before the Lord at Shiloh (1 Sam. 1:3): *"She shall surely be the Lord's"* (v. 31); consequently, *"She knew no man"* (v. 39). The reference to her knowing no man may relate to her death being a virgin or to perpetual lifelong virginity. In either case, she was permitted to bewail her virginity for two months with her companions before willingly being offered or entering into her lifelong separation unto the Lord (vv. 37-38). There was no question of her loyalty to her father – she willingly submitted to his authority in this regrettable situation. Jewish maidens lamented annually for four days in honor of her sacrifice (v. 40). Such lamenting better characterizes a memorial of her death, than just her perpetual virginity. However, in either case, she would bear no children and that was a sorrowful affair to any woman in ancient Israel (e.g., 1 Sam. 1:5-7). The reader will have to examine the record and arrive at his or her own conclusion concerning the sacrifice of Jephthah's daughter. It is noteworthy that the Jewish historian Josephus believed that Jephthah did sacrifice his daughter as a burnt offering (Antiq. 5.7.10).

"Jephthah made a vow to the Lord" (v. 31). Such swearing to validate a promise was quite common in the Old Testament. The normal Hebrew word for swearing, *shaba*, which means "to swear'" or "to take an oath," is found 180 times in the Old Testament. It was done to strongly affirm a promise or statement by using the Lord's name.

In the New Testament, however, the Lord Jesus traversed the high moral ground on the subject of swearing. He instructed His disciples, *"But let your communication be, Yea, yea; Nay, nay: for whatsoever is more than these cometh of evil"* (Matt. 5:37). The disciple of Christ does not need to swear to validate his or her words; the merit of everything said should be wholesome, accurate, needful and gracious without adding God's name to it. Hence, the Lord issued a stern warning, *"But I say unto you, **that every idle word** that men shall speak, they shall give account thereof in the day of judgment. For by thy words thou shalt be justified, and by thy words thou shalt be condemned"* (Matt. 12:36-37). Lord, please forgive us for all our idle chit-chat and for allowing our tongues to so foolishly flap in the wind!

Swearing involves tying God's name to our statements in an attempt to better validate what we say – to heighten the credibility of our words. The believer should not engage in such practices, for to do so would certainly bring low the name of God. Listen to James' warning for this sin: *"But above all things, my brethren, swear not, neither by heaven, neither by the earth, neither by any other oath: but let your yea be yea; and your nay, nay; lest ye fall into condemnation"* (Jas. 5:12). Demeaning the name of the Lord by swearing falsely is a terrible thing. As we are forgetful creatures and are rarely perfect in our speech, it behooves us to refrain from swearing oaths which we will most assuredly fall short of keeping. Certainly, the rash vows of Jephthah (Judg. 11:29-40) and Herod (Acts 12:20-23) serve as historical examples of the heavy price to be paid when one foolishly swears to God to do something.

An individual may be put into a position, such as in a court of law, where they would be placed under oath. These situations are rare, but sometimes are unavoidable. Perjury is a form of blasphemy, so if you are put "under oath," be diligent not to defame the Lord's name. *"And you shall not swear by My name falsely, nor shall you profane the name of your God: I am the Lord"* (Lev. 19:12). Swearing falsely has its consequences, for God does not forget:

> *"I will send out the curse," says the Lord of hosts; "It shall enter the house of the thief and the house of the one who swears falsely by My name"* (Zech. 5:4).

The believer should always do his or her best to convey meaningful and accurate speech and to refrain from idle talk. *"Let no corrupt word proceed out of your mouth, but what is good for necessary edification, that it may impart grace to the hearers"* (Eph. 4:29). Solomon wisely concluded regarding the operation of our speech, *"Do not be rash with your mouth, and let not your heart utter anything hastily before God. For God is in heaven, and you on earth; therefore let your words be few"* (Eccl. 5:2). May our profane speech be replaced with praise and our wasted words with silence!

Meditation

A man's life is always more forcible than his speech. When men take stock of him, they reckon his deeds as dollars and his words as pennies. If his life and doctrine disagree, the mass of onlookers accept his practice and reject his preaching.

— Charles Spurgeon

Make no vows to perform this or that; it shows no great strength, and makes you ride behind yourself.

— Thomas Fuller

Ephraim Punished, Ibzan, Elon, and Abdon
Judges 12

As after Gideon's victory over the Midianites, the Ephraimites again prove to be a cantankerous tribe by stirring up strife for no apparent reason but to preserve their pride. After the incredible success of the last chapter, the tribe of Ephraim gathered their forces and journeyed northward to threaten Jephthah with violence because he had not involved them in the battle against the Ammonites (v. 1). However, Jephthah claimed that he did request their assistance, but that they failed to respond; the narrative is silent on both points (v. 2). Jephthah explains that the situation was desperate; they were being invaded. He and his kin were forced to put their trust in Jehovah and confront the Ammonites without waiting for additional support (v. 3).

The poor spiritual condition of God's people is perhaps never more apparent than when needless contention and strife occur; such is the case before us. Even after the devil had suffered an incredible defeat, there was still the opportunity to stir up disunity among God's people. Believers are often aware of the devil's bold lion-like tactics, but fail to recognize his serpent-like subtleties among them. By enticing us to lose sight of our unifying center, Christ, the devil is able to provoke warring among believers. Paul sharply rebuked Christians in Galatia for their destructive conduct towards each other (Gal. 5:15). Regrettably, this onslaught continues to this day. The Christian community is the only army on earth which regularly permits the assault of its own soldiers, resolutely ignores their wounded, and abandons those missing in action. How can the Church represent Christ to lost souls when believers are devouring each other? For the glory of God, may we consider our ways, repent, and stop aiding the enemy!

The proud Ephraimites responded to Jephthah's explanation with insults, which led to a confrontation that resulted in the deaths of 42,000 Ephraimites (v. 4). They soon found out that battle-hardened

Jephthah was no Gideon of meekness and humility. Pride has immense consequences. So intense was the slaughter that the Gileadites, who gained control of the fords at the Jordan River killed any Ephraimite stragglers trying to return home (v. 5). This was at the same location which the Ephraimites had captured to cut off the escape route of the fleeing Midianites during the days of Gideon.

Even if the returning Ephraimites posed as non-Ephraimites, they were easily identifiable by their speech; their pronunciation of the Hebrew *sh* sound was an *s* sound – thus they could not master the correct rendering of "Shibboleth," even to save their lives (v. 6). No doubt there was fault on both sides in this matter, as often is the case in squabbles between brethren, but the lion's share of blame fell on the Ephraimities; they clearly picked a fight with the wrong man. We then read that Jephthah died after judging Israel for six years and was buried in one of the cities of Gilead (v. 7). It is doubtful that the Ephraimites would have submitted to his judgeship after such a slaughter of their clansmen, so Jephthah's influence may have been limited to the Transjordan region.

The narrative swiftly passes over the next three judges of Israel: Ibzan, Elon, and Abdon. These men, all from different tribes, were not called on to engage in armed conflict, but rather to maintain the people in the condition in which the previous victory under Jephthah had placed them. As earlier stated, during the era of the Judges, the tranquil periods of communal life in Israel also afford the fewest remarkable events. So though there were no identified periods of peace after Gideon's judgeship, these three judges were able to maintain a certain level of stability in the land for twenty-four years after Jephthah conquered the Ammonites.

Ibzan

Ibzan lived in Bethlehem and was the tenth judge of Israel (v. 8). He died and was buried in Bethlehem; his judgeship lasted seven years (v. 10). The narrative details Ibzan's work to ensure that his thirty sons and thirty daughters had spouses (v. 9). What is interesting is that he seeks only one wife for each of his sons, which upholds God's design for a monogamous marriage relationship, while he himself engaged in polygamy, as many of Israel's judges and later kings did. However, polygamy is never endorsed by God in Scripture and is generally presented negatively when mentioned. God instituted His pattern for marriage with our first parents – one man and one woman until separated by death. Having established the foundation for family life, God then commanded our first parents to procreate and fill the earth (Gen. 1:28, 2:21-24). If polygamy was better than monogamy, God would have yanked two ribs from Adam and fashioned two women for him. Certainly this would have accomplished the command of filling the earth more quickly, but Adam's need was for a singular "helper."

The first polygamist was Lamech; he also was a murderer (Gen. 4:19-23). It is no accident that Lamech is the sixth in the line of Cain. The number *six* is man's number; both polygamy and murder originated in the rebel heart of man in direct opposition to God's pattern for marriage and his command to fill the earth. The next mention of polygamy is when Abraham took Hagar as a second wife (i.e. a concubine) and she gave birth to Ishmael (Gen. 16). This union was not directed by God, but was a decision rendered by the flesh. God would fulfill His promise to Abraham through the miraculous birth of Isaac. Paul upholds the imagery of Ishmael being a picture of fallible human flesh (Gal. 4:23). The consequences of Abraham's polygamy are still wreaking havoc in the world today.

Children were crucial to Jewish family life. They were helpers, even protectors when older, and eventually the inheritors of tribal allotments in the Promised Land. Inheritance and clan leadership were passed to the next generation through male children. This is why Elkanah likely married Peninah; Hannah, his first wife, could not bear him children (1 Sam. 1:1-8). At this time, men did what was right in their own eyes (17:6). Later, kings often had multiple wives to ensure there were plenty of males who could survive, if a rival tried to seize the throne by massacring the kingly line. Though much sin occurred and grieved God's heart in ancient times, many of these offenses were not imputed as transgression because God had not yet posted His Law (Rom. 4:15, 5:13). When the Law came, it put constraints on sin, in order to show man that he was inherently sinful, condemned before God, and needed a Savior (Rom. 3:20; Gal. 3:24).

For example, God's original plan for marriage did not allow for divorce, but because of the hardness of man's heart, God permitted it in the Law with constraints (Matt. 19:8). Likewise, polygamy was not God's model for marriage, but at that time He only warned against it

116

and put constraints on it (Deut. 17:17, 21:15). Through the Mosaic Law, God proved to the Jews that they were Law-breakers and thus deserved judgment. However, with the advent of the Church age and the coming of the Holy Spirit nearing, the Lord Jesus again confirms God's standard for marriage (Matt. 19:5-6). Unless a marriage covenant is dissolved for the case of adultery (some see this caveat only applying to the Jewish betrothal), any man marrying another woman commits adultery with her (Matt. 19:9). The Lord reposted the original pattern for marriage, and thus was prohibited polygamy in the Church Age.

The fact that a man would be disqualified from church leadership if he was a polygamist tells us what marital pattern is important to God. The apostles only had one wife or no wives (1 Cor. 9:5) and those in church leadership or in the office of deacons could not be polygamists (Tit. 1:6; 1 Tim. 3:2, 12). Scripture records no example of any Christian engaging in the practice of polygamy; monogamy, however, is repeatedly shown to be the proper pattern for marriage (Eph. 5:31-33). So while many of the judges did what was right in their own eyes, and engaged in polygamy, they did not have God's blessing to do so.

Elon

Elon was of the tribe of Zebulun and judged Israel ten years (v. 11). The narrative provides no more information about him other than that he died and was buried in Aijalon in the region of Zebulun (v. 12).

Abdon

Abdon, the son of Hillel, a Pirathonite, was the twelfth judge of Israel (v. 13). His judgeship lasted eight years and he had forty sons and thirty grandsons who each rode on donkeys (v. 14). As previously mentioned, this unusual detail (i.e., the riding of donkeys) may have been included to symbolize the peaceful tenure of Abdon's rule. Abdon was buried in Pirathon in the land of Ephraim, in the mount of the Amalekites (v. 15).

Meditation

Headship is the divine calling of a husband to take primary responsibility for Christlike, servant leadership, protection, and provision in the home.

— John Piper

Let the wife make her husband glad to come home and let him make her sorry to see him leave.

— Martin Luther

Without the will, marriage is a mockery; without emotion, it is a drudgery. You need both.

— Ravi Zacharias

The Promised Nazirite Son
Judges 13

Thirty-one years had passed since Jephthah's defeat of the Ammonites and the narrative does not mention any people groups oppressing the Jews during this interim. Regretfully, chapter 13 commences with the abrupt acknowledgement of spiritual declension among God's people: *"Again the children of Israel did evil in the sight of the Lord, and the Lord delivered them into the hand of the Philistines for forty years"* (v. 13). This is the seventh time that we have read a similar statement relating to the children of Israel returning to evil in Judges. The Philistines during this period were at the height of their power, and unlike most of the previous oppressors, they were not a scourge from without, but rather dwelt in Israel's own territory.

No specifics are provided to describe the backsliding nature of the nation at this juncture, but the weight of the dispensary rod (forty years of oppression – the longest period in Judges) seems to indicate that there must have been widespread idolatry in Israel. The spiritual vitality of Israel is at an all-time low and the corporate testimony is all but lost. The spirit of complacency was so rampant among God's people that they were quite content to serve the Philistines; hence, the last judge of Israel will stand alone against their enemy.

Jehovah will call upon Samson to deliver His people from their tormentors, and in so doing will teach them that the solution to their spiritual despondency is personal *Naziriteship*: A wholehearted separation and consecration to God. H. L. Rossier explains the nature of the Nazirite vow in Jewish history:

Under the law, when all was outwardly in order, *Naziriteship* was of *temporary* duration (Num. 6); in a time of ruin it became *perpetual,* as we see in the example before us. Samson was a Nazirite from his mother's womb. This permanent character of Naziriteship reappeared in Samuel, judge and prophet (1 Sam. 1:3), but ceased with David,

119

type of the royal grace, and Solomon, type of the royal glory of Christ. Then came the ruin of the people under human responsible royalty, as had been the case in the time of the judges under the more direct government of God. After this ruin of the people and of the royalty was complete, Israel was delivered into the hands of the Gentiles, and a remnant of Judah was restored to await the Messiah.[1]

Normally, Naziriteship was entered into by a personal vow and for a distinct period of time, but in Samson's situation the state of consecration was to extend from his birth to his death.

Manoah and his wife were of the tribe of Dan that lived in Zorah; they had no children (v. 2). Manoah and his wife were among a few Danites that were still dwelling in the region allotted to them in the days of Joshua for an inheritance (Josh. 19:40-46). After the Canaan conquest some three centuries earlier, the tribe of Dan failed to drive out the remaining Amorites from their inheritance in time the; Amorites gained strength and took over much of their possession, which was not extensive to begin with. This caused many of the Danites to venture to the far north and conquer the city of Leshem and claim it as their new possession (chp. 18).

God's best was for them to seize their proper inheritance, but Leshem was within the vast region of land promised to Abraham centuries earlier, so the action was permissible. However, disobedience has its consequences and northern Danites were the first Jews in Canaan proper to engage in flagrant idolatry (18:30). Later, the city of Dan would became one of two pagan worship centers established by Jeroboam after the ten northern tribes rebelled against King Rehoboam (1 Kgs. 12:29; 2 Kgs. 10:29). Eventually, God used the Assyrians to punish Dan and the other northern tribes – many were slaughtered, and most of those who survived lost their inheritance and were exiled (2 Kgs. 17).

It is a quandary as to why the Lord chose the final judge from the tribe of Dan, given their less than illustrious history up to this juncture in time and also foreknowing their tainted future. The answer to the query is God's sovereignty. The Lord had to choose someone to be a deliverer, and to assert the necessity of Naziriteship among His people: they must learn that His communion was associated with their consecration. Perhaps the Lord was rewarding Manoah and his wife for their personal commitment to Him and for remaining in the tribal inheritance He bestowed to them.

From a practical standpoint, it is good for us to remember that the principle of God's sovereignty reaches from Genesis to Revelation. In the Church age God has given each believer spiritual gift(s), a calling, and predetermined works of righteousness to walk in (1 Cor. 12:4, 11; Eph. 2:10, 4:11-12). C. A. Coates reminds us that divine power will come out in ability when it corresponds with the position in which we are sovereignly placed:

> If we are prepared to welcome all His sovereign will, we shall welcome our assigned position in sovereignty. A brother has an assigned position; he is to be marked by readiness to pray everywhere – both at home and in the assembly; that is the sovereign will of God. Each brother and each sister is set in God's assembly, and they are set there to function in a certain manner according to the sovereign will of God, and, if we are not, we are failures. If divine power comes in, it would help me to function according to God's sovereign will. "God has set certain in the assembly" – that is a matter of gift. There are certain gifts, and they are graded; they are not all on one level. We must learn our grade in the assembly; it is no use to pretend to be an apostle if I am only a help. If I am content to be a help, power will come in in accepting the sovereignty of God. If we get out of the position in which God in His sovereignty has set us, we cannot expect power. We must not think that Naziriteship is for certain brothers and sisters only; we are under obligation to take the place of Naziriteship, and power lies in honestly accepting and answering to the obligation.[2]

We will soon see that Manoah and his wife embraced their divine calling with joy. The Angel of the Lord first met with Manoah's barren wife to inform her that she would soon conceive and give birth to a son (v. 3). She was not to drink any alcoholic beverages, nor eat any unclean thing during her pregnancy (v. 4). Because she was the vessel chosen of God to bring forth the next deliverer of Israel, she too must also take upon herself Naziriteship. Her son would be a Nazirite unto the Lord from the womb; hence, the hair on his head was not to be cut (v. 5). It would require several years for God's plan for deliverance to come to fruition, but by His prophetic word, the promised child *"shall begin to deliver Israel."*

121

The Nazirite vow was purely voluntary, normally for a distinct period of time, and permissible for either gender. Besides this narrative involving Samson, there is only one other passage in the Old Testament which mentions the Nazirite vow and what it entailed:

> *When either a man or woman consecrates an offering to take the vow of a Nazirite, to separate himself to the Lord, he shall separate himself from wine and similar drink; he shall drink neither vinegar made from wine nor vinegar made from similar drink; neither shall he drink any grape juice, nor eat fresh grapes or raisins. All the days of his separation he shall eat nothing that is produced by the grapevine, from seed to skin. All the days of the vow of his separation no razor shall come upon his head; until the days are fulfilled for which he separated himself to the Lord, he shall be holy. ... All the days that he separates himself to the Lord he shall not go near a dead body* (Num. 6:1-6).

Obviously there is nothing morally wrong with consuming grapes or raisins, or cutting one's hair, so what metaphoric principles might we glean from the Nazirite vow for today? In a good sense, wine may symbolize joy (e.g., Ps. 104:15), but in a wider view to long for the refreshing products of the vineyard can typify one's lusting for worldly pleasure. A true Nazirite was to seek after the things of God and not seek after worldly trinkets and trifles (Jas. 4:4). Furthermore, the Nazirite was not to touch any dead thing, just as believers are not to have close associations with those dead in trespasses and sin (e.g., those pursuing sin, 1 Cor. 5:9-11). Paul's warning explains why this is: *"Do not be deceived: 'Evil company corrupts good habits'"* (1 Cor. 15:33). Lastly, not cutting the hair on one's head (this included facial hair) would be an outward sign noticeable to others. Likewise, believers are to have a visible testimony of their consecration to Christ (Matt. 5:16).

For example, Paul teaches us that the male gender, the man, represents the glory of God; he therefore instructs men to keep their hair cut short and their heads uncovered in gatherings of believers for spiritual exercise. This was to ensure that the glory of God would be properly represented at such times for all to witness (1 Cor. 11:3-6). This to say, that though the Nazirite vow was clearly Jewish, Christians would do well to consider the practical benefits of what it symbolized.

God's people in any dispensation of His operations are to be committed to holiness and to serve Him faithfully. The Nazirite vow was normally terminated with a meal offering (Num. 6:15-19), but not so for Samson; he was to be a Nazirite to God his entire life (v. 7). In the application, all believers throughout biblical history are to be good Nazirites!

The meeting was brief and Manoah's wife did not ask her visitor from where he came, nor did he reveal who he was. All that she could confirm with her husband was that a man of God with angelic countenance had spoken with her and the message he had conveyed to her (vv. 6-7). After hearing his wife's testimony, Manoah prayed to the Lord: *"O my Lord, please let the Man of God whom You sent come to us again and teach us what we shall do for the child who will be born"* (v. 8). The Lord answered Manoah's prayer and the Angel of the Lord again appeared to Manoah's wife in a field. She quickly went and told her husband of their visitor and they both hastily returned to the location where the divine Messenger was waiting (vv. 9-11).

After the Angel of the Lord again confirmed that the couple was going to have a son who would deliver Israel from the Philistines, Manoah asked, *"What will be the boy's rule of life, and his work?"* (v. 12). Manoah was concerned about how to raise the child for the Lord. The Angel of the Lord responded, *"Of all that I said to the woman, let her be careful"* and then he reviewed again all the behavior limitations of the Nazirite vow (vv. 13-14). The Lord did not provide Manoah and his wife a "how to" manual on child rearing, but rather affirmed the upright conduct they should live out before the child, in this case especially the mother. The Lord had already revealed what was necessary for their family's consecration and separation and in such days of ruin, that was of primary importance to Him.

Solomon writes: *"Train up a child in the way he should go, and when he is old he will not depart from it"* (Prov. 22:6). What way should the child go – the same way parents should go. Children should readily witness parents that are devoted to the Lord in their daily conduct, which means they are: unified in serving God, praying together, showing hospitality to others, and studying their Bibles often. This is training children in the way they should go by leading the way through a good example. If children do not see their parents reading the Bible often, they will surmise that they do not need to either. If parents are not observed to have a prayer life, why should the children think conversing with God is important? If parents have a negative attitude towards the church meetings or the church leadership, the children will then pick up the same attitude. If parents are selfish, the children will tend to be selfish. If parents don't live rightly before the Lord, they should not expect their children to. An upright moral testimony speaks louder than instruction and is a rich inheritance to leave your children. Parents must absolutely live the Christian life before their children if they want to encourage them to do the same.

Conviction is worthless unless it is converted into conduct.

— Thomas Carlyle

After hearing the Angel of the Lord's message and warning, Manoah wanted to prepare a kid of the goats for him (i.e., serve him a meal). The divine Messenger responded that he would not eat anything that they prepared, but that he would tarry if they desired to present a burnt offering to the Lord. Manoah then asked their visitor what his name was so they could rightly honor the one who brought these things about. Clearly, Manoah did not understand who he was talking with, for the Messenger had not yet disclosed His identity. The Messenger inquired of Manoah: *"Why do you ask My name, seeing it is wonderful?"* (v. 18). The Hebrew word *pil'iy* translated "wonderful" is also rendered "secret." C. T. Lacey reminds us that this was the word used by the psalmist when contemplating God's personal knowledge of himself: *"Such knowledge is too wonderful for me; it is too high, I cannot attain unto it"* (Ps. 139:6). The Lord was therefore telling Manoah that his name was beyond his knowledge and understanding.[3]

Manoah did as instructed; he prepared a kid and a meal offering and then presented both as a burnt offering on a rock altar (v. 19). The Angel of the Lord then moved within the flames of the sacrifice and ascended to heaven in the smoke; He would not appear to Manoah and his wife again (v. 20). The action of the Messenger demonstrated His acceptance of their sacrifice, meaning He was the One it had been presented to. Manoah wanted to know more than what God was ready to reveal, but after the sacrifice the Lord did *"wondrously"* in their presence. It was through this awesome spectacle that Manoah understood to Whom he had been talking – the Lord Himself.

124

As previously discussed, this was a *theophany*, a pre-incarnate visit of the second person of the Godhead to the earth. Manoah feared that he and his wife would now die because they had seen the Lord (v. 22). However, his wife reminded him that their divine Messenger had accepted their burnt offering and why would He want to kill them after revealing how they were to be used in establishing the future deliverer of Israel (v. 23). The interaction demonstrates a valid principle throughout Scripture: willful sacrifice, in a manner to which God approves, results in further revelation and understanding of God Himself. A primary means of personal sacrifice in the Church Age is through unconditional obedience to revealed truth; God promises to manifest Himself to a greater degree to the one rendering such a sacrifice (John 15:21).

In the scene before us, the Lord ascended up within the flames of the burnt sacrifice to illustrate His message of consecration to Manoah and his wife, and nonetheless His own holy essence. He dwells in the heavenlies, separate from all that is evil. Commenting to the value of Manoah's sacrifice, F. C. Jennings observes:

> The flame of the offering ascends from the holy altar, and with it ascends the angel of Jehovah ... here He adds Himself to the offering; and this, we may safely say, is the only value it possesses; but who can estimate its worth now? He to whom it ascends, and only He.[4]

The Lord Jesus gave Himself completely and willingly as a sweet savor offering (representing all that delights the heart of God the Father) and a non-sweet savor offering (satisfying all that the Father demanded for the offense and damages caused by human sin; Eph. 5:2; Heb. 10:7-9). So though this was a marvelous spectacle for Manoah, the future ramifications of Christ's own Nazariteship and sacrifice during His first advent are also revealed to us. Having been rejected by the world, the Lord speaks with His Father just hours before His crucifixion:

> *As You sent Me into the world, I also have sent them into the world. And for their sakes I sanctify Myself, that they also may be sanctified by the truth* (John 17:18-19).

125

Commenting to practical aspects of this affirmation, H. L. Rossier writes:

> Set apart in heaven, He [Christ] attracts us after, and fixes our eyes upon, Himself; in order that the heavenly character of the One whom the world has rejected may be reproduced in us here below. In presence of this revelation, so instructive for us, but of which Manoah and his wife had but a faint glimpse, they *"fell on their faces to the ground"* (v. 20). And shall not we, in the midst of increasing darkness, adore in fuller measure, the God who has revealed to us, not only a heavenly and glorified Christ, but our place in Him, and has given Him to us as an object that we may reflect Him more perfectly in this world?[5]

For this reason, Paul reminds believers to be constantly mindful of their heavenly citizenship; their union with Christ demands them to be focused on and submitted to the One who is holy and above all:

> *For many walk, of whom I have told you often, and now tell you even weeping, that they are the enemies of the cross of Christ: whose end is destruction, whose god is their belly, and whose glory is in their shame – who set their mind on earthly things. For our citizenship is in heaven, from which we also eagerly wait for the Savior, the Lord Jesus Christ* (Phil. 3:18-21).

> *If then you were raised with Christ, seek those things which are above, where Christ is, sitting at the right hand of God. Set your mind on things above, not on things on the earth. For you died, and your life is hidden with Christ in God* (Col. 3:1-3).

May we too in personal consecration and adoration fall on our faces before the One who is perfectly holy and bids us to be holy too.

Manoah's wife did conceive and bore him a son, whom they named Samson. The child grew, matured, and the Lord blessed him. After reaching manhood, it was evident that the Spirit of the Lord came upon Samson at times in that he suddenly exhibited unnatural strength. Most artistic captions depict Samson as a towering man with bulging muscles – a hulk, so to speak. These are merely humanistic impressions of a strong man, but Samson's strength was supernatural; there is nothing in the narrative to suggest that Samson's frame and physique were

126

anything but normal. The fact that Scripture usually records such details is further evidence that this conclusion is valid (e.g., 1 Sam. 10:23).

David was a mere lad when he defeated the giant Goliath – great physical strength amounts to nothing when much more is required to do the impossible. Until Samson's efforts ensued against the Philistines, he dwelt with his kin, the Danites, in the region between Zorah and Eshtaol. He would later be buried at this same location.

Meditation

Do not strive in your own strength; cast yourself at the feet of the Lord Jesus, and wait upon Him in the sure confidence that He is with you, and works in you. Strive in prayer; let faith fill your heart – so will you be strong in the Lord, and in the power of His might.

— Andrew Murray

The strength of a man consists in finding out the way in which God is going, and going in that way too.

— Henry Ward Beecher

Samson's Weakness and Riddle
Judges 14

Before contemplating the judgeship of Samson, we would do well
to mark the contrast between his official exploits and his personal
character. By divine power Samson did much to honor the Lord and
assist His people, despite the moral weakness so evident in the man
himself. His personal character stands in stark contrast to his spiritual
power. William MacDonald provides this overview of Samson's
strengths and weaknesses:

> He killed a lion with his bare hands (14:6). He killed thirty Philistines
> single-handed (14:19). He broke the cords with which the men of
> Judah had bound him, and slew 1000 Philistines with the jawbone of
> a donkey (15:14-16). In escaping from a trap which the Philistines
> had laid for him, he walked away with the gates of Gaza (16:3). Three
> times he escaped the treachery of Delilah – once by breaking the
> seven fresh bowstrings that bound him, once by snapping the new
> ropes as if they were a thread, and once by pulling out the pin that
> fastened the seven locks of his hair to a loom (16:6-14). Finally, he
> pulled down the pillars of the house in which the Philistines were
> being amused by him, killing more in his death than he did in his life
> (16:30).

> He had a weakness for women, and was willing to disobey God in
> order to get a woman who pleased him (14:1-7). He also disobeyed
> his parents (14:3). He practiced deceit (14:9, 16:7, 11, 13). He
> fraternized with thirty Philistines, the enemies of God's people
> (14:11-18). He gave way to temper and vindictiveness (14:19, 15:4-
> 5). He had a cruel streak in his nature (15:4-5). He consorted with a
> harlot (16:1-2). He dallied with evil (16:6-14). He revealed the secret
> of his strength to the enemy (16:17-18). He was too cocky and self-
> confident (16:20). Last, but not least, he broke his Nazirite vow
> (14:9).[1]

We can confidently conclude that the prominent feature of Samson's judgeship was his incredible strength, not his integrity.

The Philistines occupied the coastal plain directly west of the Judean foothills. They had been the enemy of Israel since the days when Joshua led the Israelites into Canaan (3:1-4). During the era of the Judges, the Philistines repeatedly attempted to expand their dominion by invading Jewish territory. The conflict raged back and forth for hundreds of years until King David defeated Goliath and subdued Philistia (2 Sam. 8). Samson's family dwelt in the border region at the western edge of the foothills commonly known as the Shephelah. The Philistines, with their chariots, were plain warriors and knew it would be foolish to assault the Jewish fortifications in the foothills, thus the long-lasting standoff.

The narrative of chapters 14 and 15 centers in the unfortunate marriage between Samson and a Philistine woman. There can be little doubt that this marriage represents the unacceptable and unnatural relationship between God's covenant people and the Philistines at this time. The intrusion of the Philistines into Jewish society had not been accomplished through conflict per se, but rather through pagan costoms and beliefs. The opening verses of this chapter indicate the ease in which the Jews were now living among their enemy, even intermarrying with them.

Samson first saw the unnamed woman in Timnah and then promptly requested that his parents mediate a betrothal agreement on his behalf (vv. 1-2). This matter grieved Manoah and his wife and they attempted to sway Samson to choose a Jewish maiden for a wife, rather than a woman who worshipped false gods (v. 3). The Mosaic Law prohibited Jewish men from marrying foreign women, because the union would introduce heathen influences among God's people (Ex. 34:16). The children of these mixed marriages, generally speaking, did not learn the Hebrew language (Neh. 13:24). Their pagan mothers could not teach them the language of Zion, which meant the children would not receive biblical instruction, but would rather learn to worship the false gods of their mothers. Accordingly, these marriages angered the Lord; in fact, the prophet Malachi calls these mixed marriages an act of treachery and promised divine retribution on any Jewish man who married a foreigner (Mal. 2:10-12).

129

In the Church Age, believers are forbidden to marry nonbelievers, as such a relationship would also negatively influence the child of God (1 Cor. 7:39; 2 Cor. 6:14). What true spiritual harmony can a child of God and a child of the devil enjoy in such a union? Samson's determination was neither rational, nor spiritual, but rather the result of sensual lusting; "I have seen a woman in Timnah." There is nothing in the text to suggest that Samson even talked to this foreign damsel or her family; rather he observed her and wanted her – "Get her for me." Samson was requesting that his parents conduct the necessary negotiation, and pay the requested dowry to the parents of the bride.

Only Christ has fully lived absolute moral separation from the world – true Naziriteship. Morally speaking, Samson was not separate from sinners, and therefore is not a type of Christ, nor were any of the other judges for that matter, except in their mission of deliverance. Samson, as a Nazirite, should reflect the type of testimony that the Church is to also have in the world as a consecrated people empowered by the Holy Spirit and in communion with God.

There are several instances in chapters 14-16 in which Samson demonstrated tremendous strength; however, the narrative also reveals his moral weakness which ultimately caused his downfall – his lust for women. The repeated phrase *"went down"* in chapter 14 symbolizes Samson's inclination to venture outside the will of God and into the world for gratification. As Eve did in Eden, Samson also wanted what *"was pleasant to the eyes"* (Gen. 3:6). Three times the text states that he *went down* to Timnah (vv. 1, 5, 7). Timnah was about five miles directly west of Zorah, not down (i.e., south, as relating to a map). God expects a husband to desire his wife, but lusting for what is outside God's will is wrong and will lack His blessing. The Philistine woman was forbidden fruit, but Samson was determined to have her no matter how far *down* he had to go to obtain her.

We find the same terminology applied in Genesis 38:1 when Judah departed from his brethren to marry a Canaanite woman who lived in Adullam, a town located about fifteen miles northwest of their home in Hebron: *"Judah went down from his brethren."* Likewise, Abram *"went down into Egypt,"* against the will of God, to avoid the repercussions of a severe famine (Gen. 12:10). It always costs God's people something when they divert downward into Egypt (a symbol of worldliness) to resolve their problems or pursue illicit desires.

Thankfully, God intervened to return Abram to Canaan and hence we read, *"Abram went up out of Egypt"* (Gen. 13:1). Abram (later called Abraham) and his family would suffer long lasting consequences for venturing into Egypt, but God's purposes cannot be thwarted by human error. Rather, as we will see in the life of Samson, God will include Samson's foolishness within His sovereign plan to render vengeance on the Philistines for their brutality against His people.

Despite Samson's inappropriate behavior, God used it; *"He sought an occasion"* against the Philistines (v. 4). Some commentators believe that the "he" refers to Samson, but the narrative does not indicate that God's sovereign purpose to punish the Philistines is Samson's focus; rather he quite enjoys fraternizing with them. God did not cause Samson to desire the Philistine woman, but He did incorporate his lusting within His plan to provoke Samson's anger and invoke retribution against the Philistines – *"it was of the Lord"* (v. 4). When we see these words, we may be sure that the conflict is entirely according to God and without mixture.

Samson went down to Timnah with his parents to achieve a betrothal agreement (v. 5). Apparently, his parents went on ahead to meet the Philistine woman's family while Samson tarried in the vineyards of Timnah. While waiting there, he was attacked by a young lion. The Spirit of God empowered Samson to grab the lion's rear legs and pull him apart, in the same way one prepared a kid of the goats in those days (v. 6). Samson did triumph over the lion, but not in his own strength and that is the lesson that all believers must learn in confrontations with the world, the flesh, and the devil (Rom. 8:13; Eph. 6:13). Unfortunately, while victorious on one front, Samson was falling victim to the satanic device of "unnatural unions" on another – he was infatuated with a Philistine woman in Timnah. On this side of glory believers will always be in a war to overcome evil; one personal victory does not achieve the enemy's surrender, but rather provokes him to use a different stratagem.

Why did the enemy not entice Samson to eat some of the fresh or dried grapes that he was no doubt surrounded by? Apparently, because he was fortified in this area of his life and the enemy knew it. Thus, no attempt is made to cause Samson to compromise his Nazirite vow at this juncture, but rather the devil will seduce Samson through his feminine lusting to follow a path outside of God's will. Though

131

Samson may not have been tempted to violate Naziriteship that day, he was foolish to linger in the midst of what could destroy him. It is noteworthy that the lion attacked Samson in a vineyard when he was surrounded by forbidden fruit and only after Samson had isolated himself from parental accountability. Likewise, many of God's people, isolating themselves from biblical authority and personal accountability, have put themselves in a compromising position and then have fallen prey to the wiles of the devil when tested.

Satan's deception in Eden was successful because our first parents were already admiring the forbidden tree. Often believers have their defenses up to what they know is blatantly wrong, but fail to realize that Satan does not pre-warn of his cunning devices. He rarely tempts us where we are spiritually fortified, but rather in unsuspecting areas of ignorance or of consistent weakness. In Samson's case, it would not be wine, but rather a seductive woman that caused him to violate his Nazirite vow.

To this end, the roaring lion seeking to devour its prey in the vineyard is a fitting picture of Satan (1 Pet. 5:8). That day, by God's power, Samson slew the lion; hence, it was fitting that he did not mention the triumph to others (v. 6). In fact, many details of the narrative were kept private between Samson and the Lord. God's people are strong when they intimately cling to Him, but entanglements in the world hinder communion with God and impede His available strength for us. Three times we read that the Spirit of Jehovah came upon Samson. At such times he demonstrated incredible power to overcome the threatening challenge before him, whether a vicious lion or a hoard of Philistines. Yet, outward power alone was not sufficient to maintain Samson inwardly for the Lord; the same is true for us. The Lord may choose to put illustrious feats within our hands, but if our hearts are not pure, these accomplishments will be bitter-sweet experiences. To know God's power without His ongoing communion is no better than what the pagan Philistines experienced.

Without the Lord, Samson would have died, but in the might of God, Samson was victorious. In application, Samson's example is a good one to follow here: When we gain a spiritual victory over the enemy, let us not gloat about the success, but rather glorify God who granted it. It is not likely that the Lord will call upon us to slay a real lion with our bare hands, but the task of overcoming evil is every bit as challenging. James tells us how it is to be accomplished: *"Submit yourselves therefore to God. Resist the devil, and he will flee from you"* (Jas. 4:7). That is how Christians defeat the relentless lion that is seeking to devour them, i.e, the devil. The Spirit of Jehovah had moved in Samson secretly; it was a private matter; this would seem to indicate that many of the victories to be won are not public adventures, but in the solitary activities of our lives. The devil often gets a foothold in our doings through our personal longings for ease, indulgence, and amusements. True Naziriteship represents a new kind of life which enjoys inwardly what is displayed outwardly, both the death and the life of the Lord Jesus.

Samson arrives at the home of the Philistine woman that he wants to marry and converses with her privately for the first time – he was pleased with their conversation (v. 7). The marital union is agreed to and a short time later Samson returns to Timnah to receive his bride; his parents are with him. Curious as to what had become of the dead lion, he turned aside to find that a swarm of bees and honey were in the carcass (v. 8). Samson scoops up some of the honey with his hand and tastes it. He then brought back some honey for his parents to also eat, but does not tell them where it came from (v. 9). In coming into contact with something dead, the honey was defiled according to Levitical Law and should not have been eaten. Furthermore, touching the lion's dead carcass reveals Samson's careless attitude towards being a Nazirite. It is a thing to be most feared when a child of God can willfully sin without remorse. Samson's lack of moral fortitude is inching him ever so close to a catastrophic end, yet God's sovereign purpose to deliver His people would not be disturbed by Samson's inconsistency.

Samson hosted a wedding feast lasting one week (v. 10). Because no Jewish friends accompanied him to his wedding, the local Philistines provided thirty companions (i.e., purchased friends) to assist in the celebration (v. 11). Perhaps, Samson honored his Naziriteship and did not drink wine during this festive occasion, but the entire scene is pathetic; the future judge of Israel is merrily consorting with the enemy. In contrast, John reminds us that the spiritual man and the world have nothing in common:

> *Do not love the world or the things in the world. If anyone loves the world, the love of the Father is not in him. For all that is in the world*

– the lust of the flesh, the lust of the eyes, and the pride of life – is not of the Father but is of the world (1 Jn. 2:15-16).

What the world offers as satisfying and tangible is temporary – just like Samson's friends: *"The world is passing away, and the lust of it; but he who does the will of God abides forever"* (1 Jn. 2:17).

If there had been proper separation, Samson would not have been with the Philistines to offer them a wager. If he had not returned to the vineyard, the place of previous attack and temptation, he would have had no basis for gloating by telling his riddle. Until this juncture, this matter had been rightly kept private between him and the Lord. So Samson tells his riddle and offers a wager to his wedding guests: If they could solve it within seven days, he would give them thirty linen wraps and thirty changes of clothes, but if not, then they would provide him with the same (vv. 12-13). His paid companions readily agreed to the bet.

Samson then told them the riddle, which was obviously composed from his recent experiences in the vineyard of Timnah: *"Out of the eater came something to eat, and out of the strong came something sweet"* (v. 14). The Philistines could not solve the riddle and not wanting to be impoverished by losing the bet came to Samson's wife for assistance. These men threatened to burn her and her family alive in their home, if she did not obtain the answer from her husband and reveal it to them in time (v. 15).

Samson's wife apparently did not realize what her husband was capable of doing, for she feared the Philistines more than him. For seven days she continued to weep and nag Samson for the answer to his riddle, which only he knew (v. 16). We can safely assume that this was not a merry festive week for Samson – he is consorting with the enemy and his espoused wife is relentlessly nagging him.

Finally, on the seventh day, she wore down his resolve and he told her the answer, which she immediately passed on to the Philistines (v. 17). One of the Philistines conjured up a story that he was plowing with a heifer, when he stumbled upon a lion, "the eater, and the strong" whose carcass contained honey, something "sweet to eat" (v. 18). Samson was enraged that the riddle had been solved and in the power of the Holy Spirit went down to Ashkelon and killed thirty Philistines and took their clothing to pay the wager (v. 19). Samson's judgeship and God's judgment on the Philistines had now commenced.

Samson's anger was not abated; instead of consummating his marriage on the seventh day of the wedding feast, as was customary, he returned to his father's home without his wife. Enough time passed that Samson's new father-in-law perceived that the marriage was annulled, and seeking the good of his daughter gave Samson's wife to one of his paid wedding companions. The fact that he abandoned his wife in Timnah probably indicates that Samson knew that she had betrayed him by sharing the answer of the riddle with others.

Meditation

Temptations, when we first meet them, are as the lion that roared upon Samson; but if we overcome them, the next time we see them we shall find a nest of honey within them.

— John Bunyan

Unwillingness to accept God's "way of escape" from temptation frightens me what a rebel yet resides within.

— Jim Elliot

Samson's Rage
Judges 15

After having lost the riddle wager, Samson deserted his wife and returned to his father's house. This was Samson's proper place; it is never wise to depart from God's people to carouse with the enemy. During this interim the woman's father, thinking that Samson had abandoned his daughter, gave her to be the wife of one of Samson's paid companions, perhaps his best man. Later, during the wheat harvest Samson returned for his wife with a kid of the goat as a peace offering (v. 1). However, the woman's father would not permit Samson to have physical contact with her, as he explained to Samson, she had been promised to another man. Since she was still residing in her father's house, this probably meant that she was betrothed, but not yet officially married. He told Samson that his desertion showed that he *"hated"* his daughter, a term commonly connected with divorce (Deut. 24:3). The father, who had already received a dowry from Samson's father for the older daughter, then offered his younger and more beautiful daughter to be Samson's wife in an attempt to resolve the dispute (v. 2).

Samson, having been deceitfully treated and feeling the loss of his wife, became enraged. He sought for revenge, but targeted the Philistine people as a whole instead of the individuals that had wronged him. He caught three hundred foxes, likely a reference to jackals, tied their tails together with a burning torch in between the carnivores and then let them loose in fields with standing grain (v. 4). The resulting blaze was so extensive that even vineyards and olive groves were destroyed (v. 5). Once the Philistines realized who did it and why, they punished Samson's wife and her father by burning them alive (v. 6). It is ironic that the same mortal outcome that Samson's wife had tried to avoid earlier came upon her through the deceitfulness of sin. The mischief that we seek to escape through lawlessness is often what miserably overwhelms us in time.

Though Samson approved of this act of justice, his revenge was not quenched. He proceeded to single-handedly smite the Philistines with a great slaughter (vv. 7-8). F. C. Jennings observes of Samson: "Samson was a Nazirite, but a Nazirite apart from the Spirit of the Lord can do ten times more mischief than another man."[1] Samson's rage and his desire for revenge brought further adversity to him and his fellow countrymen, but God's sovereign ways were at work and all these things were permitted for a purpose. The Philistines deserved judgment for their harsh treatment of God's people, and God will use Samson's self-focused character and his abrupt anger in a wider sense to punish them. While Samson's actions seem extreme and out of balance, we must remember that God had raised Samson up to deliver Israel from the Philistine oppression (13:5, 14:4). Afterwards Samson dwelt in the wilderness, and the great rock cliffs of Etam became his home fortress.

The location of this stronghold is not known; it is not likely the same place mentioned in 2 Chronicles 11:6, as that would be too far. Given the number of local Jews that were able to quickly visit Samson, a local and well-known rock formation in Judah is more likely. A. E. Cundall describes where Samson's hideout was probably located:

> A site in the vicinity of Samson's home is much more likely and there is much to support the view that it was a cave in the cliffs above the Wady Isma'in, which was accessible only by descending through a fissure in the cliff-face, wide enough for one person to pass through at a time. This strongpoint, in an area well known to Samson, lay about two and a half miles south-cast of Zorah.[2]

Wherever this location was, Samson deemed it quite secure and yet the Jews knew right where he was.

There is not a man in all of Scripture that exhibited the physical strength that Samson did when the Spirit of God moved him. Yet, his moral weakness is equally as evident; he did not hesitate to pursue after whatever he lusted for. His actions of visiting his estranged wife with a kid were for carnal reasons – sex. When the world offered a solution to his carnality (to enjoy his wife's sister instead), his anger over what he could not have was selfish. Even after the Philistines had burned his wife and her father for their offense, Samson's illogical rage destroyed many Philistines who were not involved in the issue. Despite his obvious carnality, God chose to use both Samson's moral weakness and his physical strength to accomplish His purposes: punish the Philistines and to deliver His people from their grasp. He would also refine the character of His judge in the process.

Samson's escapades are a good reminder for us not to estimate the moral worth of a man of God by the greatness of what he does. As Jim Catron reminds us, being divinely appointed and having the power of the Holy Spirit did not make the judges infallible:

> They made mistakes. Gideon made an ephod with caused Israel to sin (8:27). Jephthah made a rash vow which involved his daughter (11:30-40), and we have already mentioned Samson who had a weakness for women (16:4-20). We as believers know as well that having spiritual gifts and the presence of the Holy Spirit in our lives does not automatically give us victory over sin and weakness. We must walk before God in faith and obedience![3]

We find another example of this principle in the New Testament concerning the church at Corinth. They did not lack for the abundance of spiritual gifts, which were wonderfully empowered by the Holy Spirit, yet they themselves were remarkably carnal (1 Cor. 1:5-7, 3:1-3). God will use whatever or whoever to accomplish His purposes. We certainly would not assert moral integrity or bestow high praise to Balaam's donkey, though being wonderfully used of the Lord to rebuke Balaam. Samson was a Nazirite, whom God mightily used to judge Israel's enemies, though he clearly failed to judge his own heart, thus, his moral condition was not in keeping with the divine gift he exercised – sadly this is true of many believers today.

The Philistines rallied their forces and prepared to attack the Jews at Lehi, which was located about ten miles east-southeast from Timnah and deep in the Judean foothills (v. 9). The Jews were startled by this ominous threat and inquired why the Philistines had gathered for war. Their response was singular: *"We have come up to arrest Samson, to do to him as he has done to us"* (v. 10). The Jews in that region were content to survive amid Philistine domination, so three thousand men from Judah went to the rock of Etam to bind Samson. Samson had been dwelling there alone; there is no one to sympathize with him, not even in all of Judah. The Jews hoped that, by delivering Samson to their enemy, war would be averted – one that they assumed they could not win (v. 11). It is ironic that the Jews put their trust into the hands of their enemy, who had just burned their own brethren in an attempt to pacify Samson's rage, instead of favoring their own kin who had already shown himself mighty in the Lord.

This is clearly one of the low junctures in the book of Judges: The Jews do not want to be delivered from oppression; rather, they were content to be the Philistines' servants. For this reason, they were disturbed by Samson's testimony and consented to help the world get rid of the very one God had sent to break their yoke of bondage. Indeed, to be encumbered by the very one destined to bring divine liberation is a mark of acute moral failure. The situation before us highlights the progressive declination of Israel between the death of Joshua and the rise of David. Unlike other judges, Samson stands alone; at least Gideon had 300 faithful comrades to help him in the work of deliverance. But, apparently, there is now no one else who will work for the good of the nation and to exalt Jehovah's name in the land.

Though Samson does not typify the moral excellence of Christ, both deliverers share common qualities in the execution of their ministry: both were rejected by those they had been sent to rescue, both were willingly bound, and both were delivered to the enemy to be put to death. The Jews in Christ's day would not have Him reign over them in righteousness, but were rather content to be servants to Rome; hence they assisted the Romans in ridding themselves of their own Savior.

Returning to the narrative, Samson explained to his own people how he had been wronged by the Philistines. Desiring not to fight against his brethren, he agreed to be bound and returned to the Philistines, if they swore not to attack him (v. 12). They agreed and Samson was bound with two new cords and taken to Lehi, where the Philistine army was waiting (v. 13).

When the Philistines saw Samson bound with cords, they triumphantly shouted – their undefeatable adversary was finally captured and would suffer their wrath (v. 14). However, their shouts of victory were premature, for at that moment the Spirit of the Lord came mightily on Samson and he easily broke out from his bonds. He eyed the discarded "new" jawbone of an ass, picked it up, and smote one thousand Philistines with it in hand-to-hand combat (v. 15). The Hebrew word for "new" is *tsari*, which means "moist, dripping, fresh," thus implying that the donkey had recently died – its carcass was not to be touched by a Nazirite.

As throughout the book of Judges, we see God using what is deemed worthless and ridiculous, an ox-goad, a tent stake, and now a jawbone of an ass, something a Nazirite was not to touch, to gain a miraculous testimony of Himself among His people. This is another example of the Lord permitting certain irregularities during times of extreme crisis which in ordinary times would not be allowed. Samson was permitted to use the only thing that God had made available to him in executing judgment on the Philistines at that particular time and place. This would ensure that the victorious outcome would then only further exalt the name of the Lord.

Samson was pleased to acknowledge his accomplishment: *"With the jawbone of a donkey, heaps upon heaps, with the jawbone of a donkey I have slain a thousand men!"* (v. 16). With the battle over, he tossed the jawbone aside, and renames the place of the slaughter Ramath-lehi, meaning "the hill of the jawbone" (v. 17). It is noteworthy that though his countrymen were nearby, that they did not assist Samson in slaying their enemy, nor did they provide him refreshment after the victory was achieved. The thirteenth judge of Israel was alone, except for the Lord; His people were obviously in deep spiritual declension. Notwithstanding, it was obvious that God was with Samson, and Israel, though previously betraying him, now submitted to Samson's judgeship.

Who would you first talk with after accomplishing some tremendous feat? Samson was very thirsty and called upon the Lord, first to give praise and then to ask for water. He was in a desperate situation: *"You have given this great deliverance by the hand of Your servant; and now shall I die of thirst and fall into the hand of the uncircumcised?"* (v. 18). This is a superb example of a man of faith uttering a prayer of faith (Heb. 11:32). Notice that Samson did not glory in himself, but honored the Lord for the victory and as the One he remained dependent on. Unfortunately, believers often honor themselves after some wonderful achievement. In doing so, they become blind by their own vain autonomy and are permitted to suffer failure by the One who will have their allegiance and dependency.

Additionally, it is important to remember that serving the Lord does not quench the believer's thirst; something else does that. If we do not want to lose the benefits of the conflict, we must seek the Word of God for our refreshment. When Samson called on Jehovah, the word of God came to him and led him to a refreshing spring of water that God had caused to flow out of a rock. Throughout Scripture, the rock speaks of Christ (e.g. Matt. 16:18) and He extended this invitation: *"If any man thirst, let him come unto Me, and drink"* (John 7:37). Beloved, may we resolve to get back into Christ's presence after conflict and be refreshed and strengthened by His word.

David demonstrates in Psalm 143 a similar reliance on the Lord, as Samson does here. Overwhelmed, desolate, and exploited, David laments his situation before the Lord. His contemplations pass over the judicial response he desires against those who have oppressed the innocent; rather, David lifts up his empty hands to the Lord to show his complete dependency and urgently begs God for help. David requests God to revive his soul and for spiritual guidance in the way of righteousness so that he would always walk according to God's will. He then concludes his prayer by requesting the Lord to cut off his enemies and deliver him from trouble. This is another example of a prayer of faith by a man of faith who desires to be in the center of God's will.

The reason many of God's people today do not see the hand of God moving in their lives is that they are not practically dependent on Him. Hence, they do not pray, or cannot do so in genuine faith, or do so with impure motives (i.e., they lust for what is outside of God's will). James puts the matter this way:

> *If any of you lacks wisdom, let him ask of God, who gives to all liberally and without reproach, and it will be given to him. But let him ask in faith, with no doubting* (Jas. 1:5-6).

> *You do not have because you do not ask. You ask and do not receive, because you ask amiss, that you may spend it on your pleasures* (Jas. 4:2-3).

Speaking to His disciples shortly before His death, the Lord Jesus promised them: *"And whatever things you ask in prayer, believing, you will receive"* (Matt. 21:22). This is not a "name it and claim it" or "blab it and grab it" reality, but rather affords assurance that our prayers offered in faith and in the will of God will be answered for the glory of God (John 14:13; 1 Jn. 5:14). Accordingly, the Lord immediately responded to Samson's prayer of faith: *"God split the hollow place that*

141

is in Lehi, and water came out, and he drank; and his spirit returned, and he revived. Therefore he called its name En Hakkore, which is in Lehi to this day" (v. 19). Our sincere prayers not only move the hand of God to act on our behalf, but through them, the Lord also revives our parched souls: *"Those who wait on the Lord shall renew their strength; they shall mount up with wings like eagles, they shall run and not be weary, they shall walk and not faint"* (Isa. 40:31). This is what the Lord did for weary Samson, who called on the Lord after his phenomenal victory.

Despite his moral weaknesses the Lord used faithful Samson to judge Israel for twenty years (v. 20). However, in the next chapter we will witness the loss of his Nazariteship and consequently the end of his judgeship.

Meditation

> The prayer power has never been tried to its full capacity. If we want to see mighty wonders of divine power and grace brought in the place of weakness, failure and disappointment, let us answer God's standing challenge, "Call unto Me, and I will answer you, and show you great and mighty things which you know not!"
>
> — Hudson Taylor

> Satan trembles when he sees the weakest Christian on his knees.
>
> — William Cowper

> You may as soon find a living man that does not breath, as a living Christian that does not pray.
> — Matthew Henry

Delilah and Samson's Revenge
Judges 16

What do Shechem, Samson, and David all have in common? Each one was enticed by the *sight* of a woman, before committing an act of fornication with her. Shechem, a Canaanite, saw Dinah and then raped her (Gen. 34:20). David saw Bathsheba bathing from the rooftop of the palace before forcing her into bed (2 Sam. 11:2). In verse 1 we read, *"Now Samson went to Gaza and saw a harlot there, and went in to her."* In chapter 14, we witnessed Samson desiring to marry a woman from Timnah after merely seeing her at a distance (14:1). Unfortunately, Samson's unconstrained sensual appetite was only subdued after his eyes were put out. It is a weakness of the male gender; we are highly stimulated to lust by the visual sense.

Solomon solemnly warned his son concerning the consequences of being enticed by a *strange woman* and that being led captive by one's own lust brings great sorrow and misery (Prov. 7). In Solomon's illustration, the strange woman appeals to all five senses of her naïve prey, but sight was used first. It seems that after one thousand wives and concubines, Solomon practically understood that unchecked gazing leads to lusting and unchecked lusting promotes immoral behavior. He said, *"The eye is not satisfied with seeing, nor the ear filled with hearing"* (Eccl. 1:8). The bottom line: our flesh is never gratified – it always wants more.

In the verse following, Solomon continues, *"there is no new thing under the sun."* Man's struggles to survive upon the earth and the outworking of his base behavior have not changed since Solomon's day, but technology has ensured that both are easier to achieve. No longer does a man have to venture out of his home to see the strange woman – through techno-filth she can be fully displayed for private viewing anytime and anywhere. The word pornography is directly derived from the Greek word *pornographous* which meant "to write

Relativity and Redemption

about prostitutes" (root words: *porne,* "harlot," and *graphos,* "writing"). The Lord Jesus said that *"whoever looks at a woman to lust for her has already committed adultery with her in his heart"* (Matt. 5:28). Accordingly, gazing on a depiction of a nude woman or actually embracing such a woman (i.e., who is not one's wife) is lewd conduct. Seeking to gratify one's lusts through any form of prostitution (actual or virtual) is against God's will and therefore has dire consequences, as Samson soon learned (1 Cor. 6:15-18; 1 Thess. 4:3).

Besides showing disdain for the moral separation that his Nazirite status demanded, Samson's lusting nearly cost him his life, as the Philistines knew that he was with a harlot and set a trap for him. They surrounded the home he was in and planned to jump him at dawn when he departed (v. 2). However, Samson only remained in the house until midnight and apparently his enemies were unprepared to attack him at that hour.

In ancient times, those living in walled cities normally secured their entrances at night. When Samson came to the perimeter of the city, he found Gaza's gate closed and locked. Samson's solution to this encumbrance was to pull the gate posts out of the ground and then shoulder the gate with its posts and carry them to a summit near Hebron (v. 3). Why Samson hauled the Gaza gate forty miles eastward across rugged terrain is unknown, but no doubt the Philistines understood that there was only one man who could do such a feat – Samson. Perhaps the gesture was symbolic, for whoever possessed the gate of a city controlled that city. Hence, by moving Gaza's gate deep into Jewish-controlled Hebron, Jehovah, the God of the Jews, was showing that He ruled over the Philistine people and He alone controlled their future.

We then read that Samson became infatuated with a woman named Delilah who lived in the valley of Sorek, which was less than three miles west of Samson's home located between Zorah and Eshtaol (v. 4). Though her name is Semitic in origin, she is likely a Philistine. Unfortunately, Samson had a weakness for forbidden pagan women: The Philistine woman of chapter 14 had been pleasing to Samson's eye; the harlot of Gaza had ensnared him but for a moment, but Delilah seized his affection: *"He loved* a woman in the valley of Sorek" (v. 4). The Lord Jesus told His disciples that it was impossible for them to love the passing things of this world and be devoted to Him: *"No servant can serve two masters; for either he will hate the one and love*

144

the other, or else he will be loyal to the one and despise the other. You cannot serve God and mammon" (Luke 16:13). Samson's misplaced affections would cause him to ultimately reveal the mysterious source of his strength; he would betray the one secret to be held in confidence with Jehovah alone.

Hearing of this ongoing relationship, the Philistine leaders came to Delilah and promised to pay her 1,100 pieces of silver if she would entice Samson to reveal the secret of his strength so they could capture and torture him (v. 5). This substantial offer, nearly two talents of silver, clearly indicates how desperate the Philistines were to rid themselves of Samson.

The plan required Delilah to seduce Samson to obtain the information, test the validity of what was revealed, and then summon the Philistines to ambush Samson if it proved accurate (v. 6). Three times Samson deceived Delilah: He told her that he would lose his strength if he were bound with seven green cords, with unused new ropes, and by weaving his hair into seven locks and fastening the entire web with a pin to a beam (vv. 7-17). Delilah implemented each of these three suggested means of depriving Samson of his power, but when she yelled to Samson, *"The Philistines are upon you, Samson,"* he easily freed himself from these various restraints.

Samson was under the heavy yoke of Delilah's manipulation: *"She pressed him daily with her words, and urged him, so that his soul was vexed unto death"* (v. 16; KJV). Notice that she had skillfully prodded him to almost reveal his secret, for in the last fabled solution Samson revealed that his strength was connected with his long hair. Samson thought himself invincible. His arrogant pride had now recklessly nudged him to the edge of a terrifying precipice: *"Pride goes before destruction and a haughty spirit before a fall"* (Prov. 16:18).

Delilah plays the scorned and dejected lover; she pouts and is unresponsive to Samson's advances (v. 15). There is a blinding deceitfulness associated with sin. Any believer can fall prey to this delusion if he or she continues engaging in what they know is outside of God's will too long (Heb. 3:13). True, no ropes could restrain Samson, but in the clutches of sin he would be as feeble as any man. The deceitfulness of sin stimulates our pride, numbs our spiritual fortitude, and allows the flesh to have its own way. At some juncture, the Lord must leave us to ourselves, to experience the horrors of going our own way. Samson was now teetering on the edge of destruction. He had to know that he was being played for the fool. Delilah continued to press him daily until he revealed to her the whole truth of his strength and that he was a Nazirite from his mother's womb (vv. 16-17). She immediately summoned the Philistine leaders, revealed Samson's secret, and agreed to assist them in capturing Samson; she was paid for her skillful treachery (v. 18).

Concerning his weakness for women, we have seen that Samson has been tested in three distinct ways, suggests C. A. Coates:

> The Philistine woman in chapter 14 represents what is natural; the harlot of chapter 16 represents what is carnal; and Delilah represents what is Satanic, for from the outset she is identified with the adversary and does her utmost to destroy Samson. God by His ways delivers His servant from each of these three snares. Samson's weakness left him open to these influences, but that which was of God in him extricated him in each case from the snare. Satan will use either the natural or the carnal or the Satanic in order to undermine the truth of Nazariteship.[1]

Besides these various tactics, sometimes the devil breaks down the resolve of the believer to do what he or she knows is right through repeated solicitations; this is especially true when we are isolated from accountability. Samson's fall in this chapter illustrates this strategy. Samson was supernaturally empowered, but succumbed to the temptation of one persuasive Philistine woman; this occurred when he was apart from his Jewish brethren. At first, Samson stood strong against Delilah's dramatic petitions to reveal to her the secret of his strength. She sought to betray him and profit from his capture. Even after three failed attempts, for some reason Samson continued to listen to her pathetic appeals. He yielded to her fourth advance and revealed the secret of his power. He was shorn while he slept and was subsequently captured, blinded, and enslaved (vv. 19-21). Samson's weakness for women and separation from accountability made him susceptible to the enemy's ploy.

It is one thing for a child of God to waste time entertaining goats instead of tending to God's sheep, and it is quite another to leave the safety of the sheepfold and to become the prey by consorting with ravenous wolves. How many Christians would have avoided shipwrecking their lives if they would have only remained in close fellowship with the Lord and His people? Matthew Henry reminds us that there is a terrible cost associated with lascivious behavior for a child of God:

> Licentiousness is one of the things that take away the heart. This is a deep pit into which many have fallen; but from which few have escaped, and those by a miracle of mercy, with the loss of reputation and usefulness, of almost all, except their souls. The anguish of the suffering is ten thousand times greater than all the pleasures of the sin.[2]

Delilah had another man shave off Samson's hair, while Samson slept comfortably in her lap. It is important to understand that Samson's long hair was not the source of his power, but rather the outward symbol of being a Nazirite, his consecration and separation to God. It was his connection with the Lord that made him strong, not his hair. When the shaving process was complete, Delilah warned Samson, as she had before, that the Philistines were upon him. Samson awoke and said, *"I will go out as before, at other times, and shake myself free!"* but the sad statement that follows would ensure that was not to be: *"But he did not know that the Lord had departed from him"* (v. 20). For over twenty years Samson had faithfully depended on the Lord and was wonderfully used in accomplishing His work. But now Samson is self-confident and has compromised his Nazirite commitment, and what is worse, he does not even know that the Lord has withdrawn from him. C. H. Mackintosh observes: "The lap of Delilah proved too strong for the heart of Samson, and what a thousand Philistines could not do was done by the ensnaring influence of a single woman."[3] From this sorrowful scene before us, J. N. Darby draws out a practical warning for the Church to heed:

> We can scarcely imagine a greater folly than that of confiding his secret to Delilah, after having so many times been seized by the Philistines at the moment she awoke him. And thus it is with the assembly: when it yields itself to the world, it loses all its wisdom, even that which is common to man. Poor Samson! His strength may be restored, but he has lost his sight forever.[4]

Samson's example of a godly leader stands in sharp contrast with that of Caleb's in the days of the Canaan Conquest (chps. 14-15). Caleb exhibited unabated divine strength in his latter years because he lacked, he knew he lacked, and he knew who alone could resolve his lack: *"If so be the Lord will be with me, then I shall be able to drive them out, as the Lord said"* (Josh. 14:12). The Lord was with him and he seized his inheritance by overcoming a fortified city held by giants. His humility and continued dependence on God were unrelenting. In comparing these two great heroes of the faith, H. F. Witherby poses the following warning to believers:

> Too many an aged Christian soldier seems to regard his long term of service as a plea for immunity from that hourly dependence on God, which at the first won him his victories; and *"if the Lord be with us"* [Caleb's response] becomes exchanged for the vainglorious and the degenerate, *"I will go out as at other times before, and shake myself"* [Samson's response] (Judg. 16:20).[5]

Caleb understood that his dependence on the Lord infused him with divine power; thus, it did not matter to him that his possession was occupied by giants. Hebron was his inheritance and he wanted to bravely claim it for God. Even though he was eighty-five years of age, he knew *the Lord was with him* and therefore he had confidence that he would drive the Anakim from his inheritance and He did!

After Samson's eyes were put out, he was shackled with bronze fetters and forced to turn a grinding stone in the prison house mill (v. 21). Samson now knew the full consequences of self-confidence and pride – sin has the power to *blind, bind,* and *grind* down the child of God. Yet, Samson's hair grew back; this was a sign of hope that God had not deserted him despite his previous failure.

As previously mentioned, there was no intrinsic power in Samson's hair, but his uncut hair was a symbol, a reminder, of his consecration to the Lord – much in the same way that male circumcision marked the Jewish people as being holy to the Lord. Samson had compromised his Nazirite fidelity, both symbolically and practically speaking, but thankfully, he would again learn the necessity of daily dependence on the Lord. In time, his hair grew back, and through suffering and humility he regained his Naziriteship (v. 22).

Thousands of Philistines gathered at the temple of Dagon to offer sacrifices and celebrate their deity's deliverance of Samson, their unbeatable Jewish adversary for twenty years (vv. 23-24). Desiring to further humiliate him, Samson was brought to the temple for their amusement (v. 25). Samson had apparently been providing them some type of entertainment because he asked to be able to rest for a moment by leaning against the pillars (v. 26). This request was granted and he was led by a boy to the two pillars of the temple. This was a coliseum-like structure supported by two main columns in the center. This was quite a spectacle; the man who had slain thousands of them in combat was led by the hand of a boy. Dagon's temple was packed, which forced about three thousand Philistines to venture up to the roof in order to see and gloat over their once legendary enemy (v. 27).

David, Daniel, and Nehemiah were men of prayer; Samson was not. Only twice do we hear him briefly calling on the Lord (15:18, 16:28). But God, still having an offense to be settled with the Philistines, was not willing to close the history of the judges with such a humiliating defeat. For the insult to His own name and the brutality rendered to His people, Samson's desire for personal vengeance is marshalled.

Samson calls on the Lord to remember him and to strengthen him one last time that he might avenge the Philistines for his two eyes and die with them (v. 28). The fact that Samson called upon the Lord indicates that a genuine work of revival had already occurred in his heart. This is not just a matter of seeking vengeance; rather Samson wanted to end his life in a way that would remove his shame and also exalt Jehovah's name among both the Jews and the Philistines. God had granted Samson's earlier prayer to preserve his life against the Philistines at Etam; now God would also honor Samson's self-effacing request to die well against them.

The strength Samson had lost by sin, he now recovers by prayer. With each of his hands upon the two supporting pillars, Samson strained and with divine power from within pushed them apart; this caused the entire structure to collapse in a colossal heap (vv. 29-30). So in his death, Samson slew more Philistines, the brutal enemy of God's people, than he did in his entire lifetime. Yet, his corpse laid beside other corpses in ruins of Dagon's temple; certainly a life of separation would have earned him a more noble death than this.

By Samson's last act, he shows us that when our self-willed-ness dies, the power of God will be revealed again in our lives. The practical ramifications of this truth must be heeded by all believers. Paul sums up the matter this way: *"I have been crucified with Christ; it is no longer I who live, but Christ lives in me; and the life which I now live in the flesh I live by faith in the Son of God, who loved me and gave Himself for me"* (Gal. 2:20). The believer must die to self to experience the power of Christ's life; only by losing one's life do we find one worth living (Luke 9:24). While it is true that Samson failed in the flesh, he finished well in God's might.

Samson was buried with his father Manoah in a location between Zorah and Eshtaol. His conception and birth had been divinely announced at this location; it was where he had been raised as a Nazirite, and it was now his resting place. After judging Israel for twenty years, his work was finished (v. 31).

Meditation

Temptations which accompany the working day will be conquered on the basis of the morning breakthrough to God. Decisions, demanded by work, become easier and simpler where they are made not in the fear of men, but only in the sight of God. He wants to give us today the power which we need for our work.

— Dietrich Bonhoeffer

I believe that you will often find that a Christian never gets to the end of himself until he gets to his deathbed. Really, his whole life has been spent in temporizing with the world, until he gets face to face with eternal issues, and there is an end of self as there is an end of life. ... The end of self should be reached at the cross, and there we should abide, always counting ourselves dead unto sin, but alive unto God in Christ Jesus.

— A. T. Pierson

Religious Confusion
Judges 17

The era of the judges concludes in the previous chapter with the death of Samson, Israel's thirteenth judge. The final five chapters of Judges serve as an addendum containing two distinct stories or examples of Israel's religious and moral apostasy occurring not long after the death of Joshua. Verse 6 reads, *"In those days there was no king in Israel; everyone did what was right in his own eyes."* The leading phrase *"In those days"* indicates that the author lived after the establishment of the kingly government in Israel, while the latter statement again confirms that moral relativity guided the nation's conduct before that time.

The evidence within chapters 17-21 would indicate that the civil war with Benjamin (chps. 19-21) happened shortly after the events pertaining to Micah and the Danites in chapters 17 and 18. The young grandson of Moses (18:30) and the older grandson of Aaron (20:28) are both mentioned in this final narrative. It is also stated that all the tribes from "Dan to Beersheba" (i.e., implying the far north and the far south) gathered to war against Benjamin (20:1). Clearly, then, the events of chapters 19-21 are subsequent to Dan moving northward in chapters 17-18 (perhaps occurring 30 to 50 years later). In summary, all the events contained within this addendum occurred within the days of Othniel and Ehud, not long after the death of Joshua and his peers.

Chapter 17 commences with a bizarre story of a man named Micah returning 1,100 pieces of silver that he stole from his mother. She had previously cursed the thief, not knowing that it was her own son. The depravity of Israel is hence illustrated by this family dynamic: a man so in love with money that he would defy natural affection and rob his own mother, and a mother so far from God that she curses instead of prays over the loss. The apple did not fall far from the tree; the woman's silver was her god; thus we should not be surprised that her son valued it beyond its proper worth also. Micah's name means, "who is like Jehovah," but clearly his spirituality was in name only; the reality of his life demonstrated his low estimation of the Lord.

Elated by the return of the silver, she says, *"May you be blessed by the Lord, my son!"* (v. 2) and then pays a silversmith 200 pieces of silver to forge an idol and also to create a carved image in Jehovah's name. The fact that she did not devote all the silver to such a just religious cause reveals her own covetous spirit. What Micah received through a fallen nature was further enhanced by the example of his mother. Children, unsurprisingly, learn to value more by what they see in their parents than by what they are told by them.

The enthusiastic connection of Jehovah's blessing with idolatrous practices shows the severity of religious apostasy at this time. False religion has always sought to mock what is divine in origin by imitating it. Micah's mother had taught her son what was idolatrous, but yet connected it with the name of Jehovah. It should be no surprise then that Micah's own home was known as a house of gods. He mimicked the Levitical system by creating a special ephod, a teraphim, and even consecrated one of his sons as a priest over pagan paraphernalia (v. 5).

This was the gravest offense that a Jew could commit: to have so thoroughly forgotten Jehovah and His Law that one could shamelessly dishonor Him by setting up a rival image and priestly system in His own name. Clearly, Micah's mother was an earth-dweller; she did not hold true to the heavenly light of God's revealed Word. Such revelation preserves God's people from all forms of substitutions which might replace the heavenly light. C. A. Coates describes how the same type of sin might occur today in the Church Age:

> If I must have an image, a picture, or ritual to make divine Persons more real to me, it is a turning aside from the spiritual. It is easy for us to get on the line of graven and molten images. A molten image would be something that could be easily multiplied. It is cast in a certain form; it is like a fixed form of service. If we get into a fixed form, in our prayers and praises, we may be in danger of molten images, instead of what is living and suitable to the light of revelation. What is not in spirit and in truth tends to either a molten image or a graven image. A molten image is a thing that can be easily multiplied; you could print it in a book so that anybody could follow it. The graven image is a little more the product of the activity of the

human mind – conceptions of God worked out in man's mind, not according to the light of revelation, but worked out according to the mind of man. I think the graven image would suggest that. We must beware of human touch in connection with the holy things of God.[1]

Unfortunately, such heathen customs were widespread among God's covenant people during much of this time period. The Law expressly prohibited the Jews from worshipping any false gods or creating any carved or forged images for religious purposes (Ex. 20:3-4; Lev. 19:4; Deut. 4:28). Jehovah was jealous of His people and threatened to destroy those who broke this commandment; at the very least He would judge offenders and their descendants even to the third and fourth generation (Ex. 20:5; Deut. 6:15). There was no king to enforce God's Law, so each man did what he thought was morally right in his own mind. When moral relativity rules human thinking, man becomes a god unto himself. Without fear and awe of the Lord, man's moral restraint becomes selective, inconsistent, and injurious – he does what he pleases with little regard for the consequences (Rom. 1:21-32).

One day Micah spotted a young Levite drifter from Bethlehem-judah sojourning in the area. This young man should have been fulfilling his duties in service to Jehovah, as supported by the tithes and gifts of the people stated in the Law. However, Israel was not following these stipulations of the Law, which forced priests and Levites to pursue whatever livelihood they could to survive. Thinking that Jehovah was signifying his approval of his gods by bringing the Levite to him, Micah invited the Levite into his home and offered him a job as his priest. Although the Levite had a connection with the house of the Lord, he had no right to its priesthood, so such an offer, no doubt, had a professional appeal. If accepted, the young man would receive clothing, room and board, and an annual salary of ten pieces of silver, plus the honor and esteem of others in the region. Those were agreeable terms and perks, and the young man was quite content to dwell with and work for Micah. In time, Micah considered him as one of his own sons.

The young Levite was unemployed, so naturally this sudden tremendous opportunity, which he had not been expecting at all, must have been provided by the Lord, right? This is a common conclusion that sadly many believers arrive at today, but clearly this was not an occupation that had Jehovah's endorsement, as it was in direct opposition to His Word. Let us be careful not to read so much into circumstances in rendering important decisions in life, such as family moves or employment changes; otherwise we might exchange what is a merely a test of faithfulness for the tragedy of compromise.

The final verse of the chapter again demonstrates the religious confusion prevalent among the Jews during much of this era: *"Then Micah said, 'Now I know that the Lord will be good to me, since I have a Levite as priest!'"* (v. 13). Micah actually expected a blessing from Jehovah because he had linked his idolatrous practices with the Levitical order commanded in the Mosaic Law. The delusional side of sin is never more evident than when man, through humanized religion, does the exact opposite of what God commands and eagerly expects God's blessing for doing so. Unfortunately, this same sin occurs today in much of Christendom; God is not honored by religious dogma that contradicts His revealed will in Scripture!

Meditation

Over the realms of pagan darkness, let the eye of pity gaze;
See the kindreds of the people lost in sin's bewildering maze;
Darkness brooding on the face of all the earth.

Thou to whom all power is given, speak the word; at Thy command
Let the company of preachers spread Thy name from land to land!
Lord, be with them always to the end of time.

— Thomas Cotterill

Danites Move North
Judges 18

During the tribal allotment process in the days of Joshua, the least desirable portion fell to Dan (Josh. 19:40-48). Joshua does not describe their tribal region because they were bounded by the already-detailed borders of Ephraim and Manasseh to the north, Benjamin to the east, and Judah to the south. The books of Joshua and Judges record that many Danites abandoned their God-given inheritance to the Amorites and moved north of Naphtali a few years after receiving their possession (v. 1). Spiritually speaking, they represent those who have nominally experienced heavenly ground, but instead of going on with the Lord and experiencing His best for them, they venture an easier way in the pursuit of satisfaction. C. A. Coates further explains this portrayal:

> This is a picture of the people of God seeking a place on earth, because heavenly territory makes too much demand on them. They speak of the land at Laish as being spacious in every direction and of there being no want of anything that is on the earth. There is a sphere of things that lies open to be seized on where people say, "We are rich and increased with goods and have need of nothing." Micah's religion just suits those conditions. The heavenly ground was not spacious enough for these Danites, and they reached a place where there was no one who possessed authority to put them to shame, where conscience was never exercised.[1]

The Danites living in Zorah and Eshtaol, which would later be the home of Samson, sent five men of valor northeastward to spy out a new land for their tribe (v. 2). When they came to Mount Ephraim, they lodged in Micah's home (v. 3). While there, they recognized the young Levite serving as Micah's priest and inquired how he came to live with Micah. The young man told the five spies that he was Micah's hired

155

priest (v. 4). Wanting to know if they had God's blessing on their endeavor, they inquired of Micah, who affirmed that they could go in peace because the Lord would prosper their way (vv. 5-6). The spies departed and going further north (beyond Naphtali's territory) they found a spacious land, lacking nothing, centered about the city of Leshem (Laish). The peaceful people of Leshem were unsuspecting, kept to themselves, and were far enough from Sidon (about 27 miles) not to be assisted if attacked. The spies concluded that this was an ideal city to seize as their new inheritance; they returned to Zorah with their recommendation (v. 8).

Shortly after receiving their inheritance, Joshua records that the Danites determined that their portion was *"too little for them"* (Josh. 19:47). Initially, this was not true, but Amorites quickly took over much of their land. While the best response would have been to drive out the inhabitants within their designated possession, as God had commanded them to do, they did decide to move north to conquer Leshem and claimed it as their new possession (v. 9). Like the Transjordan (the home of the two and a half tribes), Leshem was within the vast region of land promised to Abraham centuries earlier. God's permissive will ensures that His grace is available to us, even when we willfully stray from His best plan for our lives. God permits us to choose what we do, but He chooses the consequences of what we do.

There are consequences of choosing the *permissible* instead of the *good*, or choosing the *good* rather than the *best*, but our heavenly Father is capable of bestowing blessing as He chastens, corrects, and redirects. As the writer of Hebrews affirms, this parental discipline is an affirmation of God's love for us (Heb. 12:6). The Lord may bestow to us what we request to teach us a valuable lesson as He did with the nation of Israel after they demanded a king. It was not what He wanted for His people, but His people needed to learn this fact through experiencing the consequences of lusting for what was outside the will of God. In time the Danites would learn this lesson, but at this juncture they believed that Jehovah was with them and that He would deliver the city of Leshem to them for a new home (v. 10).

Six hundred Danites willing to engage in warfare decided to move north and resettle in Leshem (vv. 11-12). They took their families and livestock with them – this long excursion was an all or nothing venture (v. 21). Samuel Ridout explains why the Danites were vulnerable to idolatry at this time and then sounds an alarm for all God's people to avoid repeating their mistake:

> The tribe of Dan had not taken their inheritance. The Philistines occupied a large portion of it on one side, and they were not able to expel the Amorites, so they were driven up into the mountains, and cramped so closely that they had no enjoyment of their inheritance. There is a suited opportunity for idolatry to come in. The people of God who are not satisfied with the full enjoyment of their own inheritance surely are just ready for the enemy to come in and lead them astray. It is an unfilled heart, a heart that has failed to enter upon its own portion, which is open to these assaults. Just as we were seeing what was characteristic of the whole nation of Israel, it failed to enter upon possession of all that was its own; so here, and the heart that is unfilled with what is its own, that is not in the enjoyment of that, is ready for the enemy to come in and lead it into idolatry.[2]

When we choose not to go on with the Lord by faith we lose the opportunity to practically experience our full portion in Him (Eph. 1:3). It is not long before our satisfaction and joy in the Lord wane, then we lose interest in what is important to Him, and soon we become nothing more than a self-seeking clanging gong. Such were the Danites!

While en route to Leshem (which was about a hundred-mile trip), the five spies again stopped at Micah's house (v. 13). The spies informed their brethren of the ephod, the teraphim, the carved image, the melted image, and the Levite priest that abided there (vv. 14-16). The decision was made to steal all of Micah's pagan items and sequester his priest. The spies told the young Levite that it would be better for him to go with them and be *"a father and a priest"* to an entire tribe rather than to be a priest in the house of one man (vv. 17-19). The opportunity for popularity and fame appealed to the young man, who, after stealing all of Micah's pagan items, departed with the Danites (v. 20). In taking Micah's idols, the Danites had committed a double crime; it demonstrated that they neither feared God, nor had respect for their fellowman. Godliness and honesty were not to be found among them.

Verse 21 testifies to the fact that the Danites knew they had done wrong and were expecting retribution for their crime: *"Then they turned and departed, and put the little ones, the livestock, and the goods in front of them."* And they were correct, for Micah gathered as many people as he could (probably servants, family, and friends) and pursued after the Danites; his goal was to recover his gods and his priest (vv. 22-24). However, after overtaking the Danites, it became obvious that they were not going to return the stolen articles without a fight. Seeing that his contingency was no match for the Danites, Micah decided that the matter was not worth dying over and returned home empty-handed (vv. 25-26).

The Danites conquered and burned the city of Leshem (Laish), settled in that region, and rebuilt the city, calling it "Dan" (vv. 27-29). Jacob had prophesied that Dan, whose name means "judge," was going to be as treacherous as a snake by the roadside instead of being righteous and providing justice to Israel (Gen. 49:17). As we learn from this chapter, they were the first tribe in Canaan proper to engage in flagrant idolatry (v. 30). The young Levite's name is not revealed until verse 30: Jonathan. He and his descendants served as priests for the tribe of Dan until their captivity. The specific captivity is not mentioned, and given the date of writing, the author of Judges could not have known about the Assyrian invasion some six centuries after the events of this chapter. Certainly, King David would not have tolerated Dan's idolatry during his reign some three and a half centuries into the future. It is likely that the reference is to the Philistine captivity in the days of Samuel about three centuries later, which was just prior to the era of Jewish monarchs (1 Sam. 4:11).

This understanding is confirmed in the next verses: Dan's paganism rivaled God's appointed system of worship for His people the entire time that the tabernacle was erected in Shiloh (v. 31). The Lord had previously warned His people through Moses to only offer worship and offerings to Him at the specific location He chose: *"But you shall seek the place where the Lord your God chooses, out of all your tribes, to put His name for His dwelling place; and there you shall go"* (Deut. 12:5). Joshua pitched the tabernacle at Shiloh (Josh. 18:1-8) and about four centuries later David moved it to the city of David (on the southern outskirts of Jerusalem; 2 Sam. 6:12-17).

Dan's pagan priesthood would eventually come to an end during the early Monarch Period. Yet, idolatry was deep-seated in Dan, and Jonathan's pagan system was merely the forerunner of what Jeroboam would establish in Dan after Solomon's death. Dan, in the north, and

Bethel, in the south, would become the two centers of paganism for the northern ten tribes (1 Kgs. 12:28-31).

However, during the time of the judges, the tabernacle erected at Shiloh stood as a beacon of hope and truth to the nation. Unfortunately, many, like the Danites, shunned its testimony; others like Boaz, Elkanah, and Hannah sought Jehovah at the house of God in Shiloh. The two systems are in contrast: God's establishment for His people and the other which professedly honors Him, but is idolatrous in nature and a perversion of truth. The latter puts God's people under the influence of earthly things and deprives them of joyfully possessing their God-given inheritance, while the former ensures divine communion, blessing, and power.

Satan will always have his rival system to the things of God: Congregating to build a tower to heaven at Babel vs. obediently spreading out and populating the earth; idols and false gods vs. Levitical worship and obedience to the Law; Satan's harlot (false religion) vs. Christ's virgin Bride (the Church); the Antichrist vs. Christ. Satan is the counterfeit king and continually rebels and resists the things of God and causes others to do the same.

The evidence in verse 31 indicates that the tribe of Dan moved northward soon after the conquest of Canaan, likely within ten years. Young Jonathan was the son of Gershom, who was the son of Moses (Ex. 2:22). F. Duane Lindsey clarifies the apparent name discrepancy in the text:

> For Moses the Hebrew text has inserted a superlinear *n* into the name of Moses (moseh) to make it read "Manasseh" (mnasseh). This was apparently a pious scribe's attempt to relieve Moses' grandson, Jonathan, of involvement with idolatry.[3]

The Masoret scribes copied and protected the Old Testament Scriptures from the sixth to the tenth century AD. They were probably grieved that a descendant of Moses was implicated in idolatrous worship and adopted this expedient way of disguising the fact without absolutely falsifying the text. It is noted that the Vulgate reads "Moses," but the Septuagint "Manasses." Moses, not Manasseh, was clearly the father of Gershom (Ex. 2:22), thus Jonathan was Moses' grandson.

After receiving God's commission on Mount Sinai, Moses put his wife Zipporah on a donkey with their two sons, Gershom and Eliezer, and began the long journey to Egypt (Ex. 4:20). For both boys and Zipporah to ride one donkey meant that the boys were young when God delivered the Israelites from Egypt. If Gershom was, say, five years of age, that would mean that he was fifty-two when the conquest of Canaan was complete (1399 B.C.). The time of the judges began after all the elders who outlived Joshua died (2:7). If the last elder (being less than twenty years of age at the time of the exodus in 1446 B.C.) lived as long as Joshua (i.e. 110 years), then a date of 1350 B.C. for this chapter seems reasonable. If still living, Moses' son Gershom would have been approximately ninety-one and could have easily had a son named Jonathan who would have been in his twenties, thirties, or perhaps even his forties (i.e., a young man; 17:7).

It is sobering to consider that the man who spoke to God face to face and accomplished so many wondrous miracles through forty years of faithful service could have a grandson that blatantly rejected the Law of God that his own grandfather brought down from Mount Sinai. Only two generations span one of the greatest spiritual dichotomies in all of Scripture: Moses, whose face shown forth the glory of God and had to be veiled, to the time of his grandson, Jonathan, a pagan priest and idolater.

Children must be trained up for the Lord. Gershom and many of his generation did not teach their children to know God (2:10), so later they forsook the Lord and embraced false gods (2:12-13). Hence, the outcome of parental neglect resulted in God severely chastening His people. Believing parents are to train their children for the Lord (Prov. 22:6; Eph. 6:4), but it is only by the grace of God that they continue in righteousness and are able to influence the next generation for Christ! May we never cease praying for our children.

Meditation

Father, hear us, we are praying,
Hear the words our hearts are saying,
We are praying for our children.

Keep them from the powers of evil,

From the secret, hidden peril,
From the whirlpool that would suck them,
From the treacherous quicksand pluck them,

From the worldling's hollow gladness,
From the sting of faithless sadness,
Holy Father, save our children.

Through life's troubled waters steer them,
Through life's bitter battle cheer them,
Father, Father, be Thou near them.
Read the language of our longing,
Read the wordless pleadings thronging,
Holy Father, for our children.
And wherever they may bide,
Lead them home at eventide.

— Amy Carmichael[4]

Moral Degradation
Judges 19

In short, this is one of the most disgusting chapters in the Bible. The spiritual and moral declension of the Jewish nation is blatantly evident in chapter 19: disregard for God's design for marriage, devaluing the fairer gender, rampant homosexual behavior, barbaric practices, and hypocritical attitudes in justifying sin. It is sobering to think that all the filth and debauchery showcased by the narrative is derived from the same flesh nature that is within you and me (Gal. 5:19-21). Only by God's grace are we prevented from doing worse things. Paul puts it this way; *"But by the grace of God I am what I am"* (1 Cor. 15:10). Thank God for grace!

Without a central authority in Israel to enforce God's law, the Jews sank into moral anarchy (v.1). An unnamed Levite dwelt in the region of Mount Ephraim, apparently near Shiloh (v. 18), took a concubine from Bethlehem-Judah. This town was located about twenty-five miles to the south via the central ridge route through the Judean highlands. The title of concubine does not imply moral reproach, but rather a secondary position of a legal wife who did not have the same rights as a full wife.

The practice of taking a concubine (i.e., a legalized mistress) is never endorsed in Scripture, nor is it ever presented in a positive light. Unfortunately, some of the Patriarchs took concubines for humanistic reasons. Impatient Sarai opted for the legal custom of bequeathing Hagar to Abram as a concubine to bear her a son that would then be adopted by Abram with full rights of inheritance (Gen. 16:3). The competition of Jacob's wives, Rachel and Leah, to bear children forced Jacob to take their handmaids as concubines also (Gen. 30). Both families suffered serious consequences for not abiding in God's best design for marriage.

162

God created and instituted marriage in Genesis 2; His design was for one man and one woman to be bound by a lifelong covenant. Unfortunately, as Henry Morris summarizes, man has been keen to distort God's marital standard in various ways:

> It is true, of course, that with marriage as well as with all other human activities, *"God hath made man upright; but they have sought out many inventions"* (Eccl. 7:29). Polygamy, concubinage, polyandry, easy divorce, adultery, promiscuity, and other distortions of the marriage covenant have permeated many cultures; but, as the Lord Jesus said: *"From the beginning it was not so"* (Matt. 19:8).[1]

In time, the Levite's concubine abandoned her husband and returned to her father's home in Bethlehem-Judah. It is possible that the reference that she *"played the harlot against him"* simply refers to her running away, though most commentators favor that she did adopt a licentious lifestyle after deserting her husband (v. 2). After four months the Levite went to Bethlehem-Judah with a servant and two donkeys to retrieve his concubine. Rather than invoking the judgment of the Law on her (assuming that she was adulterous), he was motivated by fleshly desires to have her again for himself. There is nothing in the text to indicate that the Levite actually loved his concubine. He did speak to her kindly and her father was glad to see that his daughter was reinstated to a position of integrity (v. 3). The concubine's father detained his son-in-law several days; the longer he remained, the more public the reestablishment of his daughter would become. The desire to see his daughter's honor at least partially restored seems to verify her previous licentious behavior (vv. 4-6).

On the fifth day the Levite became incensed by his father-in-law's delay tactics and commenced the journey north to Shiloh mid-afternoon (vv. 7-10, 18). If pressed, one might be able to accomplish this entire journey in one day, but leaving Bethlehem in the afternoon meant an overnight stay somewhere along the route home. The servant pleaded with his master to lodge in Jerusalem (Jebus), but the Levite preferred to travel further north to Gibeah or Ramah to be among his own people, rather than the Jebusites (vv. 11-13). He would soon find out that his own countrymen were more vile than the heathen in Jerusalem. The sun was setting when they arrived at Gibeah (about ten miles north of

Bethlehem), so it was decided to abide there among the Benjamites for the night (vv. 14-15).

The travelers had their own provisions, but needed a resident to offer them lodging for the night (vv. 18-19). An older man, originally from Mount Ephraim but living in Gibeah, observed the strangers standing in the street and inquired of them (vv. 16-17). After learning of their plight, he offered his hospitality to them and to also care for their donkeys; his kind proposal was accepted (vv. 20-21). It is interesting that the only provider of hospitality was himself a stranger and sojourner at Gibeah. A good measurement of spiritual vitality among the Lord's people is how well they demonstrate kindness to those the Lord loves. For this reason, believers are to be *"given to hospitality"* (Rom. 12:13) and to do so *"without grumbling"* (1 Pet. 4:9). This was the example of the elderly man from Mount Ephriam, but not of others living in Gibeah; this was the first indication of a serious spiritual setback in that city.

While the older man was entertaining his guests, base men (homosexuals) from Gibeah surrounded the house, pounded on the door of the house and demanded that the old man relinquish his Levite guest for their pleasure (v. 22). William MacDonald summarizes God's disposition towards homosexuality and the moral state of those in Gibeah: "The Lord abhors homosexuality. Human depravity can hardly sink lower."[2] At the hands of these vile men it was understood that the Levite would likely perish (20:5).

Trying to protect his principal guest, the old man attempted to disperse the crowd and when that did not work, he offered the perverse hooligans his own daughter and the Levite's concubine for their enjoyment (vv. 23-24). The Levite's concubine had an appetite for lascivious things, for which she had yet to formally repent of, but the willingness of the old man to permit his virgin daughter to suffer such atrocities provides further proof of the pitiful moral condition of the nation at this time.

This story is similar to the scene at Lot's home in Genesis 19, when Lot offered his two daughters to the base men of Sodom to protect his two visitors, except in this story there were no angels to smite the opposition with blindness. Like Lot, the host of the Levite reasons at the door of wickedness and accepts one evil to avoid what was thought to be a worse one; such is the reasoning of God's people when controlled by secular philosophies and carnality. There was no calling on the Lord for help, but rather a willingness to permit that which is disgusting to the Lord to occur in order to preclude another perversion from happening. Worldliness will always find a way to rationalize sin. The wicked men of Gibeah, perhaps because they lived with the old man and his daughter, did not accept his proposal, but once the Levite handed over his concubine to them, they settled for sexually abusing her all night instead (v. 25). The actions of the Levite show that his attraction to his concubine was purely physical and not substantial. The fact that he was able to lie down and go to sleep indicates that his conscience was not bothered at all by what he had done to preserve his own life. Neither does he seem to be concerned about the excruciatingly painful and humiliating consequences to his concubine because of his cold, callous decision.

It is hard to imagine the horror this woman felt – her husband had betrayed her to save himself, knowing that she would be terribly sexually abused by a group of men; not even her previous harlotry could have prepared her for the horror of that night. What did the old man's daughter, a virgin, think of her father who was ready to hand her over to satisfy the ravenous appetites of perverse ruffians? The narrative sadly shows a general lack of respect and proper care for the feminine gender, a disposition that the New Testament confronts and corrects (Eph. 5:25). God promises to punish a believing husband who does not rightly use his God-given authority to properly protect and care for his wife (1 Pet. 3:7).

The Lord Jesus affirmed God's design for marriage – a covenant between one man and one woman until death separates them (Matt. 19:4-6). This is the pattern that the apostles, church elders, and deacons adhered to (1 Cor. 9:5; 1 Tim. 3:1-12); consequently, there are no examples of Christians engaging in homosexual relationships in the New Testament. There are, however, many warnings and prohibitions against fornication. Jude includes a history lesson in his warning: *"Even as Sodom and Gomorrah, and the cities about them in like manner, giving themselves over to fornication, and going after strange flesh, are set forth for an example, suffering the vengeance of eternal fire"* (Jude 7).

Scripturally speaking, any sexual relation other than between a husband and a wife is referred to as fornication in the Bible. This is why Paul says *"to avoid fornication, let every man have his own wife"* (1 Cor. 7:2). Fornication then includes adultery, pre-marital relationships, homosexuality (e.g. sodomy), bestiality, etc. Under the Law, any Jew engaging in these sexual sins was to be put to death (Lev. 20:10-13), except those engaging in pre-marital sex were to marry (Deut. 22:29). God gave the Law to His covenant people so that they might be a holy people unto Him and separated from the paganism and the worldliness of the nations. While Gentiles were never under the Law, and Christians will never be put under the Law, the *moral aspects* of the Law still reflect God's standard of holiness to us. For example, the Lord Jesus affirmed the relevance of nine of the Ten Commandments during His earthly ministry, the exception being the Sabbath day, as the Church would gather on resurrection day, Sunday, to show Christianity's distinction from the old system put away by the cross. Consequently, Paul says to Christians: by the Law comes the knowledge of sin (Rom. 3:20, 7:7) and the Law shows us our need for a Savior (Gal. 3:24).

When it comes to God's standard concerning sexual orientation, nothing has changed in the New Testament; the only difference is that expedient punishment for sexual sins is not demanded by God for the Church. Such sins are still an offense against God and will be punished, but immediate death is not commanded. To say that the New Testament does not condemn homosexual behavior is absurd. Paul tells us that when people exchange divinely revealed truth for a lie, God is offended; He responds by turning them over to their own reprobate thinking; homosexuality was a primary behavior that resulted when God removed His convicting influence (Rom. 1:21-28). Those who engaged in this type of conduct were worthy of God's condemnation and deep down they knew it (Rom. 1:32). Other verses that condemn homosexual conduct include: 1 Corinthians 6:9-11, 18; Ephesians 5:3-5; 1 Thessalonians 4:3; and Revelation 21:8. Being a Jewish city in Israel, Gibeah was under greater condemnation than the heathen city of Sodom (which God destroyed by fire), for the Mosaic Law sternly condemned homosexual behavior.

In the early morning hours the concubine found her way back to the home of the old man; she collapsed at the threshold of his doorway (v. 26). When the Levite awoke in the morning and opened the door to resume his journey, he found his concubine unresponsive (v. 27). His pitiless command, *"get up, and let us be going"* after seeing her lying on the ground after being abused all night is sad proof of just how hard and depraved our own hearts can become apart from the grace of God. The immoral behavior she once craved had come full circle and consumed her life.

The Levite loaded her limp body on one of the donkeys and returned to Mount Gilead with his servant (v. 28). After arriving, he entered his home, took a knife and divided her corpse into twelve pieces, which he then sent throughout the borders of Israel; this was done to summon a national inquisition (v. 29). Though the tribe of Benjamin received a portion, the men of that tribe did not respond to the summons. Even in Israel's semi-pagan state, such a grotesque act incensed the nation and prompted the other eleven tribes to gather at Mizpah to hear the matter out (v. 30).

Why the fervor to action? Was it for the outrage committed against Jehovah's name? No, otherwise the idolatry of Micah and the tribe of Dan should have met an even more zealous response. In Israel's sunken spiritual state, they did not feel anger for the libel of God's name, but were aroused to action because their personal rights had been trampled upon. However, God would use this situation to awaken the entire nation to their disgraceful insensibility towards what was important to Him; howbeit, the process to achieve their brokenness would be very costly.

Meditation

> With no fact as a referent, what is normative is purely a matter of preference.
>
> — Ravi Zacharias

Relativism poses as humble by saying: "We are not smart enough to know what the truth is—or if there is any universal truth." It sounds humble. But look carefully at what is happening. It's like a servant saying: I am not smart enough to know which person here is my master—or if I even have a master. The result is that I don't have a master and I can be my own master. That is in reality what happens to relativists: In claiming to be too lowly to know the truth, they exalt themselves as supreme arbiter of what they can think and do. This is not humility. This is the essence of pride.

— John Piper

Civil War with Benjamin
Judges 20

Four hundred thousand battle-ready men from the land of Israel, including the Transjordan region, journeyed to Mizpah to learn the meaning of the gruesome message they had received (vv. 1-3). Mizpah was located in the central highlands about ten miles directly north of Jerusalem and only four to five miles north of Gibeah. The phrase *"before the Lord"* implies that at this time the tabernacle was located nearby, perhaps at Bethel as explained later. Representatives from the eleven tribes (no one from the tribe of Benjamin responded to the summons) listened as the Levite man recounted the wicked deeds that the vile men of Benjamin in Gibeah had done, as recorded in the previous chapter (vv. 4-5). To ensure the entire nation was aware of this lewd behavior, he had cut his concubine into pieces and distributed her remains throughout Israel.

The events of this chapter indicate that we are more likely to be provoked by what offends moral decency than by something that deprives God of His proper reverence and service. While the natural conscience (even of the unregenerate man) can reckon the former as unethical, without genuine love for the Lord we will not feel the true weight of the latter offense. Such was the appalling spiritual state of Israel at this time; yet, there was still enough conscience remaining to be stunned by this wicked deed. The Levite proclaimed *"they committed lewdness and outrage **in Israel**"* (v. 6) and after hearing his testimony everyone agreed to the morality of the matter, on the right terminology *"evil **in Israel**,"* and that the action must be judged immediately. C. A. Coates suggests that despite being correct on the former two points, the third determination was a serious error having tremendous consequences:

> We often say right things without feeling them at all. They did not feel it as the sin of Israel, but as the sin of Gibeah. If they had felt it as

the sin of Israel, they would all have been on their faces before God, confessing it as their own sin. They took it up in a way God could not support; they did not feel it, though they said what was right. There was a natural indignation about what was manifestly wicked, which was not the fruit of communion with God at all. There was no sign of their being humbled before God. They did not seek direction; they decided what they would do; they say, "It cannot be tolerated; we must go and execute judgment on them at once." It was right, but they were not moving with God in it. So, while this evil was dealt with in faithfulness, yet it was only through much chastisement that the people were brought into such a state that God could be with them in what they were doing. Even then they had to go through the deepest sorrow about it, and realize that the thing had been handled in such a way that they nearly lost a tribe out of Israel.[1]

Israel had failed to drive the Canaanites from their inheritance as commanded. Now, after several decades of living among them, their idolatrous ways and immoral manners had become customary among Jehovah's people. However, it was not the rampant religious corruption among them that prompted the resilient disdain of all the people, but rather a single lascivious act. Because they did not discern the former problem, they sought to resolve the latter with improper motive and without divine prudence – the outcome was hence devastating. One cannot represent the Lord justly, if he or she is not walking closely with Him. True, they had gathered before the Lord, but He was not with them. The Psalmist explains why: *"God is greatly to be feared in the assembly of the saints, and to be held in reverence by all those around Him"* (Ps. 89:7). Israel had gathered before the Lord in a ritualistic patriotism, not in humble brokenness.

It was determined that one in ten men from their complement, as determined by lot, would acquire provisions to sustain the remaining men to fight against Gibeah, if necessary (vv. 7-11). Hoping to avoid war, messengers were sent out through the tribe of Benjamin, saying: *"What is this wickedness that has occurred among you? Now therefore, deliver up the men, the perverted men who are in Gibeah, that we may put them to death and remove the evil from Israel!"* (vv. 12-13). Rather than turning over the guilty parties to purge the evil done, the tribe of Benjamin mustered up 26,000 sword-wielding men to assist the seven hundred fighters at Gibeah (vv. 14-15). Of this contingency were seven hundred skilled left-handed stone-slingers (v. 16). The army at Gibeah was outnumbered fifteen to one (v. 17). And although they did have the city's fortifications and higher ground as a practical advantage, they would elect rather to face the larger army of Israel in open combat. To war against the army of Israel and to be allied with evil are the two most destructive mistakes any fighting force on earth can make.

While only certain base men in one city had been guilty of the original crime, now the situation had been made much worse because of the tribe's unwillingness to judge the matter. Believers may not have any control of the intrusion of evil into their local assembly, but they are fully accountable to God for judging it once it is found out. If a virus invades your body, you do not remove your heart, lungs, liver, etc. to safeguard them from infection; rather, the body works together to defeat the wrongful intruder. This is the appropriate response of a local church, which may publicly rebuke, shun, or even excommunicate a believer who chooses to continue in gross sin. Paul warns that a little yeast will leaven an entire lump of dough if its influence is permitted to spread; likewise if sin continues unchecked, it will corrupt the entire church. Thus, those in persistent sin must be purged from the church gathering (1 Cor. 5:6-7). Because Benjamin refused to uphold the righteousness of Jehovah in Israel (God's assembly of His people) and judge the evil among them, they themselves would also be judged.

Returning to the narrative, Israel journeyed to *"the house of God"* to inquire which tribe should lead the nation into battle against Benjamin. As earlier noted, the reference is to a location near Mizpah and not Shiloh, the main location of the tabernacle during the era of the Judges (18:31). Shiloh would have been about a fifteen mile trek to the northeast; and too long of a journey to go up and back after the first battle, and then engage in battle the next day (vv. 23-24). It is possible that the actual location of the tabernacle was near the town of Bethel, positioned only four miles northward of Mizpah; Bethel literally means "the house of God." The tabernacle and officiating priests had been temporarily located in the Mizpah-Bethel region, perhaps in response to this situation.

Moses had earlier instructed the nation to inquire counsel from God through the Urim and Thummim which were in the High Priest's possession (Num. 27:21). When the Lord was asked about who should lead the nation into battle, the answer was simply, *"Judah shall go up first"* (v. 18). The size and shape of the battlefield would not accommodate the entire army of Israel; it was therefore necessary to send only a portion of their forces into battle. Three things should be observed: First, Israel did not ask whether or not they should go to war with Gibeah. Second, because He had not been consulted, the Lord did not forbid them from doing so. Third, there was no promise of victory.

The eleven tribes, acting in natural indignation, had already predetermined that it was God's will to go to war; they did not consult with the Lord as to how to best handle the chapter 19 travesty. In fact, the entire nation deliberates on two separate occasions as to what to do in this situation without seeking the Lord's counsel. So, when the Lord is asked a specific question, one that presumes war, He only responds to what He was asked. This illustrates the folly and the danger of seeking the mind of the Lord for a decision in which we have already presupposed the answer. Sometimes, as in this case, the Lord permits us to learn from our own presumptuous folly.

King Jehoshaphat committed a similar error (2 Chron. 18). Ahab, the evil king of Israel, suckered Jehoshaphat, the king of Judah, into forging an alliance with him in order to pool their resources and retake Ramoth-gilead, a city of refuge thirty miles east of the Jordan River. The Syrians controlled and inhabited this city. This was a meaningless religious activity that God had not sanctioned. After agreeing to go with Ahab, Jehoshaphat thought it would be a good idea to hear from a true prophet of Jehovah, in addition to Ahab's four hundred lying prophets. Micaiah was summoned and warned Ahab and Jehoshaphat that God was not with them. Even after knowing God's will on the matter, Jehoshaphat went into battle anyway and nearly lost his life. Thankfully, he realized his mistake in time and called out to the Lord to rescue him – and the Lord did.

In the same way, perhaps Jehovah, by simply answering the question posed to Him, was permitting presumptuous Israel to suffer in their quest for gallant justice. Since the nation was predisposed to war, it would be appropriate for Judah, the largest tribe, the tribe from which the Messiah would be born, to spearhead Israel into battle. Early the next morning Israel broke camp and traveled to Gibeah and positioned themselves for battle (vv. 19-20). The smaller army came out from the city and engaged their brethren in armed conflict. F. C. Cook describes the distinct tactical advantage that the forces of Gibeah had over the larger army of Israel:

> Gibeah, being on a hill, was difficult of access to an attacking army, and gave great advantage to the defenders, who fought from higher ground, and probably defended a narrow pass, while their companions on the walls could gall the assailants with their slingstones.[2]

In the initial confrontation, the army of Israel suffered a terrible loss: 22,000 men perished (v. 21). The next day, the army of the eleven tribes put themselves in array at the same location they had the previous day, which again presupposes that God wanted them to engage in warfare (v. 22). In view of their defeat the day before, representatives from Israel went up before the Lord again (presumably to Bethel), and wept (v. 23). This time they inquired of the Lord if they should engage Benjamin in battle. This question showed that Israel was deepening its dependence on the Lord, but as of yet, they were still not examining the integrity of their own hearts; they were rather all about judging others for their waywardness. The answer to their question was affirmative, but there was no promise of victory.

However, the second battle was also a disaster for Israel; 18,000 men were killed (vv. 24-25). Why had God instructed them to confront the Benjamites and then permitted such an agonizing loss? J. N. Darby suggests that the Lord permitted the initial defeats of the nation against a much smaller army so that the people might learn where they really were spiritually speaking:

> The evil which required chastening had so blunted their spiritual state that they had not the thought of waiting in the first place on Jehovah to know what was to be done. Their course of action is determined before they consult Him, for they were far from him. They merely ask who is to go up first. Jehovah points out Judah, but Judah is defeated. Twice beaten when they expected an easy victory, the people humbled and in tears have recourse again to Jehovah, and inquire if they shall go up. Jehovah then gives them the victory. Gibeah well deserved this discipline; but, to execute it, Israel itself needed discipline, and God allowed all to take part in it in order to make it take effect upon all.[3]

The nation had neglected proper worship of God as decreed by the Mosaic Law. It took the deaths of 40,000 men to realize that though they were attempting to cleanse the land of blood, they had lost sight of a more important matter – their love, respect, and awe for Jehovah. After all, Jehovah ruled over Israel, and He had not been approached in mourning and brokenness concerning the sin of Benjamin, who was their brother. Paul told the Corinthian believers that this was the right thing to do when grieved over a particular sin, but yet not knowing how to best deal with the one committing it (1 Cor. 5:2). The nation rightly hated the immorality in Benjamin, but had wrongly approached Jehovah in the matter and therefore did not have His endorsement in judging the sin, though indeed it needed to be dealt with.

After the defeat of the second day, the *entire* nation traveled to the house of the Lord. While fasting and in a spirit of utter brokenness, the people remained before the Lord all day. The priests offered burnt offerings and peace offerings to Jehovah in the evening (v. 26). Phinehas, the High Priest and the grandson of Aaron, stood before the Ark of the Covenant and asked the Lord whether they should battle the Benjamites or cease from conflict. The Lord then affirmed the right action and the result – go to battle and victory will be achieved (vv. 27-28). Why did Jehovah promise Israel victory now, but not before? The attitude and motive for approaching Jehovah was now correct, suggests C. A. Coates:

> When they went to Phinehas, they brought the burnt-offerings and peace-offerings. A remarkable cluster of ideas is brought forward; the Ark of the Covenant and Phinehas are there. Now Phinehas was a man who in his day executed summary judgment on what was evil. No man in Scripture was more noted than Phinehas for judgment of evil; he judged it unsparingly, but God says of him, "He was jealous with my jealousy," Numbers 22:11. We have to be brought to this, that we are not jealous with natural indignation, but with God's jealousy. We have to ask when we judge any kind of evil, Is this my jealousy or God's? If we have God's jealousy, we shall have a blessed sense of the burnt-offerings, the peace-offerings, and the ark of the covenant.[4]

The next day Israel returned to Gibeah and arrayed their army, but also set an ambush (vv. 29-30). The smaller army of Gibeah came out from the city and engaged the men of Israel as before, initially slaying about thirty men (v. 31). The army of Israel then faked a retreat to draw the men of Gibeah further away from their city (v. 32). The men of Gibeah fell for the ruse and the ambush consisting of ten thousand men was sprung (vv. 33-37). Though the battle was severe, the city was overrun, the inhabitants slaughtered, and the city set ablaze (vv. 38-40).

After seeing the smoke rise up from their city and realizing their dire situation, the men from Gibeah attempted to flee northeasterly into the wilderness (vv. 41-42). However, they were sandwiched between the ambushers in the south, having withdrawn from blazing Gibeah and the full army of Israel to the north, who had reversed their purposed retreat (vv. 43-45). About 18,000 were slain on the battlefield and another 7,000 were slain in the ridge highways all the way to Gidom; in total, 25,000 of 26,700 soldiers from Benjamin died that day. We thus can surmise that only eleven hundred Gibeah soldiers perished in the first two days of fighting. In the end, only 600 men were able to outrun their attackers and survive the onslaught by reaching the cliffs of Rimmon. Rimmon is thought to be modern day Rammun, which is located about six miles northeast of Gibeah. H. L. Rossier summarizes why the final battle was successful in removing the evil done in Israel, and the practical lesson to be gleaned for the Church today:

> Benjamin was defeated by a humbled people who showed themselves weaker than he. It is the principle of all discipline in the assembly. Without love, without dependence on God and His word, without self-judgment, discipline will always be defective, and it is only under such conditions that an assembly can purge out the old leaven.[5]

Believers cannot properly deal with a sinning brother or sister unless they are first humbly before the Lord in innocence, have pure motives, and are dedicated to obeying His Word. Only through this type of attitude can the work of rebuke and restoration be effectively accomplished: *"Brethren, if a man is overtaken in any trespass, you who are spiritual restore such a one in a spirit of gentleness, considering yourself lest you also be tempted"* (Gal. 6:1). Paul reminds us that we are all of like passions, and if it were not for the grace of God, each of us would be capable of doing the most vile works of unrighteousness. Realizing that should keep us broken before the Lord.

The six hundred survivors lived in the safety of the Rimmon rock formation for four months, until they received terms of peace by the nation (v. 47, 21:13-14). With the main Benjamite army destroyed, the remaining cities of their tribal region were easily captured and destroyed by fire (v. 48). The moral depravity of Benjamin was widespread, as marked by their refusal to turn over a few guilty culprits connected with the hideous crime in chapter 19; therefore, the slaughter spared no one, not even the animals. The entire tribe of Benjamin was wiped out, except for the 600 men securely garrisoned in the cliffs of Rimmon.

Meditation

> When we forget God, we lose the only true basis for morality and ethics, and we are cast upon the shifting sands of moral relativism in which anything goes, including lying, cheating and stealing.
>
> — Judge Roy Moore

> The man who commits immorality does so because he thinks it will maximize pleasure if he can minimize the pain by keeping it secret.
>
> — Erwin Lutzer

Mourning for the Lost Tribe
Judges 21

We learn in this chapter that before engaging the Benjamites in battle, the other eleven tribes entered into a corporate vow: Everyone swore, on the penalty of death, that they would not give their daughters to any Benjamite survivor in marriage (vv. 1, 5). After the fighting and cleansing was over, Israel realized they had gone too far in their holy zeal to rid blood-guiltiness from Israel. Because they had slain all the women of Benjamin, there were no wives for surviving men, which ultimately meant the extinction of one of the twelve tribes of Israel.

This regretful realization caused the nation to again come before the Lord and to weep bitterly. Yes, there had been victory in purging evil from Israel, but there was no rejoicing. This somber tenor was mainly because the people had recovered in part their affections for Jehovah and for their brethren, who were now nearly extinguished from the earth. C. A. Coates writes:

> What a dreadful thing it would have been if one stone had to be torn out of the high priest's breastplate… when they came to look at things according to God, they could not bear to think of Benjamin being lost. It should be more of a real sorrow to have to part company with anyone we can recognize as a true saint.[1]

Amen! In the way a body suffers from a lost limb, Israel mourned, for there was a tribe missing among them. It was before the Lord that the nation had previously found victory and so having realized their error, they return again to seek guidance. They erected an altar and offered burnt offerings and peace offerings to Jehovah (vv. 2-3).

The nation was in a doleful quandary: They did not want the tribe of Benjamin to be wiped out forever, but because of the vow, they could not supply wives to the remaining six hundred Benjamites, nor did the Law permit these men to marry heathen women (vv. 4-7; Deut.

177

7:3). Their solution was to obtain Jewish wives for the remaining Benjamites from those who did not participate in the campaign and thus were not bound by their oath. Notice that Jehovah is acutely silent throughout this chapter; His people had engaged in a vow and in a slaughter that He had not endorsed; hence He would not be assisting them in righting the wrong. They had come before the Lord to merely weep for the lost tribe, but as Matthew Henry suggests, they should have confessed their guilt in uttering a rash vow and offered sin offerings to the Lord in restitution:

> Israel lamented for the Benjamites, and were perplexed by the oath they had taken, not to give their daughters to them in marriage. Men are more zealous to support their own authority than that of God. They would have acted better if they had repented of their rash oaths, brought sin-offerings, and sought forgiveness in the appointed way, rather than attempt to avoid the guilt of perjury by actions quite as wrong. That men can advise others to acts of treachery or violence, out of a sense of duty, forms a strong proof of the blindness of the human mind when left to itself, and of the fatal effects of a conscience under ignorance and error.[2]

It was then learned that none of the inhabitants of Jabesh-Gilead had answered the summons to investigate and judge the lewd crimes of Benjamin (vv. 8-9). Jabesh-Gilead was located about two miles east of the Jordan River and some thirty miles northeast of Shiloh. When God's name has been willfully dishonored, indifference to judge that evil is the same as accepting it; this is what led Gideon to judge the men of Penuel. However, the facts were not known: perhaps Jabesh-Gilead did not receive an initial summons, or perhaps a few people heard about it, but the entire town did not, or perhaps a few Jabesh-Gilead soldiers did come, but were killed in battle. The leaders of Israel, in a hurry to fix the terrible problem they had created, were not using good judgment. They decided to send 12,000 choice warriors to that city to punish their apparent complacency and to secure young virgin women as wives for the Benjamites (v. 10). It was barbarous act to slaughter men, women, and children in this way, just to obtain four hundred young females to be wives for the surviving Benjamite men (vv. 11-12). The traumatized damsels were brought to Shiloh until the men of Benjamin hiding at Rimmon could be called to peace talks and receive their new wives (vv. 13-14).

The matter was agreeable to the Benjamite men, but there was a shortfall of two hundred women (vv. 15-16). To ensure that the tribe maintained its inheritance, this shortfall must be resolved. But since all Israel had given their vow on this matter, no man could give his daughter in marriage to a Benjamite man (vv. 17-18). A solution was devised relating to a local harvest feast in which the daughters of Shiloh annually ventured into the grain fields of Lebonah (three miles north of Shiloh) to thank the Lord with celebratory dancing (v. 19). The scheme was simple; the Benjamite men were to hide in the woods and the vineyards near the highway running between Bethel to Shechem and then capture a dancing maiden as the opportunity presented itself (v. 20). Shiloh was about halfway between Bethel and Shechem on the highland route.

The vow prevented any Jewish man from *giving* his daughter in marriage, but not if she was *taken* as a wife without parental consent. Obviously, representatives from Shiloh were not present when this decision was affirmed. The Benjamite men were then promised the cooperation of tribal leaders, if the fathers of the kidnapped daughters rejected this venture and attempted a rescue (vv. 21-22). Given the devastating response Jabesh-Gilead suffered in this matter, where supposedly the nation was righting a wrong, it is doubtful that any father raised a serious objection.

Each of the two hundred Benjamite men caught himself a wife and returned to their tribal inheritance and began rebuilding the cities that had been destroyed by war (v. 23). With the problem of preserving the tribe of Benjamin resolved, the army of Israel dispersed and every man returned to his own home (v. 24). The book concludes by acknowledging the moral relativity that governed God's people during the era of the judges: *"In those days there was no king in Israel; everyone did what was right in his own eyes"* (v. 25). This is the fourth and final time in these five concluding chapters that the author has made this statement. Though the people thought they were in the right, we have seen that their conduct was completely unacceptable to God. What then did God accomplish through the thirteen judges? H. L. Rossier answers this question:

God did not change the deplorable state of things; He simply states the fact; but He led His own away from the confused light of conscience, which while it judged never guided them; and brought them back to the pure light of His own infallible word which was able to conduct them, to build them up, and to give them an inheritance among all them which are sanctified (Acts 20:32).[3]

Sadly, if there was ever the right moment for revival to break out, it would have been in the painful aftermath of civil war, when the people were weeping and broken before the Lord. Yet, sorrow for the consequences of one's doings is not the same as repentance, and without true repentance spiritual revival will elude God's people. Without repentance, there can be no proper worship of God, proper fellowship with God, nor can the power of God be experienced in a refreshing and constructive way. Without inward conviction and brokenness, God's people cannot effectually reach heavenward for help and guidance.

The Jewish nation had erred terribly in their execution of judgment on the tribe of Benjamin. However, they did not obtain Jehovah's counsel on how to best remedy the disaster they had created; rather, they contrived a ghastly solution of their own ingenuity. Consequently, the eerie silence of Jehovah is a distinguishing characteristic of this entire narrative.

The gruesome stories of these final chapters of Judges, which relate to the earliest period of the Judgeship era, confirm just how far God's people had wandered from Him. But, as revolting as Israel's apostasy is in chapters 17-21, things actually got worse in time.

This portion of Scripture plainly declares that God does not endorse human activity and reasoning apart from His expressed will (1 Jn. 5:14). Indeed, we must reason together with Him to make sense of life (Isa. 1:18). When God's presence and fellowship are not sensed, it is best for believers to cease from all their doings and humbly seek the face of the One whom they have neglected and offended. Otherwise, we likely will realize only too late that we were acting outside of God's will, and thus further grieving the heart of our wonderful Savior, the Lord Jesus Christ. This is the sad travesty of Judges.

Following on the heels of Judges is the inspiring book of Ruth, which has its setting *"in the days when the judges ruled"* (Ruth 1:1). Mercifully, as C. T. Lacy points out, the story of Ruth illustrates that the Lord is able to redeem the humble in spirit even during the darkest days of moral relativity:

> It is encouraging to know that during the dark and gloomy days of the judges, beautiful characters like Boaz, Naomi, and Ruth could be found. They tell a story of redemption, grace and new life, which culminates in the birth of a son, and testify to the fact that, in spite of their rebellion, there is a future for Israel. God's plan of salvation can never be thwarted by the waywardness of his people or by the opposition of mankind in general.[4]

Meditation

> God always gives His very best to those who leave the choice with Him. ... When God's work is done in God's way for God's glory, it will not lack for God's supply
>
> — Hudson Taylor

> Revival is a renewed conviction of sin and repentance, followed by an intense desire to live in obedience to God. It is giving up one's will to God in deep humility.
>
> — Charles Finney

Ruth

Introduction to Ruth

The Author

The author of Ruth does not identify himself, but Hebrew tradition asserts that Samuel was the writer of the book. The Babylonian Talmud (Tractate Baba Bathra 14b) states: "Samuel wrote the book which bears his name and the books of Judges and Ruth." The internal evidence in the book of Ruth indicates that that book was written just before or during the reign of David (4:17, 22). If this supposition is correct, this timeframe ensures that Samuel is a strong candidate for authorship. Samuel was the leading prophet at that time, was well-respected in Israel, and was also a renowned writer (1 Sam. 10:25). If Samuel is the author of Ruth, the book would have been written in the latter years of his life; a date of 1040 B.C. (the birth of David) to 1014 B.C. (the approximate date of Samuel's demise) seems appropriate. If the author is not Samuel, he was likely a contemporary of David, and penned the book prior to Solomon's coronation, as he is not mentioned in the closing genealogy.

The Date and Setting

The setting for the book of Ruth occurred during the days of the Judges: *"Now it came to pass, in the days when the judges ruled."* As Ruth was also the great grandmother of King David, a setting approximately one hundred years prior to his ascent to the throne seems appropriate. At the age of forty, just after Saul's death, David began to rule from Hebron in 1010 B.C. This means that the actual events recorded in the book would have occurred towards the end of the twelfth century B.C. This timing would correspond to a date just after the forty years of peace under Gideon, perhaps during the judgeships of Tola (the position of several Jewish commentators), or Jair, or even the onset of Jephthah's rule.

A severe draught in Judah caused Elimelech to move his wife Naomi and their two younger sons to the land of Moab (1:1-2). Later, Elimelech died and his sons married Moabite women (1:3-4). In time both sons died, leaving Naomi with her two daughters-in-law, Ruth and Orpah (1:5). There are no children mentioned, meaning both Moabite women were not likely married very long. Naomi lived in Moab about ten years before she and Ruth returned to her native land (v. 4). The storyline would then span a period of about twelve years, concluding with the marriage of Ruth to Boaz and the birth of their first child, Obed.

Outline
1:1-5: Introduction
1:6-22: A New Beginning
2:1-23: Gleaning Grace
3:1-18: Seeking Redemption
4:1-13: Blessings of Redemption
4:14-21: Conclusion

The Theme
Spiritual corruption and idolatry became rampant among the Jews during the era of the Judges, beginning with the generation directly after Joshua's. This angered the Lord, who repeatedly punished His covenant people through military invasion. After years of oppression, the Jews would repent and cry out to the Lord for deliverance. On these occasions the Lord raised up judges to remove the oppressors from the land and to guide the nation in righteous conduct. Amidst this long and gloomy backdrop of failure and chastening, a bright ray of redemptive hope is conveyed in the lovely story of Ruth, a young Moabite widow who is sacrificially devoted to her mother-in-law Naomi, also a widow.

From a redemptive standpoint, the book of Ruth offers a striking contrast to the preceding book of Judges, says C. A. Coates:

> In the book of Judges not only did no redeemer appear great enough to restore fully according to God that which had been departed from, but, on the other hand, moral conditions suitable to divine recovery were not present in the people. What marks Judges is the statement that every man did what was right in his own eyes. There could be no true recovery or reinstatement in such a condition; and, alas! it is a

condition that very largely bars the way to recovery of the inheritance at the present time amongst the people of God. Movement on the line of recovery is brought about by such dealings of God as are seen in Ruth 1. Brokenness of spirit – a broken and contrite heart under the dealings of God – is an absolute necessity, and it is the preparation for all recovery.[1]

Accordingly, from a typological sense the story of Ruth pictures the fulfillment of all God promises in connection with Israel, on the ground of sovereign grace, after the nation (portrayed in Naomi) had lost all claims to God's blessing because of moral and spiritual failure (as witnessed in Judges). Judges displays the ever increasing depravity of Israel, despite divine chastening and intervention, which ultimately leaves God's people in a thick hue of spiritual deadness. Thankfully, the activities of God's grace are not overcome by human failure; this leaves us with a wonderful scene of joy and blessing at the conclusion of the book of Ruth.

Naomi, representing the chastened nation of Israel, is a backsliding believer, who returns to the Lord after experiencing the consequences of departing from God's will. She departed Judah "full," but willingly "returns" (a key word in Ruth) "empty," after God stripped everything away by disciplinary action. Having been emptied of all self-ambition and self-fortitude, she again experiences God's delight and blessing in her life.

Through her connection with Naomi, Ruth steps forward in faith to reject the deep-seated pagan heritage of her own people to become a Jehovah worshipper. After approaching a potential kinsman-redeemer, Boaz, and requesting to be redeemed, she receives his pledge to do so. Later, she will experience the redeeming love of Boaz through marriage and be not only brought into the commonwealth of Israel, but also the genealogy of Christ. The sentiments of Hamilton Smith well summarize the captivating appeal this book has for all those who read it:

It is a love story of other days in which sorrow and joy, failure and devotedness, life and death, are intermingled, all leading at last to the day of the marriage and the birth of the heir. The very setting of the story is restful to the spirit; for we are carried into pastoral scenes to find ourselves in company with harvesters and gleaners. For the

Christian, however, reading the sacred page with Christ before his soul, the story of Ruth has a deeper interest, and a richer meaning, for therein he discerns, as "in all the Scriptures," "the things concerning Himself."[2]

In Boaz, Ruth's kinsman redeemer, we see the Lord Jesus typified as the future Savior, who is both willing and able to redeem all who desire to be saved and blessed by Him. The Lord is also our Kinsman-redeemer. H. L. Rossier concisely captures the marvelous character of the book:

> Ruth is a book of grace; it is necessarily also a book of faith. Grace and faith ever go hand in hand, for it is faith that lays hold of grace and appropriates it, and that cleaves to the divine promises and to the people who are the subjects of these promises, and it is faith that finds its delight in Him who is the bearer of the promises and their heir.[3]

Though evil spreads and human depravity expands, the testimony of grace develops and progresses in an ever-increasing proportion to attain God's purposes. Grace originated in the heart of God and centers in the person of the Lord Jesus Christ. For believers, then, the book of Ruth will be appreciated as a tender and beautiful love story of genuine humility, steadfast faithfulness, and God's redeeming mercy as pictured in the Lord Jesus.

Devotions in Ruth

A New Beginning
Ruth 1

The story of Ruth occurred during the days of the Judges: *"Now it came to pass, in the days when the judges ruled."* Ruth was the great grandmother of King David, which places the setting of the narrative towards the end of the twelfth century B.C. It is possible that Ruth lived during the latter portion of Gideon's judgeship, but it seems more likely that Tola, or Jair, were overseeing Israel at the time; it is even possible that Jephthah had just defeated the Ammonites.

The book commences with the introduction of Elimelech and his family who lived in Bethlehem-Judah. Years earlier, Bethlehem-Judah was the home of Jonathan, the pagan Levite (Jud. 17:8) and the Levite's concubine in Judges 19. A severe draught in Judah caused Elimelech to move his wife Naomi and their two younger sons, Mahlon and Chilion, to the idolatrous land of Moab to find adequate food (vv. 1-2). The land of Moab would be fifty miles east of Bethlehem and on the eastern side of the Dead Sea. Hence, Ruth begins where Judges ends, a conscious decision by God's people to depart from His expressed will and intimate presence.

As in the days of Abraham and Isaac, famines represent a test for God's people. Faith cannot be trusted if it is not tested. Given the demeanor and theme of the book of Judges, this famine was likely disciplinary in nature. Solomon would later acknowledge what Moses said would happen if Israel became idolatrous: *"When the heavens are shut up and there is no rain because they have sinned against You"* (Deut. 11:17; 1 Kgs. 8:35). Famine was God's calling card to His wayward people to repent and return to Him.

Would Elimelech remain in the land divinely conferred to him for a possession and seek the Lord or abandon everything? Would he tarry and seek God's assistance through the trial, or would he seize personal control of the crisis and attempt to resolve it his way? Would Elimelech rest in God's sovereign ways? Regrettably, the man from Bethlehem chose to divert into Moab to alleviate his difficulty. He did not live up to his name, which means "My God is King." His behavior pictures the disposition of the entire nation at this time; the Jews might say "Jehovah rules," but they certainly did not live as if He did. Like Abraham before him (Gen. 12:10), Elimelech did what we are all prone to do; he sought to relieve his difficulties, rather than to seek the Lord's benefit in the trial.

The tabernacle, the priests, and the altar were all visible evidence that Jehovah's presence was in Canaan among His covenant people, not in Moab. When God's pilgrims venture out of the Promised Land (i.e., out of His will and presence) to resolve their problems, it is for carnal reasons. Exploring a cursed world filled with corruption for aid and comfort can only lead a child of God into misery – this is where selfish ambition and fickleness always lead us. Elimelech doubted God's faithfulness and tried to avoid the test of chastening. In doing so, he led his family into a spiritual wasteland resulting in heartache and many squandered years. Elimelech was quite willing to dwell in the land of God's appointment in the time of plenty, but not so during the hardship of a famine; he abandons his God-given inheritance and the blessings of his God associated with it.

The Moabites were descendants of Lot and his oldest daughter and were to be excluded from the congregation of Israel (Deut. 23:3-6). Lot was a child of God, but he was not content with a life of obedient dependence and separation; rather he chose to live in Sodom, apart from God's people for its obvious worldly advantages. Hence, Lot's descendants, the Moabites, represent a carnal people that have an outward connection with God (i.e., knowledge of Him), without an inner reality of His presence. It stands to reason, then, that though the Jews were not forbidden to marry Moabites, as they were the Canaanites, it was not advisable (Num. 25:2).

Things did not work out in Moab as Elimelech thought; in fact, he dies there only a few years after arriving. No longer under their father's authority, Elimelech's sons chose to marry Moabite women (vv. 3-4). In time both sons died, leaving Naomi with her two young daughters-in-law, Ruth and Orpah, all being widows (v. 5; 4:10). Neither Ruth nor Orpah had children, which likely means they had only been briefly married before their husbands died. Since Ruth was married to the older brother, Mahlon, she may have been married a bit longer than Orpah and perhaps was slightly older than Orpah. In Ruth's case childbearing may have been divinely inhibited in order to accomplish her later redemption and induction into the tribe of Judah through the marriage of Boaz.

Naomi learned that the famine was over in her native land and that Jehovah was again blessing His people with agricultural prosperity (v. 6). God promised His people that the land would flow with milk and honey as long as they were obedient. This signaled that repentance had been achieved, His disciplinary judgment was past, and perhaps a new judge was overseeing Israel.

The abundance of food in Judah was enough to convince Naomi to return to Bethlehem; there was nothing for her in Moab, but lingering regrets and three graves. She was an unprotected widow, a stranger in a land whose people disdained Israel; at least she had kin in the land of her nativity who could help her (v. 7). It was the lack of food that first moved Elimelech out of the Promised Land and now the promise of food that excites Naomi about returning there. Elimelech pictures the way of the backsliding believer enticed away from the Lord by what he does not have, but thinks he deserves. Naomi, however, shows us the way of restoration: rightly reckoning the depravity of her position, rejecting her false association with Moab, and then trusting in Jehovah for future blessing. In Moab, *"she had heard"* that Jehovah was blessing His people and she wanted in on it. God's grace was working to draw her back and she chose to act on faith, hence *"she went out from the place where she was"* (v. 7).

Initially, perhaps out of a sense of family loyalty, both daughters-in-law traveled with Naomi, but she encourages them to return and remain among their own people (v. 8). Naomi knew that being Moabites, their prospects for remarriage were slim in Israel. Yet, even after she kisses Orpah and Ruth good-bye, and instructs them to return and to remarry, they refuse to leave her (vv. 9-10). Marriage meant security for a woman in ancient near-Eastern days and Naomi wanted them to be cared for, something she could not do. Naomi again tries to convince them to return to their Moabite families, claiming that there were no more sons in her womb for them to marry at a later date (v. 11). Naomi confirms that she is past childbearing age.

191

In verse 12, Naomi tries a third time to persuade her daughters-in-law to abandon her, claiming that even if she could bare sons as soon as possible, would they really want to wait until they became old enough to marry (vv. 12-13)? Naomi referred to the levirate custom in Israel in which a brother was responsible to marry his deceased brother's wife to father a son, who could then perpetuate his brother's name and inheritance (Deut. 25:5-10). Obviously, this was not going to happen; her logic was sound. It is an intensely emotional moment for all three women; *"Orpah kissed her mother-in-law, but Ruth clung to her"* (v. 14). Orpah lived out the meaning of her name: "her back" – she turned her back on Naomi and deserted her mother-in-law in her greatest time of need.

Orpah's kiss was merely an expression of affection without devotion; Ruth's allegiance to Naomi, however, was much more than emotional; it was genuine. Samuel Ridout suggests that Ruth did honor the meaning of her name: "Ruth most probably means, 'having a shepherd.' Her faith here shows that she is one of the sheep, though a Gentile, who is to be brought into the fold."[1] This reminds us that the natural heart may attach itself to God's people, but for the wrong reasons; only those who belong to the true Shepherd will be motivated and able to adequately demonstrate love in the way He approves.

Orpah returns to Moab; it is unlikely that she will ever see Naomi and Ruth again. Ruth, out of genuine concern for her mother-in-law, is willing to sacrifice everything, including the security and children that would be associated with a Moabite husband, in order to ensure Naomi's welfare. Hamilton Smith contrasts the responses of the two daughters-in-law:

> How different the history of Ruth; she becomes the witness of the grace of God. Ruth also makes a good profession; she too utters fair words; she too is deeply moved, for, like Orpah, she lifted up her voice and wept. But with Ruth there is more, for with her are found the "things that accompany salvation," faith, love and hope (Heb. 6:9-12). With Orpah there was only the outward expression of love. She could kiss and leave Naomi, even as, at a later date, Judas could kiss and betray the Lord. Of Ruth it is never actually said that she kissed Naomi; but if there was no outward expression of love there was the reality of love, for we read Ruth "clave unto her" (v. 14). Love if real,

cannot give up its loved object, and must be in the company of the one that is loved.[2]

Orpah abandons the course which seems to have no possible beneficial outcome; Naomi was ruined, bitter, stricken of God, and furthermore, had nothing to offer her. Orpah did by reason what was natural and logical; Ruth does by faith what is unnatural and sacrificial. After Orpah's departure, Naomi again commands Ruth to return to her own gods and her own people, citing Orpah's example of obedience as a further justification for her to depart (v. 15). Ruth's sincere refusal for deserting Naomi is deeply moving (vv. 16-17):

- Do not force me to leave you.
- I will go where you go.
- I will lodge where you lodge.
- Your people will be my people.
- Your God will be my God.
- I will die where you die.
- I am committed to you; only death will separate us.

H. L. Rossier summarizes the wonderful aspects of faith and sacrifice that Ruth displays in her rejection of Naomi's charge to return to Moab:

> What precious faith she displays: full of certainty, resolution, and decision! No objection can change her mind. How clearly faith sees its goal! She listens to Naomi's words but her decision has been made, for she knows only *one* path, which for her is the *necessary* path. What are nature's *impossibilities* before faith's *necessities*? Ruth neither allows herself to be deterred by the prospect of not finding another husband, nor even by the Lord's hand stretched out against her mother-in-law; in the obstacles that mount up she sees only so many new reasons for clinging to her decision. Naomi is everything to Ruth, and Ruth *cleaves* to Naomi.[3]

Naomi could no longer argue against such genuine devotion, or with Ruth's resolve to be a Jehovah worshipper. The two forlorn women, one smitten of God for rebellion and too old to remarry, and the other, able to remarry, but a foreigner with no claims to Israel's promises or blessings, departed the land of Moab in hopes of a new beginning in the Promised Land. The dispensational design of sovereign grace is here portrayed for us to notice: Naomi represents God's covenant people of old, who though rebellious have been chastened, refined, and restored to Him; Ruth, as the future wife of Boaz is the recipient of all God's promises in Christ, which includes not just the Jewish nation, but a Gentile bride who is also grafted into the commonwealth of Israel. Some commentators, like W. J. Hocking, believe that Ruth prefigures only the refined Jewish remnant of the latter days of Israel. He argues that Ruth's Gentile lineage is used to show God's covenant people dispersed among the Gentile nations for rebellion:

> Ruth's Gentile origin makes her the more fitting to be a type of the restored nation. Now the ancient people of God are in the "Lo-ammi" condition (Hos. 1:9), and for their sins are regarded as a Gentile people, but eventually they will no longer be outcasts, for, in accordance with prophecy, Jehovah will say to Israel, "Thou art My people" (Hos. 2:23).[4]

Regardless of which typological view of Ruth is correct, both women benefit from the gracious deeds of Boaz (which pictures Christ's future redemptive work). Boaz is the kinsman-redeemer, who will restore the lost inheritance of Naomi and bring Ruth into the good of it also. It is then fitting that both Naomi and Ruth arrived safely at Bethlehem at the beginning of the barley harvest (vv. 18, 22). Barley is used to symbolize redemption in Scripture (e.g., Lev. 23:9-14; Hos. 3:2) and both these women would experience the blessings of redemption. It is always a joyful harvest of souls when a wandering sheep returns to the fold or an unregenerate sinner turns to the Lord, as the parables in Luke 15 so wonderfully illustrate.

Bethlehem, which means "the house of bread," would be the earthly birthplace of the Jewish Messiah and our Savior (Mic. 5:2). It is fitting that poverty stricken and spiritually destitute souls willing to exercise faith would experience God's grace at Bethlehem, the hometown of God's heavenly manna. Over eleven centuries later, that Bread of Life spoke directly to a hungry Jewish crowd who had eaten from His miraculous hand the previous day:

"Most assuredly, I say to you, Moses did not give you the bread from heaven, but My Father gives you the true bread from heaven. For the bread of God is He who comes down from heaven and gives life to the world." Then they said to Him, "Lord, give us this bread always." And Jesus said to them, "I am the bread of life. He who comes to Me shall never hunger, and he who believes in Me shall never thirst" (John 6:32-36).

"Most assuredly, I say to you, he who believes in Me has everlasting life. I am the bread of life. Your fathers ate the manna in the wilderness, and are dead. This is the bread which comes down from heaven, that one may eat of it and not die. I am the living bread which came down from heaven. If anyone eats of this bread, he will live forever; and the bread that I shall give is My flesh, which I shall give for the life of the world" (John 6:47-51).

Indeed, Ruth and Naomi would taste the goodness of the Lord after arriving at Bethlehem. The concluding narrative shows that they are in complete agreement with David: *"O taste and see that the Lord is good: blessed is the man that trusts in Him"* (Ps. 34:8). In a coming day, the entire nation of Israel will be satisfied by their Messiah: *"I will abundantly bless her provision; I will satisfy her poor with bread"* (Ps. 132:15). The Lord Jesus Christ, "the Bread of Life," is the only One who can satisfy every spiritual yearning of the famished human soul.

So in grace, the Lord was working through this situation to honor Himself and to demonstrate His redeeming mercy; to this end, Psalm 146:8-9 is most fitting: *"The Lord raises those who are bowed down; the Lord loves the righteous. The Lord watches over the strangers; He relieves the fatherless and widow."* Ruth would qualify on all five counts; she was humble, righteous, a stranger, fatherless (no natural family association), and a widow. From the lowest of human plights, God's abundant grace would be observed by all in the life of this young and faithful Moabite woman.

All Bethlehem was stunned to see Naomi and to learn of her plight. Remembering her status before, some just could not believe it was the same woman. "They" is in the Hebrew feminine gender, meaning that the women of Bethlehem inquired among themselves: *"Can this be Naomi?"* (v. 19). No doubt many were also astonished by the foreigner Ruth's dedication to her mother-in-law. The people of Bethlehem were greatly disturbed by Naomi's tragic story, but also rejoiced to see her return to her rightful home. In our present day, the Church has a marred testimony; many wayward saints are wandering in the land of Moab. May we too be excited to see backsliders return to their rightful place, that is, to be in close communion with the Lord. Some saints have become disillusioned by hardship; others have fallen into sin; there are many soldiers of the cross who are MIAs (missing in action): May we too be moved with compassion to see each of them restored to the Lord and be faithful to pray for them in the interim!

The loving reception that she received by her own people seems to have opened her heart to confess the reality of her situation, though her heart is yet restored to gladness. Though she had failed the Lord and suffered for doing so, the Lord had not abandoned her: *"The Almighty has dealt very bitterly with me. I went out full, and the Lord has brought me home again empty"* (vv. 20-21). Though difficulties and doubts may cause us to withdraw from the Lord's presence, He will not withdraw from us: *"If we are faithless, He remains faithful; He cannot deny Himself"* (2 Tim. 2:13). Naomi was of the tribe of Judah, the kingly tribe and the largest of God's elect nation among nations; she had wandered away from a great inheritance in the Lord. Now, Naomi could testify through circumstances that "the Almighty" was a powerful God who could not be resisted. Indeed she had experienced the power of His hand, but also the grip of His faithful love in a way that she never had before. The Almighty loved her too much to leave her where she was. The writer of Hebrews tells us that God's disciplinary rod is a proof of His love for His children:

> *If you endure chastening, God deals with you as with sons; for what son is there whom a father does not chasten? But if you are without chastening, of which all have become partakers, then you are illegitimate and not sons* (Heb. 12:7-8).

Naomi knew that Jehovah had brought about all her hardship and misery to cause her to separate from pagans and abide with her own people in the land of Jehovah. He had dealt with her "very bitterly" (v. 20), which reminds us that: *"Now no chastening seems to be joyful for the present, but painful; nevertheless, afterward it yields the peaceable fruit of righteousness to those who have been trained by it"* (Heb. 12:11). Accordingly, she asked to be called *Mara* meaning "bitter," rather than Naomi, which means "sweetness" or "pleasantness." She does not blame Jehovah for her missteps, but rather acknowledges His powerful response to her wrong action: *"I went out."* She chose to leave Canaan and had lost everything in Moab; her solace now was, *"the Lord has brought me home"* again.

Finally, it is noted that Naomi says she came back from Moab *"empty."* There can be no other condition in which a believer can be brought back to the Lord other than empty and broken – only then can we benefit from His grace. A backsliding believer makes no spiritual progress in the days of his or her wandering from the Lord. No doubt Naomi and her family thought that only if they worked harder they could persevere in the land of Moab. But a child of God can never thrive in the world apart from abiding in Christ – for without Him we can do nothing (John 15:5). Desperation prompted Naomi to seek the Lord, and like all who do, she was blessed by Him for doing so.

In reality, it is only the Lord who can get the attention of a wandering sheep; many may call and warn, but only He knows how to shepherd a dissenting heart. He skillfully strips away self-confidence and personal ambition and whatever is hindering the soul's affection heavenward. Naomi had been divested of everything, she was empty, and now she could start again with Jehovah. Hence, it is no coincidence that she arrives in the land of plenty *"at the beginning of barley harvest"* (v. 22). For Naomi, it indeed would be a new *"beginning"* – she would reap the abundant blessings of being restored to her God.

Meditation

Farewell, then, to doubts and fears. No more comings and goings – no more gleanings and beatings. Farewell to the land of Moab – farewell to a deceitful world. Thou art one, redeemed sinner, with yonder Christ in glory. That home above – that scene of love – is thine forever. There, set thy affections. There, poor desolate wanderer is thine everlasting rest.[5]

— Nineteenth-century
evangelist Charles Stanley

197

Gleaning Grace
Ruth 2

We are introduced to Boaz, a mighty man of wealth and near kin of Elimelech (v. 1). In ancient times the poor and strangers in Israel were permitted to glean the corners of fields during harvest time – it was God's provision for them (Lev. 19:9-10, 23:22). Ruth realizes what she must do for the two women to survive and asks Naomi's leave so that she might glean grain for them. Ruth is hopeful that someone will show her grace in this matter (v. 2). The word "glean" in its various forms is found twenty-two times in all of Scripture and twelve of those occurrences are in chapter 2. We can safely conclude that the spiritual features associated with gleaning are the main theme of this chapter. For believers, we learn that gleaning inseparably connects God's sovereign grace with human responsibility.

There are many aspects of salvation illustrated in the story of Ruth. In the previous chapter, we witnessed Ruth exercising faith in Naomi's God, Jehovah, and then her willingness to separate from the corruption of her old life in Moab (picturing the world). This walk of moral consecration is something that God expects from all His pilgrims journeying heavenward though still strangers sojourning in this wicked world. Those trusting in Christ as Savior are both saved by His cross and carved out of the world by it for the expressed purpose of fulfilling His good pleasure.

In this chapter, we find Ruth seeking grace in order to labor in the most prosperous way for the good of Naomi. This is the attitude that all God's people should have. The Lord Jesus told His disciples that God plants his children in the world where He chooses so that they will be the most fruitful; the devil then tries to negate their testimony of God's grace (i.e., their witness and influence) by positioning his evil workers right next to them (Matt. 13:24-28). This is the reality of laboring for the Lord – it is not easy and indeed would be impossible without Him.

Thankfully, God co-labors with His people to both bless them and ensure their fruitfulness: *"For we are God's fellow workers; you are God's field"* (1 Cor. 3:9). Faithful Ruth was placed right where God would accomplish the most good from her laboring.

So was it a mere coincidence or divine guidance that led Ruth to glean in a field owned by Boaz? The narrative reads, *"She happened to come to the part of the field belonging to Boaz"* (v. 3). The text confirms that the location of Ruth's laboring was not contrived by Naomi, as she did not know where Ruth had been gleaning until later (v. 19). As the story progresses, it becomes apparent that what seems to be a series of random events is actually God's providential care. Jehovah wants to restore Naomi to the joy of her salvation, to redeem Ruth and bring her into the commonwealth of Israel, and to exalt the character and ability of Boaz in bringing it all about. Even Naomi, who previously recognized that the hand of "the Almighty" was against her, now sees His hand of blessing in their situation: *"Blessed be he of the Lord, who has not forsaken His kindness to the living and the dead!"* (v. 20).

Ruth began to glean barley in the morning. Boaz arrives from Bethlehem to check on the progression of the harvest and spots Ruth laboring in the field (vv. 4-5). Was it a coincidence that Boaz just happened to come to that particular field and just happened to notice Ruth that day? After greeting his reapers in the name of Jehovah, he inquired from his foreman about the mysterious gleaner who obviously was not a daughter of Israel. Can you image how this impoverished and desperate stranger, perhaps only a teenage girl, felt laboring in that field? She was a despised Moabite and with each curious and perhaps disdaining glance she was forced to keenly feel her own isolation. But the eye of our Lord seeks those poor souls who desire His help, and His eye was upon Ruth.

Behold, the eye of the Lord is on those who fear Him, on those who hope in His mercy, to deliver their soul from death, and to keep them alive in famine. Our soul waits for the Lord; He is our help and our shield. For our heart shall rejoice in Him, because we have trusted in His holy name. Let Your mercy, O Lord, be upon us, just as we hope in You (Ps. 33:18-22).

The reaper foreman reported to Boaz that she was Naomi's daughter-in-law who had just come out of Moab with Naomi (v. 6). She had asked him for permission to glean and he had granted it to her. He observed that she had worked in the field diligently all day, except for a brief visit to "the house" (i.e., a shed or shelter of some kind) for personal reasons (v. 7).

From a spiritual standpoint, we might well entitle this chapter "Faithful Gleaners Obtain Grace." Ruth, a new convert, so to speak, had just arrived in the Promised Land, which was bursting with abundance (picturing God's grace). Just as crops must be harvested to have value in nourishing the needy, God's grace benefits others when those who have experienced it are willing to exercise faith and work to more fully appropriate its abundance:

> *For I am the least of the apostles, who am not worthy to be called an apostle, because I persecuted the church of God. But by the grace of God I am what I am, and His grace toward me was not in vain; but I labored more abundantly than they all, yet not I, but the grace of God which was with me. Therefore, whether it was I or they, so we preach and so you believed* (1 Cor. 15:9-11).

Ruth wants to benefit from God's abundance in the same way that all believers should long to practically appropriate *"every spiritual blessing in the heavenly places in Christ"* (Eph. 1:3) and to *"grow in grace"* (2 Pet. 3:18). *"Faith if it has not works is dead being alone"* (Jas. 2:17) and Ruth's faith is active and expectant. She desires to further experience God's grace through gleaning. She says to Naomi, *"let me go to the field to glean";* to the foreman she pleads, *"let me glean";* and Boaz responds to Ruth *"do not go to glean in another field,"* and he instructs his young men, *"let her glean";* and then verse 17 informs us *"so she gleaned."* In doing so, she did more than satisfy the need of her own soul; she blessed Naomi as well. This situation teaches us that God's grace is never to be hoarded, but rather laid hold of by faith and shared with others. Why? The Psalmist answers this question: so that others may *"taste and see that the Lord is good"* (Ps. 34:8).

Boaz, who was already aware of Naomi and Ruth's plight, had now witnessed for himself Ruth's diligent devotion. He addressed her kindly, *"my daughter,"* which confirmed both his gentle nature and the significant age difference that existed between them. Furthermore, he is moved with compassion to show Ruth favor. He directs that:

- Ruth should not glean in any another fields, but remain with his maidens (v. 8).

- His young men, the reapers, should not take advantage of her in any way (v. 9).

- Ruth should drink from the water that the young men had drawn from the well (v. 9).

- Ruth should eat with the reapers for her protection (v. 14).

- Ruth should glean from the sheaves already gathered (v. 15).

- His young men should purposely let some of the harvest fall so Ruth could glean it (v. 16).

Boaz' first instructions to Ruth are imperative: *"Do not go to glean in another field."* In application, this is a primary decree of the Lord Jesus for His Church today also. It is the same ill that Paul warned the church at Corinth of, that is, do not desert your privileged place of communion and blessing at the Lord's Table to venture into the world for things which cannot satisfy: *"You cannot drink the cup of the Lord and the cup of demons; you cannot partake of the Lord's table and of the table of demons. Or do we provoke the Lord to jealousy? Are we stronger than He?"* (1 Cor. 10:21-22). The Lord's Table in this passage is not the same as the Lord's Supper (1 Cor. 11:17-34). The latter is a remembrance meeting of the Church where there is a physical table with bread and wine. The Lord's Table is spiritual in nature, and speaks of the sum total blessings and provisions that are ours when we remain in fellowship with the Lord at His table. Just as Ruth was not to glean in any other field, all that we need is provided for at the Lord's Table. Hence, Paul warns that believers are not to venture to the table of demons (i.e., into the world) to seek pleasure and gratification apart from Christ. Therefore, the warning given Ruth is also one that we should heed, says Samuel Ridout:

"Go not to another field." Many are the temptations to do this, both for the seeking soul now, and for the remnant in the coming day. How the enemy would allure away or drive away the soul from the word of God, the fields of grace. There are other and easier ways of getting peace; reformation, happy feelings, religious professions — thousands of substitutes are offered for the simple way of God. Or the soul is terrified, there is no hope for one so guilty and hardened, the day of grace is passed, why throw away even the few days that remain of life in futile efforts to get what never can be ours? Ah, who that has been under exercise of soul can forget how many and often were the temptations to go to some other field.[1]

Besides not gleaning in other fields, Ruth is further instructed by Boaz to remain near his household maidens. F. C. Cook explains the practical nature of this request: "The fields not being divided by hedges, but only by unplowed ridges, it would be easy for Ruth to pass off Boaz' land without being aware of it, and so find herself among strangers where Boaz could not protect her."[2]

Boaz sought to provide Ruth immunity from all molestation; she would be under his authority and protection. She was permitted to eat with the reapers, even to dip her bread in a communal bowl of vinegar with them, and most exhilarating, she ate from the hand of Boaz: *"So she sat beside the reapers, and he [Boaz] passed parched grain to her; and she ate and was satisfied"* (v. 14). This is a tender scene: the revered Jew, Boaz, personally passes to the young Moabite woman a bountiful helping of parched or roasted corn.

Like the Lord, Boaz knows that food and rest must go together to properly care for his servants. The beasts of the field eat standing, but the servants of the Lord enjoy the Master's provision and fellowship while resting from their labors. But we must choose to come aside to adequately feed on His Word and receive the nourishment He provides from it. Unfortunately, many believers today are so busy that they do not provision the time to come into the Lord's presence to be refreshed; as a result, they do not enjoy the full benefits of His communion.

How does Ruth respond to the goodness of Boaz? *"So she fell on her face, bowed down to the ground, and said to him, 'Why have I found favor in your eyes, that you should take notice of me, since I am a foreigner?'"* (v. 10). Should not this be the response of all who have

202

experienced the unmerited favor of God in Christ? Why then should believers feel it necessary to exalt themselves or maintain crusty, dried up hearts which cannot wring out any joy or praise to the Lord? Ruth, a recipient of grace, demonstrates in her initial response to Boaz the proper attitude that all believers should have concerning God's grace. H. L. Rossier agrees:

> Ruth opens her mouth. "Why," she asks, "have I found favor in thine eyes, that thou shouldest regard me, seeing I am a foreigner?" I love this "why" that demonstrates the deep humility of this young woman: "I have no right," she says, as it were, "to such favor." She is not concerned with herself except to confess her unworthiness, but how she appreciates him! "You took notice of me when I was nothing to you!"[3]

Indeed, God noticed us when we were still His grievous enemies deserving judgment, and then righteously acted in judging His Son for our sins to offer us complete salvation forged in His grace:

> *For when we were still without strength, in due time Christ died for the ungodly. For scarcely for a righteous man will one die; yet perhaps for a good man someone would even dare to die. But God demonstrates His own love toward us, in that while we were still sinners, Christ died for us* (Rom. 6:7-8).

Dearly beloved, no matter how long we have been saved, may we never get beyond Ruth's first question in our spiritual journey: "Why have I received God's unmerited favor?" Like the psalmist, may we always *"Give thanks to the Lord, for He is good! For His mercy endures forever"* (Ps. 106:1).

Boaz was fully aware of Ruth's conversion and good deeds towards her mother-in-law (v. 11). He then responded to Ruth's quandary with this promise: *"The Lord repay your work, and a full reward be given you by the Lord God of Israel, under whose wings you have come for refuge"* (v. 12). Why could Boaz confirm the goodness of God to Ruth? Because he was the instrument of God's grace in this story, just as Christ is for humanity: *"For all the promises of God in Him are Yes, and in Him Amen, to the glory of God through us"* (2 Cor. 1:20). For faithfulness and abiding in truth, Ruth received God's grace and promise of protection and care – all believers have the same provision in Christ. Let us remember Ruth's gracious example, she had sowed sacrificial love and kindness and was now reaping the same from the Lord. The Lord is faithful to ensure that whether we sow (good or bad), we will reap what we sow (Gal. 6:7-8)!

With the setting of the sun, Ruth's gleaning efforts ceased, but there was still work to be done; the grain needed to be separated from the chaff. Ruth beat out the chaff from the barley sheaves she had reaped (i.e., what she had not eaten of). Believers often miss this important aspect of gleaning spiritual food from God's Word. It is not enough to just read Scripture; there must be the follow-on work of prayer and meditation to fully benefit from what God has for us. We cannot irreverently rush into the presence of the "Ancient of days" and expect Him to conform to our daytime planner. Rather, we are to *"wait upon the Lord our God, until that He have mercy upon us"* (Ps. 123:2; KJV).

What was the measure of God's grace for Ruth's first day of laboring? After beating out the grain, she gathered up about an ephah and then returned to Naomi with it (v. 17). The exact amount cannot be verified, as the amount of a biblical ephah varied over time. The equivalence at this time was probably about six-tenths of a bushel, or about 5 $\frac{1}{2}$ English gallons, which would have weighed about 30 pounds (13 kg). It is noted that a day's wage will only buy a measure of wheat or three measures of barley during the desperate days of the Tribulation Period (Rev. 6:6). Three measures is an ephah, which is what Ruth obtained after laboring an entire day.

It is also noted that one omer (one-tenth of an ephah) of manna was a day's food allotment during Israel's wilderness experience (Ex. 16:36). This meant that in one day Ruth had gleaned a five-day food supply for both women. The weight of the grain Ruth harvested was manageable in one trip back to Naomi. Samuel Ridout reminds us of an important application drawn from Ruth's eating and beating activities:

> Ruth must first be sufficed before she can give to Naomi. … Faith must feed on its gathered store before it can impart to others. In John's gospel we see this strikingly illustrated in the "Come and see" of those who had themselves already come and seen the Christ. It is the poor Samaritan, who in her position resembles Ruth, who can take the message to the people of the town. We are living in days not only of great activity, but when the doctrine of activity is put in the place

of feeding upon the truth of God. We are told that the way to grow is to work; but how can we work without strength and guidance and all else suggested in that word "communion"? We can only give the overflow to others …We eat and are sufficed, and out of a full heart we minister to the needs of others.[4]

When Naomi saw the unusual amount of gleaned grain for a single day's effort, she was astonished (v. 18). She immediately inquired from Ruth: *"Where have you gleaned today? And where did you work? Blessed be the one who took notice of you"* (v. 19). Though still bitter in her soul, she knew enough from her earlier "full" life to recognize the undeniable marks of God's providential care. God's grace! The grain now before her was much more than what a woman could have gleaned and beat out on her own without receiving assistance. Ruth then relates to Naomi the wonderful events of the day and how a man named Boaz showed much kindness to her.

Naomi knows Boaz, and in fact she has been connected with him for a long time; Boaz is kin of her dead husband Elimelech (v. 20). In Naomi, we again see Israel's long connection with Christ, but in her waywardness she lost God's blessings available through Him. Now understanding the potential of obtaining redemption through her kinsman Boaz, she instructs Ruth to heed his invitation and return only to his fields to glean and also to remain among his maidens (vv. 21-22). It is doubtful that Ruth, being a stranger in Israel, fully understood what Naomi was talking about (i.e., Levitical Laws pertaining to redemption). Regardless, she obeyed the instruction of her mother-in-law and labored hard for the next six to eight weeks: from the commencement of the barley harvest to the conclusion of the wheat harvest (v. 23).

Ruth was a faithful gleaner who was greatly blessed by God's grace. Considering her testimony, Hamilton Smith wonders why Christians at this time are such poor gleaners. He then suggests that profitable gleaners of grace must have certain conditions with which they must be willing to comply:

First she was marked by a spirit of *humility and subjection.* ... She did not act independently of others who were older and more experienced than herself. She did not despise guidance and counsel. She did not

205

suffer from an unbroken will, leading her to do that which was right in her own eyes. ...

Secondly, Ruth was marked by *diligence.* ... in verse 17 we read, "She gleaned in the field until even." Is there not a great lack of diligence with believers in the things of God? We are diligent enough in the things of this world, but alas, the things of the Lord too often have only the odd moments of our lives. Are we diligent in the study of the Word? Are we diligent in prayer?

Thirdly, Ruth was *persevering.* She was not diligent one day and slothful the next ... day after day she gleaned until the end of both the barley and the wheat harvest. It is easy to be diligent for one day, but to be diligent day after day calls for perseverance. Daily is a hard and testing word. Let the disciple "take up his cross daily," said the Lord.

Finally, we read that Ruth *"beat out* that she had gleaned" (verse 17). It is not enough to glean the barley and the wheat; it must be beaten out. The truth we gather whether through our private study, or from the ministry of others, must become the subject of prayer and meditation if it is to promote spiritual growth.[5]

In summary, for us to grow in grace and experience spiritual progress there must be conditions in our soul that are marked by subjection, diligence, perseverance, and meditation.

Notice the two groups of people laboring in the field with Ruth: first, the larger group of laborers, and second, the smaller group which is more closely associated with Ruth, the maidens. These maidens are mentioned three times in this chapter (vv. 8, 22, 23). There can be little doubt what these laboring companions of Ruth symbolize: the fellowship and encouragement of other like-minded believers who are co-laboring together in the same local church. Each believer is growing in grace to the extent that he or she practically gleans in faith and in so doing blesses not just their own soul, but their companions in the faith also.

The reapers also have an important service in connection with Ruth (4-7, 9, 21). These represent leading servants in the wider body of Christ who are laborers in various capacities, but in the same field as the maidens and Ruth. Notice that Boaz greets them with what should be the desire of every believer: *"the Lord be with you"* (v. 4). Without personal intimacy with the Lord, the servant of God will have no joy or wherewithal to labor with the Lord and for Him. The reapers clearly demonstrate their respect for Boaz' authority and are subject to his commands – another must for any believer desiring to honor the Lord in service.

These reapers also went ahead of Ruth, after which she was blessed by their efforts (they left grain behind for her). Ruth was also to keep in close company with them for her protection. Likewise, those who are more mature in Christ must lead by example and ensure that their ministry both benefits and protects those younger in the faith. Lastly, these reapers drew water from the well to refresh Ruth in her laboring. God's Word rightly administered to believers is as cool water drawn from a well, but Peter warns that false teachers are empty wells and clouds without rain (2 Pet. 2:17). These workers of iniquity provide nothing to enhance and energize the believer for service. Mature reapers have a duty to apply the Word of God in such a way as to invigorate others to serve the Lord also. Ruth, a new believer, had the wonderful encouragement of fellow working maidens and also the practical example, protection, and assistance of the reapers, all of which were under Boaz' authority, as directed by his foreman. Some commentators suggest he pictures the Holy Spirit, who directs believers and works within them to honor Christ through spiritual fruitfulness.

This is a lovely scene for the Lord to view from His exalted position in heaven: His people working together in harmony to further His kingdom. Just as the reapers did not know when Boaz might arrive to review their work, believers today do not know when Christ might suddenly appear and judge their labors either. Therefore, *"let us consider one another in order to stir up love and good works, not forsaking the assembling of ourselves together, as is the manner of some, but exhorting one another, and so much the more as you see the Day approaching"* (Heb. 10:24-25). For the glory of Christ, may we all be faithful gleaners together and enjoy God's abundant grace!

Meditation

When Ruth a-gleaning went, Jehovah was her guide;
To Boaz' field he led her straight, and she became his bride.

Relativity and Redemption

Jesus my Boaz is; my strength and portion too;
His word of grace the precious field, where I a-gleaning go.

O what a heavenly field! What handfuls it contains!
What strength and comfort gleaners get, to recompense their pains!

Ye gleaners, one and all, let Christ be all your song;
He is your strength and portion too, and you to him belong.

— W. Gadsby

Seeking Redemption
Ruth 3

When Naomi was departing Moab, she instructed her two daughters-in-law to return to their own people and to remarry that they might obtain *rest* (1:9). Where "gleaning" was the main subject matter of the last chapter, the theme of "rest" occupies the final two chapters. In ancient near-Eastern times, marriage provided security for a woman. Naomi informs Ruth that it is still her desire for her to marry: *"My daughter, shall I not seek security for you, that it may be well with you?"* (v. 1). The same Hebrew word translated "security" in this verse is also rendered "rest" in Ruth 1:9. Naomi desires Ruth to have this type of rest. However, Naomi also sees the opportunity to have her own inheritance redeemed through a Levirate marriage agreement between Ruth and a near kinsman, that is, if there is a willing and able kinsman-redeemer, such as Boaz.

For a Jew at this time, the matter of possession (land inheritance) and rest were inseparably connected; this reality is repeatedly shown in the book of Joshua. By faith and obedience, God's people entered Canaan – their inheritance. They could not engage in conquest until they entered the land, they could not possess the land without conquest, and they could not enter God's rest in the land without first possessing it:

*Remember the word which Moses the servant of the Lord commanded you, saying, "The Lord your God is giving you **rest** and is giving you this **land**"* (Josh. 1:13).

But you [the two and half tribes] *shall pass before your brethren armed* [i.e., cross over the Jordan first], *all your mighty men of valor, and help them, until the Lord has given your brethren **rest**, as He gave you, and they also have taken **possession of the land** which the Lord your God is giving them* (Josh. 1:14-15).

> *So Joshua took the whole **land**, according to all that the Lord had said to Moses; and Joshua gave it as an **inheritance** to Israel according to their divisions by their tribes. Then the land **rested** from war* (Josh. 11:23).

In the Church Age, believers do not labor for a *place* of rest; our rest and inheritance are in a *Person* – *"Christ in heavenly places"* (Eph. 1:3). Thus, Paul could pray for fellow believers, *"The Lord of peace Himself give you peace in every way"* (2 Thess. 3:16) and also share his life's aspiration with them:

> *Not that I have already attained, or am already perfected; but I press on, that I may lay hold of that for which Christ Jesus has also laid hold of me. Brethren, I do not count myself to have apprehended; but one thing I do, forgetting those things which are behind and reaching forward to those things which are ahead, I press toward the goal for the prize of the upward call of God in Christ Jesus* (Phil. 3:12-14).

Christ is the believer's inheritance and resting place. The practical blessing of those present possessions granted the believer in Christ will be experienced through faith and obedience as one engages in active conquest and is enabled to do so by resurrection power. For Ruth, the ultimate rest would be obtained through redemption and the marriage to Boaz, which she requested by faith. She shows us through the events of this chapter that all depends upon Christ; only He can exercise grace and only He has the right to redeem that which is dead and is hence without rights. C. A. Coates further explains this reality as pertaining to Israel:

> Ruth, though a Moabitess, was the representative of the dead, but she could not claim the inheritance in her own right, nor secure a seed to hold it on behalf of her dead husband. If taken up at all, the inheritance had to be taken up according to the ancient statute of the right of redemption. Israel never truly had the inheritance in any other way, and never will have.[1]

While in this author's mind Ruth is a lovely picture of the Gentile Church, the bride of Christ, the book of Ruth is primarily Jewish in nature and should be understood as a message of God's providential love to His covenant people. In this sense the childless, widowed Moabite is dead in every sense of the word concerning the commonwealth of Israel, the position of Israel without redeeming grace. God provides abundant mercy to those who humbly seek Him with empty hands:

> *I love those who love me, and those who seek me diligently will find me. Riches and honor are with me, enduring riches and righteousness. My fruit is better than gold, yes, than fine gold, and my revenue than choice silver. I traverse the way of righteousness, in the midst of the paths of justice, that I may cause those who love me to inherit wealth, that I may fill their treasuries* (Prov. 8:17-21).

In Naomi, we see a different aspect of Israel being typified: she represents the once chastened and dispersed Jewish nation that will in the future be forever restored to the Lord through the work of redemption. By grace, Israel will possess all the land promised to Abraham (Gen. 15:18-21). As witnessed in the book of Joshua, this earthly inheritance is Jehovah's reward for faithfulness and relates to His rest for His people (i.e., His provision for sustaining life).

Returning to the narrative, Naomi proceeds to inform Ruth of her legal claim upon Boaz, but she must act promptly to prepare herself in order to request Him to perform it. Time was short, for the harvest was over and all the work was nearly complete, but Naomi knew that Boaz could still be found at his threshing floor winnowing barley (v. 2). She instructed Ruth to lay aside the garments of her widowhood, to wash and to anoint herself, and to dress in attire that would be fitting to present herself as a willing bride to Boaz (v. 3). She was then to journey to the threshing floor but remain concealed (v. 3).

After the men had eaten and drunk, she was to mark the spot in which Boaz laid down to sleep. After he fell asleep, Ruth was then to uncover his feet and lie down at his feet (the place of humility). This act would eventually cause Boaz to discover Ruth's presence: When Boaz discovered that his feet were chilled, he would bend down to cover his feet and find Ruth. Naomi told Ruth that Boaz would tell her what to do after she made her Levirate marriage request to him (v. 4). Ruth agreed to do exactly what Naomi instructed her to do, and does so (vv. 5-6). At the end of verse 7, we find Boaz asleep at the end of a pile of grain (to protect it from being plundered) – and his feet are getting cold.

At midnight, the plan unfolds; Boaz awakes and is startled to find a woman lying at his feet (v. 8). It was dark so Boaz asks who the woman was. Ruth responds, *"I am Ruth, your maidservant. Take your maidservant under your wing, for you are a close relative"* (v. 9). Under Mosaic Law, if a brother died and did not have a child to pass his inheritance down to, then his brother was to marry his widow and bear children in his name by her. This type of union was called a Levirate marriage. The firstborn male of that relationship would be the heir to the dead brother's estate. All this to say that there is nothing immoral about the scene before us; as C. I. Scofield explains, Ruth's actions must be interpreted in light of the customs of that day:

> It was clearly a way of letting a near kinsman (goel) know that he had, not only the right but also the request to proceed with the legal steps necessary to the exercise of his responsibility. That Ruth's conduct was above reproach is indicated in Boaz' reception, protection, and tacit agreement with the general evaluation of her character (vv. 10-11).[2]

Boaz understood Ruth's marriage proposal to mean that she was refusing all others to have and to follow after him. In response, Boaz assures her of blessing, *"blessed are you"* (v. 10). Then he removes all fear from her heart by saying *"fear not"* and promises: "I will do for you all that you request" (v. 11). One way or another Ruth would be redeemed, either by the nearer-kinsman or Boaz (vv. 12-13). Boaz tells Ruth that he is honored by her request; she could have married a younger man and been taken care of, but the fact that she desired to pursue a Levirate marriage with him was flattering (v. 10). Given his status and wealth, Boaz was probably old enough to be her father, so her actions were noble and pure, not sensual in nature – she sought to restore Naomi's dead husband's inheritance to a son born from their union. Her selfless act was to resurrect a man's family name from dying out and remove reproach from Naomi, for to be childless in Israel was regarded as a mark of God's displeasure.

Boaz agrees to Ruth's request, but also acknowledges a difficulty in what she has proposed. There was a kinsman who was nearer to Naomi (Elimelech) than himself, and the Law granted him the first opportunity to redeem the land and honor the Levirate duty (vv. 11-12). Ruth had earned quite a reputation with the local people as a hardworking, virtuous woman, and Boaz acknowledges that and also applauds her fine character himself.

To avoid possibly shaming Ruth, Boaz instructs her to wait until first light in the morning to return to her home (v. 14). It would be safe then to travel and yet, dark enough that no one would recognize her or see her leaving the threshing floor. If Ruth was discovered at a remote location where various men were sleeping, it would likely taint her reputation. Boaz told Ruth that he would approach the nearer-kinsman about the matter later in the morning (v. 13). How much sleep either Ruth or Boaz enjoyed after this exciting interchange is unknown, but Ruth could rest in the reality of redemption, and Boaz could rejoice in Ruth's devotion.

Before Ruth departed the threshing floor, Boaz put six measures of barley (or two ephahs, about 60 pounds of grain) into the cloak (or long veil). As previously mentioned, barley symbolizes redemption in Scripture and this barley was a secret pledge of what Boaz would do for Ruth, a token that Naomi would recognize and rejoice in (v. 15). Ruth labored all day for one ephah in chapter 2, but this barley is fostered in grace, and is double that portion. In faith, Ruth laid open her cloak and received Boaz' promise of more bounty to come, even himself – the master of the harvest.

The barley would also be an abundant provision for Ruth during the interim while she waited (rests in faith) to hear the outcome of the matter. H. L. Rossier explains that the book of Ruth teaches us much about working for the Lord and also resting in Him:

> Work and rest in service, the work and rest of faith, and the work and rest of grace. The reapers work and rest; so does the lord of the harvest; so does Ruth, the bride of his choosing. How peacefully she rests at Boaz' feet during the hours of the night! And how she rests afterwards while waiting for her redeemer's efforts to prepare for her the rest of which chapter 4 speaks![3]

It is observed that the time between the provision of his pledge and when Ruth would become Boaz' wife was only a few hours. Likewise, for the One who inhabits eternity, the passing of centuries in the

Church Age are mere moments, but for the bride awaiting her Groom, time passes much more slowly.

At first light, Ruth returns to Naomi with the barley and relates to her all Boaz stated (vv. 16-17). Naomi then instructs Ruth to wait at home, *"sit still,"* as she knows that Boaz *"will not rest until he has concluded the matter this day"* (v. 18). Having received Boaz' provision of barley, Ruth had what she needed to "sit still" in the knowledge that Boaz would not rest until he has finished what he had begun. Dear believer, we do well to remember this important truth; Paul put it this way: *"Being confident of this very thing, that He who has begun a good work in you will complete it until the day of Jesus Christ"* (Phil. 1:6). Though we have been purchased in our entirety by the blood of Christ, our bodies have yet to be redeemed (Eph. 1:14, 4:30; 1 Pet. 1:18). On that day, the Lord will come for His Church and our salvation in Him will be complete – we will receive an immortal body like His (1 Cor. 15:51-52; Phil. 3:21). Until that day occurs, it is comforting to know that He has provided everything we need to both labor for Him and rest in Him.

Boaz' diligent fervor to assist the poor and destitute wonderfully pictures the Lord's steadfast resolve to be crucified in place of guilty vile sinners, and then to redeem and to continue assisting those who petition Him for mercy. The prophet Isaiah conveys the Lord Jesus' determination to expend Himself on our behalf despite the human brutality and divine judgment He knew He would suffer:

> *And I was not rebellious, nor did I turn away. I gave My back to those who struck Me, and My cheeks to those who plucked out the beard; I did not hide My face from shame and spitting. For the Lord God will help Me; therefore I will not be disgraced; therefore I have set My face like a flint, and I know that I will not be ashamed* (Isa. 50:5-7).

Thankfully, two thousand years ago, the Lord Jesus did not enter into His rest until He had secured ours, through the shedding of His own blood. As this chapter closes, we leave Ruth waiting to know the outcome of her request: Will she be redeemed? Will Boaz be able to marry her? Will she enter into his rest? We will see in the next chapter that Boaz did not rest until he secured Ruth's rest through marriage.

Meditation

Oh, Jesus, Lord, who loved me like to Thee?
Fruit of Thy work, with Thee, too, there to see
Thy glory, Lord, while endless ages roll,
Myself the prize and travail of Thy soul.

Yet it must be, Thy love had not its rest
Were Thy redeemed not with Thee fully blest;
That love that gives not as the world, but shares
All it possesses with its loved co-heirs.

— John N. Darby

Blessings of Redemption
Ruth 4

As we commence the final chapter of Ruth, let us consider the story of grace that God is conveying to us in the narrative. Hamilton Smith notes the lovely progression of salvation's features throughout the book of Ruth:

- In chapter 1, Ruth sets forth the faith, love and devoted energy of a newly converted soul.
- In chapter 2, Ruth presents a picture of the growth in grace by which the believer makes spiritual progress.
- In chapter 3, Ruth is seeking the rest of heart that will alone bring satisfaction to the believer.
- In chapter 4, the story of Ruth closes with the rest secured, setting forth the way that God's rest is reached for Christ and the believer.[1]

Ruth gleaning in the fields of Boaz and receiving provisions from his hand, however lovely and gracious, will not suffice for either Boaz or Ruth. Nothing will provide rest and full satisfaction to the heart but to possess the one that is loved. In chapter 3, we witnessed Ruth seeking to have Boaz, and in chapter 4, we will see Boaz working to possess Ruth. He is busy acting on Ruth's appeal for a Levirate marriage, while Ruth anxiously awaits with Naomi to hear the outcome of her request. She cannot enter in this work – it is Boaz' responsibility alone. True love cannot be satisfied with mere gestures and gifts; it must have the giver – this is the theme of this chapter. Christ, and only Christ, can satisfy our heart's deepest desire, and He longs to do so.

Boaz goes to the gate of the city and gathers trustworthy observers in addition to ten elders of the city to witness the legal proceedings (vv. 1-2). In Jewish society, the presence of at least ten elders was required to constitute a lawful public assembly (today modern Jews still require ten, a *minyon*, to constitute a synagogue). The gate of the city is where judgments were passed and only Boaz can do this work; all others, including the elders, can only sit and observe. This scene reminds us that at Calvary, the place of God's judgment for human sin, only the Lord Jesus could accomplish the redemptive work, while the Jewish nation and Gentiles alike witnessed the transaction.

Boaz and the witnesses waited at the gate of Bethlehem until the other nearer-kinsman came into town. This kinsman is then informed by Boaz about a parcel of land that Naomi had sold (probably when her family moved to Moab) and now desired that it be redeemed on her behalf (v. 3). The other kinsman was willing to redeem this land (v. 4). Boaz then informs the unnamed kinsman that if he does redeem the land, he must also take Ruth as his wife, so she can bear children to maintain the inheritance active that belonged to Naomi's family (v. 5). After hearing this detail, the man declined to redeem Naomi's land.

Leviticus 25 declares God's right to "eminent domain" in the Promised Land. Because this land was the Lord's, it could never be indefinitely lost from those by which His grace had placed it. All was to go free in the year of jubilee, or could be redeemed and restored by a near kinsman (as valued in association with the time remaining until the year of Jubilee). In Naomi's case, there was no heir to pass down the inheritance, so redeeming the land for Naomi was a noble and merciful gesture, but one that he would profit from eventually, after the death of Naomi and Ruth, the rightful heirs of the land. However, when the matter of marrying Ruth was broached, the nearer-kinsman did not want to redeem a land that he would not own for long (i.e. Ruth's children, not his present family, would possess Naomi's land and perhaps some of his existing land also). This suggests that this man was of limited means, whereas Boaz was wealthy and fully able to do all Ruth had requested. Perhaps he was already married and did not want the strife that a Levirate marriage might cause in his home-life. Samuel Ridout suggests another reason why the nearer-kinsman did not want to redeem Naomi's land:

> The law, even with the most merciful construction, could no longer interpose. "An Ammonite or Moabite shall not enter into the congregation of the Lord; even to their tenth generation shall they not enter into the congregation of the Lord forever" (Deut. 23:2). The apostate people had deliberately given up all claim, and so far as the

law was concerned, were cut off. This explains why the kinsman, no matter how willing he might be to restore the heritage to Naomi, could not take it to raise up by *Ruth* the name of the deceased kinsman. His own inheritance would be marred. How truly that law, "holy, just and good," would be marred if the smallest jot or tittle of its righteous demands were abated. ... They are in the place of the Moabite.[2]

The Law was inflexible in demonstrating grace to a Moabite, and the nearer-kinsman did not want to impoverish himself and mar his own inheritance. He therefore agreed to relinquish his right to redeem what he could not and did so before the elders of the city (v. 6).

There were three requirements for a redeeming kinsman: close family tie, enough wealth to redeem, and willingness to redeem. The unnamed man possessed the first two, but not the third. He represents the Law, which by divine decree made righteous demands on Israel; it was close kin, per se, but it was unable to redeem anyone, for no one could keep the Law. God's purpose for the Law was to show sin (Rom. 3:19-20) and point man to God's solution – a Savior:

Therefore we conclude that a man is justified by faith apart from the deeds of the law (Rom. 3:28).

But the Scripture has confined all under sin, that the promise by faith in Jesus Christ might be given to those who believe. But before faith came, we were kept under guard by the law, kept for the faith which would afterward be revealed. Therefore the law was our tutor to bring us to Christ, that we might be justified by faith (Gal. 3:22-24).

Therefore, the unnamed nearer-kinsman could not redeem anyone; the mechanics of the situation would not permit him to. However, his valid claim and right to redemption must first be legally set aside – the Law cannot affect a work of grace to redeem what it has condemned. The Law, having been shown its honorable resolve, now transfers all its rights to Christ. The Law has no more claim on the destitute; this then permits the fruitless to become abounding through a new relationship made possible through Christ's resurrection. Boaz represents, to us, Christ risen, alive, and personally able to redeem.

Under Levitical Law, if the next of kin refused the Levirate marriage request of a widow, she was then to take off the shoe of that man and spit in his face (Deut. 25:5-10). The latter detail is passed over, as Ruth is not present and Boaz is representing her. However, the nearer-kinsman does give Boaz his shoe as a visible testimony that he was abdicating his legal right in the matter and transferring it to Boaz. In type, the demands of the Law must concede its rights to the risen Christ, who fulfilled the Law and bore its judicial penalty for those who could not.

Being the next closest kin to Elimelech, Boaz agrees to redeem the land that belonged to Naomi's dead sons, Chilion and Mahlon, and to take Ruth as his wife (vv. 9-10). The witnesses and the elders all give their consent in the matter. They desired God to bless Boaz with a great posterity through Ruth, as He blessed Rachel and Leah (the wives of Jacob) with children, and Tamar, who had twins (Pharez being the oldest, as fathered by Judah; vv. 11-12). Their statement in verse 11 is worthy of further examination: *"The Lord make the woman who is coming to your house like Rachel and Leah, the two who **built** the house of Israel"* (v. 11). Solomon clarifies that: *"Every wise woman **builds** her house: but the foolish plucks it down with her hands"* (Prov. 14:1). The Hebrew word translated "built" and "builds" in these two verses is *banah*, which simply means "to build" or "to make." A wise woman builds up her home. She orders it, keeps it and makes it better. This is what Leah and Rachel did and what the people hoped that Ruth would do.

Interestingly, the first occurrence of *banah* in the Bible also relates to a woman: *"And the rib, which the Lord God had taken from man, **made** He a woman, and brought her unto the man"* (Gen. 2:22). Scripture first applies *banah* to God's creative act of fashioning a woman. The second biblical usage of *banah* in relation to a woman is found in Genesis 16 where we find the barren Sarah desperately seeking children to "build up" her house (Gen. 16:2). Abraham pitched tents and erected altars, but building the home was Sarah's job. From the earliest pages of Scripture, we see God's plan for the family. The husband is to be the head of and the provider for his family, while the wife is to bear children, nurture them, and keep and maintain the home. The wise mother rests in God's wisdom and strength to build and to keep her home, for *"except the Lord build the house, they labor in vain that build it"* (Ps. 127:1).

Boaz moved quickly to redeem the land and marries Ruth and the Lord did bless them with a son, Obed (v. 13). Obed will be the father of Jesse, who will be the father of King David, the king of Israel (v. 17). Perhaps to quell any future doubts concerning Messianic lineage, the narrative provides the genealogy for the tribe of Judah from Tamar's son Perez to David (vv. 18-22). Ruth, the poor and despised Moabite, will be King David's great grandmother and thereby also in the lineage of the Lord Jesus Christ (Matt. 1:3-6).

Under the chastening of the Almighty, Naomi desired to be called Mara, or bitter. However, the Lord did not leave her without a provision for full restoration into His joy and blessing – there was a kinsman-redeemer (Boaz) who rescued her. Concerning the child Obed in relationship to Naomi, the women of Bethlehem avowed: *"May his name be famous in Israel! And may he be to you a restorer of life and a nourisher of your old age"* (v. 14). Being outside the will of God, Naomi had suffered the deaths of her husband and two sons; now she tightly holds Ruth's son in her own bosom and became a nurse to him (v. 16). In this sense, the son of grace comes forth, like the Messiah from God's barren people. God had redeemed Naomi, given her a new life, and a new son: *"There is a son born to Naomi"* (v. 17). H. L. Rossier explains the meaning of the baby's name and the significance of what it represents:

> Obed means "He who serves." This is the Lord's title of glory before all His other marvelous titles. This *Servant* is the Root and Offspring of David, the bearer of royal grace. Do not all our hearts beat with joy when we call Him by this name? He the Counselor, the Mighty God, has served, is now serving, and will remain a Servant forever for the benefit of those whom He loves! Our highest blessings are comprehended in this title of Servant[3]

Christ's devotion to His Father, His sacrificial love and work for us, His present grace, and His eternal service of love after we are in His presence in glory – "He who serves," indeed.

With the birth of Obed, the reproach of Naomi's childlessness was removed, her family's name resurrected, and the inheritance associated with that name restored in full. Naomi was no longer bitter; the joy of her salvation had returned and she was abundantly living out the meaning of her name. In chapter 1, the original state of Israel, as the elect of God, is demonstrated in Elimelech's name, "whose God is King," and His favor to Israel in Naomi's name, "My pleasantness." Through willful sin, the blessing of that divine status was lost, but through weeping and brokenness, all had been restored in grace.

Centuries later, the psalmist would declare what Naomi and many of us know to be experientially true: *"Those who sow in tears shall reap in joy. He who continually goes forth weeping, bearing seed for sowing, shall doubtless come again with rejoicing, bringing his sheaves with him"* (Ps. 126:5-6). In the prophetic sense, Naomi in chapter 4 pictures the refined and fully restored nation of Israel enjoying the blessings of the future Millennial Kingdom with her Kinsman-Redeemer, the Lord Jesus Christ. Rejoicing with her will be once-destitute Gentiles, now the bride of Christ, and joint-heirs with Him in all things (Rev. 21:7). Whether Jew or Gentile, all those desiring to be redeemed by the only One willing and able to do so will rejoice in that day!

Ruth's example of faithfulness, loyalty, and sacrifice is an inspiring example to follow. After the birth of Obed, the local women commend Ruth to Naomi: *"Your daughter-in-law, who loves you, who is better to you than seven sons, has borne him"* (v. 15). The Lord remembered her selfless and arduous service to Naomi and rewarded her for it. Believers today have the same promise of God. He is watching. He knows. He cares. He remembers. He will reward appropriately and abundantly:

For our light affliction, which is but for a moment, is working for us a far more exceeding and eternal weight of glory (2 Cor. 4:17).

For I consider that the sufferings of this present time are not worthy to be compared with the glory which shall be revealed in us (Rom. 8:18).

For God is not unjust to forget your work and labor of love which you have shown toward His name, in that you have ministered to the saints, and do minister. And we desire that each one of you show the same diligence to the full assurance of hope until the end, that you do not become sluggish, but imitate those who through faith and patience inherit the promises (Heb. 6:10-12).

We do not know when our Boaz will return for us and remove us to His abode, but He has provided everything that we need until that time. We can be assured that He will not rest until all believers are brought into His full inheritance and eternal rest!

Beloved, now we are children of God; and it has not yet been revealed what we shall be, but we know that when He is revealed, we shall be like Him, for we shall see Him as He is. And everyone who has this hope in Him purifies himself, just as He is pure (1 Jn. 3:2-3).

Then, we all will be shocked to learn how little we practically appreciated the reality of *"all spiritual blessings in heavenly places in Christ."* Dear believers, let us not live like paupers, but rather appropriate, in full measure, the grace of God afforded to us now in Christ! May we use our inheritance in Christ for His glory now, rather than squander the opportunity through disbelief and disobedience!

Meditation

The reason why many fail to enjoy their inheritance is that they have never realized that they are not enjoying it; they lack the deep exercises seen in Naomi. Their spiritual standard is low; they believe that their sins are forgiven, and that they will go to heaven when they die or when the Lord comes, but they have very little conception that there is a vast wealth of spiritual blessing which they might be enjoying now. On the other hand, how often is there a lack of affectionate interest in God's things such as was seen in Ruth. She had never personally been in the land, so that she could not have quite the sense of having departed from it. Perhaps many of us have opportunity to come into things as she did. Under the influence of Naomi her affections went out fully to what was of God. If this is so with us, it will lead to reaching Him who can fully secure to us the blessedness of the inheritance. There is often desire at the bottom of the heart, but no definite purpose to go in for what is desired, and when this is the case, there is danger of being diverted by all kinds of things that are not Christ.[4]

— C. A. Coates

Endnotes

Introduction to Judges

1. F. Duane Lindsey & Dallas Theological Seminary, *The Bible Knowledge Commentary: An Exposition of the Scriptures* (Victor Books, Wheaton, IL; 1983-1985), p. 172
2. http://www.cresourcei.org/exodusdate.html
3. John D. Hannah & Dallas Theological Seminary, *The Bible Knowledge Commentary : An Exposition of the Scriptures* (Victor Books, Wheaton, IL; 1983-1985), , op. cit., pp. 104-108
4. J. N. Darby, *Synopsis of the Books of the Bible: Genesis – 2 Chronicles, Vol. 1* (Stow Hill Bible and Tract Depot, Kingston, England; 1948), p. 289
5. Steve Rudd, *Chronology of the Judges Timeline*: http://www.bible.ca/archeology/bible-archeology-exodus-route-date-chronology-of-judges-1350-1004bc.jpg
6. William Kelly, *Lectures on the Book of Judges*, STEM Publishing (intro.): http://stempublishing.com/authors/kelly/1Oldtest/judges.html

The Joshua-Judges Connection

Warring in Review

1. John Hannah from J. F. Walvoord, R. B. Zuck, & Dallas Theological Seminary, *The Bible Knowledge Commentary : An Exposition of the Scriptures* (Victor Books, Wheaton, IL; 1983-1985), p. 152
2. H. L. Rossier, *Meditations on the Book of Judges*, STEM Publishing (chp. 1): http://stempublishing.com/authors/rossier/JUDGES.html
3. Matthew Henry, MHCC derived from *Matthew Henry Commentary Vol. 2* (MacDonald Pub. Co., Mclean, VA), p. 126
4. H. L. Rossier, op. cit.

Preamble to the Judges

1. Jules Gomes, *The Sanctuary of Bethel and the Configuration of Israelite Identity* (Walter de Gruyter, 2006), p. 117
2. Samuel Ridout, *Lecture 2: From Gilgal to Bochim*, STEM Publishing: http://stempublishing.com/authors/S_Ridout/SR_Judges02.html
3. C. A. Coates, *C. A. Coates Commentary – Judges* (Kingston Bible Trust, West Sussex, UK), chp. 2
4. F. C. Jennings, *Judges and Ruth* (Believer's Bookshelf Inc., Gospel Pub. House; 1905), chp. 2
5. F. C. Cook, *Barnes' Notes Bible Commentary – Exodus to Ruth* (Baker Book House, Grand Rapids, MI; 1981), p. 419

Idolatry Ensures Slavery

Othniel, Ehud, and Shamgar
1. H. L. Rossier, op. cit., chp. 3
2. William Kelly, op. cit., chp. 3
3. C. T. Lacey, *Judges – What the Bible Teaches* (John Ritchie LTD, Kilmarnock, Scotland; 2006), p. 305
4. F. Duane Lindsey, op. cit., p. 387

Deborah and Barak
1. H. L. Rossier, op. cit., chp. 4
2. C. A. Coates, op. cit., chp. 4
3. http://www.messengers-of-messiah.org/Tour/JezVal.html
4. F. C. Cook, op. cit., p. 429

The Song of Deborah and Barak
1. Matthew Henry, op. cit., p. 145
2. C. A. Coates, op. cit., chp. 4
3. William MacDonald, *Believer's Bible Commentary* (Thomas Nelson Publishers, Nashville: 1989), p. 270
4. Hamilton Smith, *The Psalms*, STEM Publishing: http://stempublishing.com/authors/smith/PSALMS.html
5. H. L. Rossier, op. cit., chp. 5

The Call of Gideon
1. C. A. Coates, op. cit., chp. 6

Gideon's Call Confirmed
1. Samuel Ridout, *Lecture 5: Gideon*, STEM Publishing: http://stempublishing.com/authors/S_Ridout/SR_Judges05.html
2. C. T. Lacey, op. cit., p. 333

Too Many for God
1. H. L. Rossier, op. cit., chp. 7
2. Matthew Henry, op. cit., p. 168
3. William MacDonald, op. cit., p. 273
4. C. H. Mackintosh, *Genesis to Deuteronomy* (Loizeaux Brothers, Inc., Neptune, NJ; 1972), p. 122.

Victory, Rest, and Confusion
1. Matthew Henry, op. cit., p. 170
2. C. A. Coates, op. cit., chp. 8
3. Matthew Henry, op. cit., p. 172
4. F. C. Cook, op. cit., p. 438
5. H. L. Rossier, op. cit., chp. 8
6. F. C. Cook, op. cit., p. 438

The Career of Abimelech
1. A. R. Fausset, *A Critical and Expository Commentary on the Book of Judges* (Banner of Truth; 1999), chp. 9
2. C. A. Coates, op. cit., chp. 9
3. H. L. Rossier, op. cit., chp. 9
4. Irving L. Jensen, *Judges and Ruth* (Moody Press, Chicago, IL; 1968), p.12
5. Matthew Henry, op. cit., p. 183

Tola, Jair, and Slavery Again
1. Matthew Henry, op. cit., p. 185
2. C. T. Lacey, op. cit., p. 365
3. Matthew Henry, op. cit., p. 188

Jephthah Victory and Tragic Vow
1. Samuel Ridout, op. cit., chp. 11
2. C. A. Coates, op. cit., chp. 11
3. Donald Campbell, *The Bible Knowledge Commentary Vol. 1: An Exposition of the Scriptures* (Victor Books, Wheaton, IL; 1983-1985), p. 326
4. William Kelly, op. cit., chp. 11

Ephraim Punished, Ibzan, Elon, and Abdon

The Promised Nazirite Son
1. H. L. Rossier, op. cit., chp. 13
2. C. A. Coates, op. cit., chp. 13
3. C. T. Lacey, op. cit., p. 400
4. F. C. Jennings, op. cit., chp. 13
5. H. L. Rossier, op. cit., chp. 13

Samson's Weakness and Riddle
1. William MacDonald, op. cit., p. 279

Samson's Rage
1. F. C. Jennings, op. cit., chp. 14
2. A. E. Cundall, *Judges – An Introduction and Commentary* (Tyndale & Inter-Varsity Press, London, England; 1968), chp. 15.
3. James L. R. Catron, *Old Testament Survey: Law and History* (Emmaus Bible College, Dubuque, IA; 1996), p. 58

Delilah and Samson's Revenge
1. C. A. Coates, op. cit., chp. 15
2. Matthew Henry, op. cit., p. 220
3. C. H. Mackintosh, *Genesis to Deuteronomy* (Loizeaux Brothers, Inc., Neptune, NJ; 1972), p. 465
4. J. N. Darby, op. cit., p. 309
5. H. F. Witherby, *The Serious Christian Series: The Book of Joshua* (Books for Christians, Charlotte, NC; no date), p. 184
6. A. T. Pierson, *Lectures on the Book of Judges* (T & T Clark, Enidburgh, Scotland; 1895)

Religious Confusion
1. C. A. Coates, op. cit., chp. 17

Danites Move North
1. C. A. Coates, op. cit., chp. 18
2. Samuel Ridout, op. cit., chp. 18
3. F. Duane Lindsey, op. cit., p. 410
4. Kathleen White, *Amy Carmichael* (Bethany House Publishers, Minneapolis, MN; 1986), p. 72

Moral Degradation
1. Henry M. Morris, *The Genesis Record* (Baker Book House, Grand Rapids: 1976), p. 102
2. William MacDonald, op. cit., p. 284

Civil War with Benjamin
1. C. A. Coates, op. cit., chp. 20
2. F. C. Cook, op. cit., p. 465
3. J. N. Darby, op. cit., p. 310
4. C. A. Coates, op. cit., chp. 20
5. H. L. Rossier, op. cit., chp. 20

Mourning for the Lost Tribe
1. C. A. Coates, op. cit., chp. 21
2. Matthew Henry, op. cit., p. 250
3. H. L. Rossier, op. cit., chp. 21
4. C. T. Lacey, op. cit., p. 466

Introduction to Ruth
1. C. A. Coates, *C. A. Coates Commentary – Ruth* (Kingston Bible Trust, West Sussex, UK), chp. 1
2. Hamilton Smith, *The Book of Ruth*, STEM Publishing (intro.): http://stempublishing.com/authors/smith/RUTH.html
3. H. L. Rossier, *Meditations on the Book of Ruth*, STEM Publishing (intro.): http://stempublishing.com/authors/rossier/RUTH.html

A New Beginning
1. Samuel Ridout, *Ruth*, STEM Publishing (chp. 1):
   http://stempublishing.com/authors/S_Ridout/SR_Ruth1.html
2. Hamilton Smith, op. cit., chp. 1
3. H. L. Rossier, op. cit., chp. 1
4. W. J. Hocking, *Ruth*, STEM Publishing (intro.):
   http://stempublishing.com/authors/WJ_Hocking/WJH_Ruth0.html
5. Charles Stanley, *Ruth: Blessing and Rest,* STEM Publishing:
   http://stempublishing.com/authors/stanley/Ruth.html

Gleaning Grace
1. Samuel Ridout, op. cit., chp. 2
2. F. C. Cook, op. cit., p. 475
3. H. L. Rossier, op. cit., chp. 2
4. Samuel Ridout, op. cit., chp. 2
5. Hamilton Smith, op. cit., chp. 2

Seeking Redemption
1. C. A Coates, op. cit., chp. 2
2. C. I. Scofield, *The New Scofield Study Bible* (Oxford University Press, New York: 1967), p. 319
3. H. L. Rossier, op. cit. chp. 3

Blessings of Redemption
1. Hamilton Smith, op. cit., chp. 3
2. Samuel Ridout, op. cit., chp. 4
3. H. L. Rossier, op. cit. chp. 4
4. C. A. Coates, op. cit. chp. 4

www.ingramcontent.com/pod-product-compliance
Lightning Source LLC
LaVergne TN
LVHW051625080426
835511LV00016B/2186